Music, Technology, and Education

The use of technology in music and education can no longer be described as a recent development. Music learners actively engage with technology in their music making, regardless of the opportunities afforded to them in formal settings. This volume draws together critical perspectives in three overarching areas in which technology is used to support music education: music production; game technology; musical creation, experience and understanding. The fourteen chapters reflect the emerging field of the study of technology in music from a pedagogical perspective. Contributions come not only from music pedagogues but also from musicologists, composers and performers working at the forefront of the domain. The authors examine pedagogical practice in the recording studio, how game technology relates to musical creation and expression, the use of technology to create and assess musical compositions, and how technology can foster learning within the field of Special Educational Needs (SEN). In addition, the use of technology in musical performance is examined, with a particular focus on the current trends and the ways it might be reshaped for use within performance practice. This book will be of value to educators, practitioners, musicologists, composers and performers, as well as to scholars with an interest in the critical study of how technology is used effectively in music and music education.

Andrew King is Senior Lecturer in Music at the University of Hull, UK, where he has held numerous senior leadership roles such as Deputy Dean (Learning & Teaching) and Associate Principal. He is editor of the *Journal of Music, Technology & Education* and *The Routledge Companion to Music, Technology, and Education*.

Evangelos Himonides held the University of London's first ever lectureship in music technology education. He is now Reader in Technology, Education and Music at University College London, UK, where he co-leads the Postgraduate Programme in Music Education. Evangelos is a Chartered Fellow of the British Computer Society.

SEMPRE Studies in The Psychology of Music

Series Editors
Graham Welch, *University of London, UK*
Adam Ockelford, *Roehampton University, UK*
Ian Cross, *University of Cambridge, UK*

The theme for the series is the psychology of music, broadly defined. Topics include (i) musical development at different ages, (ii) exceptional musical development in the context of special educational needs, (iii) musical cognition and context, (iv) culture, mind and music, (v) micro to macro perspectives on the impact of music on the individual (from neurological studies through to social psychology), (vi) the development of advanced performance skills and (vii) affective perspectives on musical learning. The series presents the implications of research findings for a wide readership, including user-groups (music teachers, policy makers, parents) as well as the international academic and research communities. This expansive embrace, in terms of both subject matter and intended audience (drawing on basic and applied research from across the globe), is the distinguishing feature of the series, and it serves SEMPRE's distinctive mission, which is to promote and ensure coherent and symbiotic links between education, music and psychology research.

Recent titles in the series:

Communities of Musical Practice
Ailbhe Kenny

Creative Teaching for Creative Learning in Higher Music Education
Elizabeth Haddon and Pamela Burnard

The Tangible in Music
Marko Aho

Artistic Practice as Research in Music: Theory, Criticism, Practice
Edited by Mine Doğantan-Dack

Advanced Musical Performance: Investigations in Higher Education Learning
Edited by Ioulia Papageorgi and Graham Welch

Collaborative Creative Thought and Practice in Music
Edited by Margaret S. Barrett

Coughing and Clapping: Investigating Audience Experience
Edited by Karen Burland and Stephanie Pitts

Embodied Knowledge in Ensemble Performance
J. Murphy McCaleb

Music, Technology, and Education

Critical Perspectives

**Edited by
Andrew King and
Evangelos Himonides**

Routledge
Taylor & Francis Group

LONDON AND NEW YORK

First published 2016
by Routledge
2 Park Square, Milton Park, Abingdon, Oxon OX14 4RN

and by Routledge
711 Third Avenue, New York, NY 10017

First issued in paperback 2017

*Routledge is an imprint of the Taylor & Francis Group, an informa
business*

British Library Cataloguing in Publication Data
A catalogue record for this book is available from the British Library

Library of Congress Cataloging-in-Publication Data
Names: King, Andrew (Music researcher) | Himonides, Evangelos.
Title: Music, technology, and education : critical perspectives / edited by
    Andrew King and Evangelos Himonides.
Description: [2016] | Series: SEMPRE studies in the psychology of
    music | Includes bibliographical references and index.
Identifiers: LCCN 2015038069 | ISBN 9781472426208 (hardcover : alk.
    paper) | ISBN 9781315596945 (ebook)
Subjects: LCSH: Music–Instruction and study–Technological innovations. |
    Sound recordings–Production and direction–Instruction and study.
Classification: LCC MT1. M98732 2016 | DDC 780.71–dc23
LC record available at http://lccn.loc.gov/2015038069

ISBN 13: 978-1-138-50502-5 (pbk)
ISBN 13: 978-1-4724-2620-8 (hbk)

Typeset in Times New Roman
by Apex Covantage, LLC

To Elaine
To Cynthia

Contents

Figures

Tables

Contributors

Monty Adkins is a composer, performer, and Professor of Experimental Electronic Music at the Centre for Research in New Music at University of Huddersfield. His work is characterised by slow, shifting organic textures often derived from processed instrumental sounds. Exhibiting a post-acousmatic sensibility, his compositions draw together elements from ambient, acousmatic, and microsound music. He has written extensively on the aesthetics of electronic music, presenting papers at conferences worldwide. In 2013, he co-edited the *Ashgate Companion to Roberto Gerhard* and has since written on the electronic music of Christopher Fox and aspects of British sonic art.

Matthew C. Applegate is a professional multidisciplinary artist and lecturer, a patron of the Access to Music Centre in Norwich, a Science and Engineering Ambassador for Suffolk and member of STEMNET (Science, Technology, Engineering and Mathematics Network). As PixelH8, he is known internationally for programming some of the world's oldest and rarest computers as well as rewiring children's toys to make new musical instruments and musical compositions. He has produced music software used by Grammy-winner Damon Albarn and Grammy-nominee Imogen Heap.

Andrew R. Brown is an educator, researcher, musician, author, and programmer. He holds a doctorate in music and is Professor of Digital Arts at Griffith University, Brisbane. His academic expertise is in technologies that support creativity and learning, the creation of computational music and art, and the philosophy of technology. Andrew's creative activities focus on real-time audio-visual works using generative processes and live coding performance. He has performed live coding and interactive music in many parts of the world and his digital art works have been shown in galleries across Australia, the USA, and China. He is the author of *Music Technology and Education: Amplifying Musicality*, co-author of *Making Music with Computers: Creative Programming in Python*, and the editor of *Sound Musicianship: Understanding the Crafts of Music*.

Gianna Cassidy is senior lecturer in interactive entertainment design and psychology at Glasgow Caledonian University, having gained a doctorate on the effects of music on game play and a Master of Psychology and Music Composition from the University of Glasgow. Cassidy's research focuses on the impact of music on user performance and experience and the design and evaluation of music-game technologies for health and well-being in a range of contexts, including education, neuro-rehabilitation and Alzheimer's care.

Martin Fautley was a secondary school teacher for many years before returning to full-time study at Cambridge, where his work involved assessment, the creative process, and the interfaces between the two. He then worked at Manchester Metropolitan University before moving to Birmingham City University. He is now Professor of Education, and coordinates the work of the Centre for Research in Education.

Evangelos Himonides held the University of London's first ever lectureship in music technology education. He is now reader in technology, education, and music and teaches music education, music technology, and information technology at post-graduate level at the UCL Institute of Education and also leads the post-graduate course 'Music Technology in Education'. He holds a Music Diploma from the Macedonian Conservatoire of Thessaloniki, Greece, a Bachelor of Science in information technology (multimedia) with starred first-class honours from Middlesex University, a Master of Education with distinction from the University of Surrey and a doctorate in information technology and psychoacoustics from the University of London. He is Chartered Fellow (FBCS CITP) of the British Computer Society.

Andrew King is senior lecturer in music in the School of Drama, Music, and Screen at the University of Hull. He was the Deputy Dean (learning and teaching) and Associate Principal between 2009 and 2013 also at the University of Hull. He is the editor of *Journal of Music, Technology, and Education* and *The Routledge Companion to Music, Technology and Education.* His research interests include the use of technology in the music curriculum. He is particularly interested in the recording-studio environment, especially the types and use of technology, how learners interact in the environment, and the roles undertaken in group work. He has worked as a professional recording engineer for the BBC.

Phil Kirkman is the course director for initial teacher education at the University of Cambridge. He previously taught music in several comprehensive schools across the UK. Alongside these roles he has spent much of his time directing and performing with choirs and bands, as well as working as a church music director. Kirkman is often engaged as an international consultant on technology mediated learning and music education. His current research interests include innovative pedagogy, educational technologies, musical development, and dialogic education.

Don Knox is senior audio lecturer at Glasgow Caledonian University. He completed his doctorate in audio signal processing in 2004 in collaboration with the Centre for Music Technology at the University of Glasgow. His research interests include audio and music processing and analysis, music emotion, and music psychology. He is director of the GCU audio-research group, founding member of the Scottish Music Health Network, member of the Audio Engineering Society, the Institute of Electrical and Electronics Engineers, and SEMPRE, a fellow of the Higher Education Academy, and associate editor of *Psychology of Music*.

Marc Leman is a research professor in systematic musicology and director of the Institute for Psychoacoustics and Electronic Music at the University of Ghent. His research interests include methodological and epistemological foundations of musicology; perception-based analysis of music and musical audio; digitalisation, restoration, and archiving of musical audio-archives; interactive (dance/music/video) multimedia technology and its application in the arts; musical audio-mining; emotions and movements in response to music; neuroscience and music; and forensic musicology. His approach is based on computational and empirical methods, which include the use of acoustical/sonological, perceptual/motor, cognitive/emotive, and social/cultural approaches to music analysis.

Luc Nijs is a musician, teacher, and researcher. He holds a Master of Music Performance (Royal Conservatory of Brussels, 1996), a Master of Philosophy (Ghent University, 2008) and a doctorate in art sciences (Ghent University, 2012). His research focuses on the role of the body in instrumental music learning and on how interactive educational technologies contribute to an embodied-constructivist approach to music teaching and learning. For his research project on the Music Paint Machine, he was awarded the European Association for Practitioner Research on Improving Learning Best Research and Practice Project Award 2012. Furthermore he does research on teacher reflectiveness. Currently he is a postdoctoral researcher at Institute for Psychoacoustics and Electronic Music at the University of Ghent, researcher and lecturer at LUCA School of Arts (music education and therapy), and clarinet teacher in specialized music schools.

Adam Ockelford is Professor of Music at the University of Roehampton, London, where he is director of the Applied Music Research Centre. His principal research interest is in cognitive musicology – music theory with a psychological slant. He has worked extensively with children on the autism spectrum, and his students include the internationally acclaimed musical savant, Derek Paravicini. Recent books include *Applied Musicology* and *Music, Language and Autism*.

Anna Paisley is doctoral student at Glasgow Caledonian University, having received an Master of Research from the University of Strathclyde. Anna was research assistant on the Engineering and Physical Sciences Research Council project 'Music-Games: Supporting New Opportunities for Music Education', and her doctoral research focuses on designing and evaluating music and music-technology interventions for health and wellbeing, with a focus upon the social, emotional, and cognitive benefits of music across the lifespan.

Amandine Pras graduated from the Paris Conservatory Music and Sound Recording programme in 2006 and completed her doctorate at McGill University, Canada in 2012 on the best practices to produce musical recordings in the digital era. She conducts postdoctoral research on free improvisation at the New School for Social Research and teaches musical recording techniques at New York University. In parallel to her academic activities, she works as a record producer and a sound engineer in different countries and for a great variety of artistic projects. She has specialised in contemporary and experimental creation, often involving new technology.

Jonathan Savage is reader in education at the Education and Social Research Institute, Manchester Metropolitan University, where he is a deputy director of the CREATE research group. He teaches on various PGCE courses and doctoral studies programmes and is an active researcher in a wide range of areas. He is published in a number of field, including using technology in education, supporting gifted and talented students, the arts, creativity, assessment, and cross-curricular approaches to teaching and learning. He is a series editor for Routledge. More information can be found on his blog at <www.jsavage.org.uk>.

Mark Slater is a lecturer in music in the School of Drama, Music, and Screen at the University of Hull. He is a composer, songwriter, producer, and musicologist with particular interests in popular and experimental music, and the links between them. Improvisation and the accidental play a large part in the music he studies and makes. Music from two recent projects – 'Middlewood Sessions' and 'Nightports' – has been broadcast internationally. His research explores processes of musical creativity that involve technologies in some way.

Simon Zagorski-Thomas is a reader at the London College of Music, University of West London. He is a director of the annual Art of Record Production Conference, co-founder of *Journal on the Art of Record Production* and co-chairman of the Association for the Study of the Art of Record Production (<www.arto frecordproduction.com>). His publications include *The Art of Record Production* (co-edited with Simon Frith) and *The Musicology of Record Production*. Before becoming an academic he worked for 25 years as a composer, sound engineer, and producer with artists as varied as Phil Collins, Mica Paris, the London Community Gospel Choir, Bill Bruford, the Mock Turtles, Courtney Pine, and the Balanescu Quartet. He continues to compose and record music and is currently conducting research into the musicology of record production, popular music analysis, and performance practice in the recording process.

Series editors' preface

The enormous growth of research that has been evidenced over the past three decades continues into the many different phenomena that are embraced under the psychology of music 'umbrella'. Growth is evidenced in new journals, books, media interest, an expansion of professional associations (regionally and nationally, such as in Southern Europe and Latin America), and with increasing and diverse opportunities for formal study, including in non-English-speaking countries. Such growth of interest is not only from psychologists and musicians, but also from colleagues working in the clinical sciences, neurosciences, therapies, in the lifelong health and well-being communities, philosophy, musicology, social psychology, ethnomusicology and education across the lifespan. As part of this global community, the Society for Education, Music and Psychology Research (SEMPRE) celebrated its fortieth anniversary in 2012 and continues to be one of the world's leading and longstanding professional associations in the field. SEMPRE is the only international society that embraces formally an interest in the psychology of music, research and education, seeking to promote knowledge at the interface between the twin social sciences of psychology and education with one of the world's most pervasive art forms, music. SEMPRE was founded in 1972 and has published the journals *Psychology of Music* since 1973 and *Research Studies in Music Education* since 2008, both now produced in partnership with SAGE (see www.sempre.org.uk), with a new online journal *Music and Science* due to be launched in late 2016. We continue to seek new ways to reach out globally, both in print and online as we recognise that there is an ongoing need to promote the latest research findings to the widest possible audience. Through more extended publication formats, especially books, we are more likely to fulfil a key component of our mission that is to have a distinctive and positive impact on understanding, as well as on policy and practice internationally, both within and across our disciplinary boundaries. Hence, we welcome the strong collaborative partnership between SEMPRE and Routledge (formerly Ashgate).

The Routledge series *SEMPRE Studies in The Psychology of Music* has been designed to address this international need since its inception in 2007. The theme for the series is the psychology of music, broadly defined. Topics include (amongst others): musical development and learning at different ages; musical cognition and context; culture, mind and music; creativity, composition, and collaboration; micro to macro perspectives on the impact of music on the individual (from neurological studies through to social psychology); the development of advanced performance skills; musical behaviour and development in the context of special educational needs; and affective perspectives on musical learning. The series seeks to present the implications of research findings for a wide readership, including user-groups (music teachers, policy makers, parents and carers, music professionals working in a range of formal, non-formal and informal settings), as well as the international academic teaching and research communities. A key distinguishing feature of the series is its broad focus that draws on basic and applied research from across the globe under the umbrella of SEMPRE's distinctive mission, which is to promote and ensure coherent and symbiotic links between education, music and psychology research.

It is with particular pleasure that we include this new volume *Music, Technology, and Education: Critical Perspectives*. The text, edited by senior colleagues in the field – Dr Andrew King (University of Hull) and Dr Evangelos Himonides (University College London) – is conceived in three main sections, music production, game technology, and music creation, and brings together the writings of key national and international authors who are at the forefront of theoretical and empirical research into the use of technology in music-making and learning. The reader will enjoy the rich variety of perspectives on offer, whilst having the opportunity to reflect on how many of our modern experiences of music are mediated through technological means and in ways that consumers, listeners, and makers are probably singularly unaware. They also posit the question as to how technology is not just a tool in supporting an established music pedagogy, but also how what counts as experience can be expanded or different because of the use of digital technologies.

We are delighted to have this volume within the SEMPRE Studies in The Psychology of Music series, not least because the text highlights the need for greater critical insights into the experiences of music through digital technologies. We believe that the inclusion of this new volume continues to demonstrate SEMPRE's commitment to the holistic celebration of academic excellence in music research, policy and practice.

Graham Welch, University of London, UK;
Adam Ockelford, Roehampton University, UK;
and Ian Cross, University of Cambridge, UK

Introduction

Andrew King and Evangelos Himonides

Music, technology, and educational research draw upon a rich diversity of different disciplines. Pedagogues in the field often find themselves researching and practising across different thematic areas such as engineering, acoustics, psychology, education, composition, performance, and sound design. This book aims to rehearse current perspectives about the domain, as informed by the latest theoretical and empirical research.

The use of technology in music-making can no longer be classified as a new or recent development. A contemporary view of this phenomenon in music-making is centralised around the microprocessor. This innovation has spawned a number of electronic devices and computer software that have become widespread in the musical community. Some would argue that technological innovation in music has a long tradition in the historical development of musical instruments (the development of valves for brass instruments is one of the obvious examples). Himonides (2012) even argues that 'musicking' humanity's trajectory has been parallel to that of 'technological' humanity's. However, many would agree with Théberge's (1997) assessment that it is to the latter part of the twentieth century that we look for many of the technological innovations in music-making. The electric guitar, keyboards, and samplers came into prominence and afforded musicians a different sound world. However, all of these innovations – it could be argued – fall into the category of instrument development. Although electronic in nature, synthesisers use an organ style keyboard and most of the early synthesiser development concentrated on attempts to produce realistic replicas of standard acoustic instruments (usually quite unsuccessfully).

This book explores current issues of music, technology, and education from three main perspectives: music production; game technology; and musical creation, experience, and understanding.

Overview: Critical perspectives

Part I of this book examines pedagogical approaches to recording-studio practice. It begins with Mark Slater in Chapter 1 highlighting how technology has become miniaturised and how new locations for creativity are now possible away from the traditional recording studio. Experiences are drawn from a five-year longitudinal project that include why learning takes place, what is learnt, and provides a perspective of how such learning takes place. This provides a useful starting point for this volume since it acknowledges that the place of creativity has changed, and there is perhaps a direct link here to how many learners may engage with technology within informal contexts. In Chapter 2, Amandine Pras similarly acknowledges the changes in the music industry and the rise of the project studio (outlined earlier by Théberge). However, rather than examine the context of the creative work Pras provides some understanding of the roles in the studio, such as producer and engineer. This chapter has a particular focus on the management of a recording session and the relationship between the artists and the technicians, although admittedly there is considerable overlap between the technical and artistic elements of music production demonstrated by the rise in the study of the art of record production.

The theme of record production is further investigated by Andrew King who presents perspectives from three leading producers concerning recording-studio pedagogy. The views of experts who had worked through the transition from analogue to digital recording technology were gathered, providing historical context, and the phenomenological analysis of the interview data identified the superordinate themes of 'knowledge and skills' and 'human perspective'. The number of affordances now possible using digital technology is discussed and an important viewpoint is put forward that could have implications for how we approach the study of sound recording.

The final chapter in Part I addresses the question of theoretical research and challenges in teaching record production. Simon Zagorski-Thomas draws upon three examples in this chapter: performance in the studio, record production in musicology, and cognition versus psychoacoustics. Zagorski-Thomas suggests that these are three of the key research areas that need to progress in order to help educate students in sound recording. In the third area it is proposed that there should be a stronger link between theoretical work in the psychoacoustics of record production and processes such as dynamic compression and frequency equalisation. This chapter brings Part I to a useful conclusion, as it signposts potential future developments.

Part II centres on game technology, music, and education. This is an often neglected aspect of music and technology, the impact of which is presented by Don Knox, Gianna Cassidy, and Anna Paisley in Chapter 5. The authors place an emphasis on the communication of emotion and the role of musical attributes in the process, establishing music's fundamental role and impact on players' (and maybe learners') overall experiences.

Chapter 6 presents a very exciting use (and abuse) of an established gaming technology (video-game control pads). Matthew Applegate, a very successful coder, hacker, and developer of new technologies, rehearses the possibility of skill transfer from gaming to musical creativity, using an agile model of software development dynamically during his investigation. His research provides some evidence that systematic exposure to and engagement with video gaming has a direct impact on muscle memory, hand–eye coordination and familiarity with a directional control pad. Applegate proposes that all of these skills are transferable to the real world outside video games.

In Chapter 7, Andrew Brown offers an inspiring exploration of key aspects of game technology in the music classroom, a field that is under-researched as well as under-rehearsed. Brown's review of the literature, critical thinking, and stimulating synthesis of theoretical and empirical evidence is a much-needed examination of how creating sound and music for video games can be part of the music classroom but also how design patterns in music and audio can be taught using computer-game development as a paradigm. Three areas of video-game audio are explored in this chapter: sound design, non-linear music, and creative coding. This diversity highlights the richness of opportunities in game music and sound. For each area a related music education case study is described. These case studies shed light on the pragmatic reality of how concepts can be put into practice.

In Chapter 8, the concluding chapter of Part II, Anna Paisley and Gianna Cassidy present the findings of a research project funded by the UK's Engineering and Physical Sciences Research Council (EPSRC) titled 'Music-Games: Supporting New Opportunities for Music-Education'. This is a very stimulating contribution, as it rehearses key issues raised throughout Part II and provides clear evidence, drawn from multimodal systematic research, about the potential benefits of employing music games in the classroom. This is, of course, something that needs to be further addressed, as it not only requires changing established musico-pedagogical practice, but also common polarised views of learning as either formal or informal.

Musical creation, experience, and understanding is the third theme of the volume. In Chapter 9 Phil Kirkman explores constructions of technology in relation to a postmodern notion of the 'hyper-real'. Kirkman bridges philosophical, epistemological, and praxial aspects of music technology and provides a critical lens through which technology can be viewed as a framework that underpins the formation of new relationships with music and how it functions within time and space, sound and silence. Through a number of real-world exemplars, Kirkman also offers a critical discourse about the potential caveats of placing technology in the centre of educational spaces.

Chapter 10 presents Evangelos Himonides' and Adam Ockelford's view of the role of music technology within the field of special educational needs (SEN). The authors invite the reader to consider music technology as something much broader than a set of tools for music-making. They provide evidence about why this tool-centric approach is a threat to music education and highlight the importance of adopting a critical approach in addressing the important role of technology within this unique educational context. The paradigm of 'sounds of intent' is a real world, research-informed, exemplar in support of the authors' view about how the creative use of technology can foster the musical (as well as other) development of young people with complex needs.

In Chapter 11, Monty Atkins offers an exploration of how musical creativities can be facilitated and engendered within academic environments. Atkins introduces the notion of 'experience design', the integration of which has the potential to foster social integration and the development of communities of compositional practice in an academic milieu that is stimulating, relevant and supportive. Similar to the conclusion of modern educational research regarding the social location of learning, Atkins extends the argument by emphasising the social location of creative practice and how this is shaped by technology and music technology.

Jonathan Savage and Martin Fautley address the very important aspect of assessment within the novel (or as they argue, not that novel) context that digital technologies have introduced. Chapter 12 forms a critical and suggestive link between the somewhat fluidly defined sections of the volume. The authors offer a critical discourse about what they call the 'uncritical adoption and use of technologies' and how this might become a negative catalyst for high-quality music education. Savage and Fautley demonstrate how the exaggeration of the novel character of 'the present moment' usually seeks to radically rethink assessment, theory, and practice and attempts to forget systematically acquired knowledge about assessment that is not necessarily tool related, tool specific, affordance specific, or even context specific. In their highly critical and refreshing text the authors bring the focus back on the learner. Savage and Fautley suggest that regardless of whether technology is present or not (or if at all possible) the 'additionality' offered by the technology also needs to be considered within the context of the specific work of the student.

In Chapter 13 Luc Nijs and Marc Leman present an embodied approach to educational technology and music-making and performance. This is manifested by the Music Paint Machine (MPM), an interactive music educational technology that has been developed to support the acquisition of music performance skills and, in particular, of musical creativity and expressiveness. Grounded in an in-depth investigation of the musician–instrument relationship, the concept and development of the MPM were shaped by an embodied–constructivist approach to music teaching and learning and by an elaborated empirical framework. The authors present systematically acquired evidence about the effectiveness of such a machine and the creative potential that it introduces to learners by challenging certainties and fostering new developmental and creative opportunities.

In the concluding chapter of this volume, Evangelos Himonides offers his opinion on the future of education in general and music education specifically as shaped by the newly introduced concept of 'big data'. Himonides offers a brief overview about what big data entails and how this might shape attitudes, theory, and practice in the years to come. Very much in line with Savage and Fautley's stance, Himonides attempts to place the focus on critical thinking and how a new technology (or sets of new technologies and affordances) might enhance and foster the development of critical thinking. Himonides believes that big data will be pivotal in the establishment of evidence-based educational practice and an invaluable tool in safeguarding and enhancing the quality measures in place for generating educational theory and practice.

A refreshing novelty for this volume is that its contributing authors are not monothematic theorists, but rather multidisciplinary researchers, practitioners as well as scholars, with an impressive breadth of expertise in technology, education, and music. This volume is an attempt to move the conversation on from what we are doing with technology onto examining the why and also create debate from a philosophical perspective of how we are achieving this.

We are delighted to have had the opportunity to lead such an exciting initiative and are very grateful to all the contributors, the publishers, and SEMPRE for their support and enthusiasm.

References

Himonides, E. (2012). 'The Misunderstanding of Music-Technology-Education: A Meta-Perspective'. In G. McPherson and G. Welch (eds), *The Oxford Handbook of Music Education*. New York: Oxford University Press.

Théberge, P. (1997). *Any Sound You Can Imagine: Making Music / Consuming Technology*. Middletown, CT: Wesleyan University Press.

Part I
Music production

1 Processes of learning in the project studio

Mark Slater

The emergence of the project studio is a story of increasing access to ever more powerful technologies that allow music to be produced in increasingly diverse circumstances. In 1973 *Melody Maker* responded, somewhat tongue-in-cheek, to an emerging trend by offering basic advice about setting up a home studio: 'about half the garages and basements in England must be echoing to the siren song of rock music by now; everybody's building their own recording studios' (Blake 1973). Théberge identifies the same year as a milestone in the emergence of a viable market for consumer music technologies because sales of electronic synthesisers were first tracked as a separate category (1997: 52–3). Technological innovation, economic viability, and the socio-cultural impetus to make music with technology coincided in the early 1970s to create the conditions for the eventual emergence of the domestic project studio.

While technologies had been deployed in domestic settings from the 1930s (and earlier), they were relatively expensive and only capable of documenting events (Brock-Nannestad 2012). More sophisticated technologies were developed in the 1950s and 1960s, though these were often idiosyncratic and highly specialised (Théberge 2004), built by 'tinkerers' from a lineage of mechanical and electrical engineers (Horning 2004: 721). From the early 1960s the nascent electronic musical instrument and music technology industries developed more standardised designs and processes of manufacture, which brought down costs and expanded the potential market. At the higher end of the market, 'star performers' assembled home studios 'to experiment and create while relatively unfettered by the constraints of time and money' imposed by professional studios (Théberge 1997: 231–2). The equipment aimed at the lower end of the market could only produce demo-quality material and as such posed no real threat to the professional establishment (Wadsworth 2007: 53). The integration of microprocessors and music devices during the late 1970s was a reciprocal innovation between computer and music technology industries that delivered cheaper, more flexible devices. In the 1980s a new studio environment emerged, the 'so-called "project studios" – often little more than large home installations' (Théberge 2004: 773). This new form of studio environment had a significant impact on recording practices and the commerciality of the recording studio industry (Leyshon 2009). The story continues into the 1990s, with increasing processing power giving rise to better integration of digital audio and MIDI sequencing capabilities along with ever-expanding track counts (Théberge 2004: 774), and the 2000s, when miniaturised, mobilised, and ubiquitous technologies allowed 'extended movement of social actors into geographic locations previously unusable as places for sonic creativity' (Slater and Martin 2012: 72).

The terms 'home studio' and 'project studio' are often used interchangeably, perhaps because of the historical root of such technological 'assemblages' (Born 2005: 8) being situated in the home. I prefer the term 'project studio' because it avoids designating one particular type of place and maintains the dynamic possibility of active location (Slater, 2016, p. 173). The 'project studio', as an umbrella term, encompasses an unknowable range of possibilities and variations. There is no neat designation: project studios can produce professional-standard material (though they might also be the realm of amateur hobbyists); there can be a flow of people and materials between project studios and professional studios in the overall process of bringing music into being; project studios may be as stable as professional studios (architecturally, economically, and in reputation) but they may also be in a constant state of flux in terms of the technologies that constitute them and the practices and materials that are explored there.

Proliferation of technologies leads to a proliferation of creative practices across expanding socio-demographic and geographic planes (Crowdy 2007; Greene 2001). Given this context – outside formal institutions, in spare rooms, bedrooms, and garages – how do people learn what they need to know? Specialist music technology programmes are now a well-established part of the music education landscape, providing access to expertise, equipment and architectural spaces beyond the reach of most individuals. But engagement with musico-technological creativity is a significantly broader field, ranging from basic equipment to professional set-ups often (but not necessarily) situated in the home, supported by specialist print publications, forums, websites, and consumer textbooks. This non-institutional context, in which people learn what they need to know as they need to know it, is where the gaze of this chapter falls.

The ideas presented here are derived from a case study of a collaborative music project – Middlewood Sessions – that existed for a little less than eight years. Prior to the release of a nine-track album in February 2012, Middlewood Sessions had three singles released (with two remixes) on two established record labels,[1] achieved support from international radio and club DJs, and performed six live UK gigs – all of which received some critical acclaim (formal and otherwise). Such a case-study approach provides a detailed, idiographic insight into one manifestation of collaborative creativity in a project studio setting. In the final part of the chapter, I will present findings relating to what was being learned and how this learning took place, by identifying and describing four categories and four general processes. Prior to that, and prompted by the need to find ways of talking about learning from a standpoint external to formal institutions and curricula, I present a review of music education literature that explores the relationship between formal and informal styles of learning (eventually to reject this binary) giving rise to a proposal for five dimensions of learning. The goals of this chapter are twofold: to present something of the particular case study in an attempt to derive some insight into the possible processes of learning at play in the lived-out context of the project studio and to engage with music education literature in the formulation of a theoretical tool to facilitate a deeper, more nuanced, understanding of the nature of particular instances of learning activity.

Researching Middlewood Sessions

The research project began in 2006 just as Middlewood Sessions' first track, 'Fall Back', was beginning to receive national (UK) and international radio play. Data were collected through participant diaries and four semi-structured interviews (May 2007 to November 2011), which were analysed according to principles of thematic identification derived from interpretative phenomenological analysis (Smith, Flowers, and Larkin 2009) and organised using an adaptation of Spradley's (1980) nine-point model for carrying out descriptive participant observations. Starting tentatively in August 2004, there were originally two members constituting Middlewood Sessions (including myself). This tally grew over the subsequent years to include an additional 28 contributors (musicians, visual artists, and technicians) plus, importantly, a sound engineer who became the third 'core' member. Each 'core' participants' background is summarily sketched here to indicate something of the histories and prior experiences.

- Core Participant 1 invokes a range of subgenres (hip-hop, trip-hop, broken beat, drum-n-bass, acid jazz) and DJs (Gilles Peterson, Patrick Forge, Coldcut, DJ Food, Mr. Scruff), which reveals an experiential basis as listener and practitioner, rooted in DJ culture. This constitutes the primary knowledge base brought to bear on Middlewood Sessions alongside some basic training in studio production techniques.
- Core Participant 2 cites particular eras of jazz music (late big-band swing, bebop, cool jazz, modal jazz, funk) and electronica (Massive Attack, Portishead). These influences are set against a backdrop of formal university education in music, during which modernist and experimentalist composers were encountered (Cage, Cardew, Feldman, Finnissy, Stravinsky). Music technologies and associated practices did not figure in this participant's prior experience.
- Core Participant 3 abandoned jazz trumpet during his degree studies in favour of a career in music production, motivated by an interest in the crossover between music and physics. As the third core member, joining in the final third of the life of Middlewood Sessions, this participant brought technical expertise in recording techniques and post-production processes.

Participants came to the project with different levels and types of musical and technical expertise, but all were starting from scratch with one another in this particular creative endeavour. While there was some combined prior experience with composition and music production technologies, there was no pre-determined objective (except to try to make some good music) and there was no pre-existing technological configuration. Given this starting position, considerable effort was needed to learn all of what was required to put the project studio together, to get the music made and, eventually, out to an audience.

The research project focused on the three core members as a means of tracing the aspirations and activities that drove the creative endeavour from the perspective of the most central and continuous participants. The use of interviews and diaries was instrumental in capturing something of the story of Middlewood Sessions as it was unfolding; but, of course, my status as participant and researcher (and now author) must be acknowledged. Despite the objectifying processes of data capture and analysis (and the passage of not an insignificant amount of time), some remnants of my predilections and biases are bound to remain (not to mention my influence on events at the time [see Yin 2009: 101–3, 111–13]). This position is at once valuable (because of the 'insider perspective' it permits) but limited (in that it will inevitably lead to a particular reading of the data).

Dimensions of learning

Those making music in a project studio discover what skills and knowledge they need as they go along. This self-directed process of learning, taking place outside educational institutions and formal curricula, resembles informal learning, which 'has been defined as "the lifelong process by which every person acquires and accumulates knowledge, skills, attitudes, and insights from daily experiences and exposure to the environment"' (Coombs and Ahmed 1974, cited in Jenkins 2011: 181). Self-motivation is a predominant factor in determining an informal learning style, along with how that learning is sequenced. Folkestad states that in 'the *formal* learning situation, the activity is sequenced beforehand . . . [by] a person who takes on the task of organising and leading the learning activity' (2006: 141, original emphasis). Participants in a project studio motivate themselves to make music, though there might not be any pre-determined pattern for how this will happen and the eventual goal (whether to make a single track, an EP, or an album or what technology and musical materials to use) might not be known in advance. Furthermore, there may be no clear distinction between carrying out the creative activity and learning how to carry it out: they can be one and the same.

While the terms 'informal' and 'formal' turn out to be problematic, the related body of music education research is instructive in how it acknowledges and critiques the potential value of absorbing so-called informal practices into formal pedagogy. There is a direction of flow – from practice to praxis – in the music education literature, which has a centre-point around rock-based performance practices at high-school level (Davis 2005; Fornäs, Lindberg, and Sernhede 1995; Green 2002; Jaffurs 2004). In other words, there is a clustering of interest around style (rock), mode of engagement (performance), age group and educational context (high school), which sets up the strands that are variously inflected and extended.

Väkevä (2010) explored the impact of 'digital musicking' by anyone with a computer with 'entry-level software like GarageBand' with reference to remix and mash-up cultures. Savage (2005) assessed the impact of the presence of music technologies in the classroom for compositional activity. Söderman and Folke-stad (2004) observed how two hip-hop 'communes' create music using technologies in a studio setting. Finney and Philpott (2010) expounded on the integration of informal learning into initial teacher training prior to the classroom context. Robinson (2012) explored how instrumental teachers' learning histories, including experience of informal and formal approaches, influence their eventual teaching practice. Partti and Karlsen (2010) build on an earlier case study by Salavuo (2006) exploring online 'communities of practice' in which knowledge about music is shared and discussed. Two studies by Waldron (2009, 2013) explore the interaction between offline and online folk music communities. For practitioners beyond compulsory education, Feichas (2010) explored university students' attitudes towards studying music and Karlsen problematised informal pedagogy in a rock-based higher education programme in Sweden by questioning the ability of informal approaches to 'remain informal when included in formal education' (2010: 36). Thompson (2012) presented an enquiry into the learning strategies of DJs, turntablists, and dance and hip-hop producers with a view to extending the repertoire of learning practices in higher education to include electronic musicianship as well as instrumental rock-based approaches.

Against this groundswell of support for understanding what informal learning is and what it offers, Jenkins warns that 'approaches that have fallen under the banner of "informal" have often been subject to bandwagon over-enthusiasm, with proponents inflating their virtues beyond what the concept appears to warrant' (2011: 180). He asks: 'If informal learning is so pervasive, why is there a need for formal learning?' (ibid.: 181). Cain addresses a similar question by presenting a case study of formal pedagogy in comparison with the informal pedagogy developed by Green (2008). Cain asks why informal approaches should be regarded as ideal, liberatory, authentic, true, and good compared with the supposed rigidity and artificiality of boring formal approaches. In concluding his empirical study, he calls for the bipolar view of formal and informal as existing at opposite ends of a continuum to be abandoned in favour of other ways of thinking about the higher-level aims of a pedagogical approach (such as 'transmission' and 'authentic reproduction' [2013: 89]).

The general consensus is that a rounded music education will feature a mixture of formal and informal approaches to learning, and that this pedagogical mixture has been established for quite some time now. This subsumption of previously (and falsely) dichotomous approaches into one pedagogical outlook collapses any clear distinction between the formal and the informal. An effect compounded by the prevalence of technology that provides access to tools, information, materials, and communities – the same technology that propagates the creative music practices of interest here. Given this collapse, attempts to define one or the other are at best definitions of learning styles that are subsumed into a broader mixed pedagogy. While attempts to define informal and formal learning are flawed because the implicit contradistinction through comparison of contexts (the garage versus the classroom) and agents (teacher versus student) has been thoroughly undermined by information technologies, a meta-analysis of work by Jenkins (2011, citing Beckett and Hager 2002), Folkestad (2006), Green (2008) and, antithetically, Cain (2013) provides a theoretical basis for tracing and describing the nature of learning processes at a given point. This framework consists of five dimensions of learning that emerge once each set of definitions is remapped to show how common strands align. Table 1.1 juxtaposes the four sets of definitions in the top half and reorganises these according to the emergent five dimensions of learning in the bottom half. The five dimensions are ordered non-hierarchically and non-chronologically (each dimension is implicated in all learning) though there is some logic in the flow between them: intentionality (whether learning is the primary focus or not) is dependent upon agency (identifying who motivates the learning), which in turn affects the patterning of activities that afford opportunities for developing experience or conceptual knowledge that have a socio-architectural dimension (happening at a particular time, in a particular place).

Intentionality

Intentionality concerns the direction of the mind either towards learning itself or towards the core activity. In Jenkins' model, learning is not the main aim because the primary focus is on making music (2011: 186–7); conversely in Cain's case study, developing knowledge about music (the pursuit of knowledge) is the primary focus (2013: 16). Folkestad's distinction of intentionality (from whom I draw this term) as the direction of the mind towards either 'learning how to play or towards playing' (2006: 142) is reflected in the 'emphasis on personal creativity' that Green's approach advocates (2008: 10). When talking about learning in the project studio, we might be describing learning as an explicit process but it might equally be incidental and implicit, occurring as a consequence of some other activity.

Intentions can change in an instant. While experimenting with reverb plugins in the flow of creating a part for a string ensemble, stumbling across a particular preset might trigger a curiosity about how to control specific settings to achieve different effects. What began as a session geared towards exploring musical material might veer off into a conscious pursuit to learn aspects of technical detail (including recourse to online instructional materials or a question posed on a social network or dedicated forum). Furthermore, intention has scale: the decision to embark on the grander scheme of building a project studio might be partly driven by the desire to learn how to do it, but once the studio is up and running, the intention or the direction of the mind is towards creating music.

Agency

Agency describes how intention comes about, who decides to embark on the project as a whole or who activates particular tasks within it. Folkestad describes this as 'ownership', encompassing who makes the decisions about what, how, where, and when to participate in some activity that could lead to learning (2006: 142).

Table 1.1 Five dimensions of learning

	INFORMAL			FORMAL (antithetical)
	Jenkins (2011), citing Beckett and Hager (2002)	Folkestad (2006)	Green (2008)	Cain (2013)
	Organic/holistic Contextual Activity-based Learning not main aim Activated by individuals Collaborative/collegial	Situation Learning style Ownership Intentionality	Selection of material Copying by ear Friendship groups Holistic rather than sequential Personal creativity	Conceptual (analytic and discursive) Knowledge about music Unfamiliar repertoire Differentiation (tasks match skills) Additionally: Not so practical Self-expression/collaboration reduced
A	4. Learning not main aim	4. Intentionality	5. Personal creativity	2. Knowledge about music
B	5. Activated by individuals 6. Collaborative/collegial	3. Ownership	1. Selection of material 3. Friendship groups	3. Unfamiliar repertoire 6. Self-expression/collaboration reduced
C	1. Organic/holistic		4. Holistic rather than sequential	4. Differentiation
D	3. Activity-based	2. Learning style	2. Copying by ear	1. Conceptual 5. Not so practical
E	2. Contextual	1. Situation	1. Selection of material	1. Conceptual 3. Unfamiliar repertoire
	A: Intentionality	**B**: Agency	**C**: Patterning	**D**: Experience/concept **E**: Socio-architectural dimension

The selection of material by learners in friendship groups to foster familiarity, enjoyment, and the exchange of skills and knowledge in Green's model (2008: 10) has its correlate in the activation by individuals and collaborative/collegial pairing in Jenkins' construct (2011: 187). Agency delineates both individuals and social groupings, so it accounts for how people might be interacting to instigate and progress some kind of creative endeavour, whether solo or collaborative.

Patterning

Patterning describes the order of learning, which could be organic and holistic, in that making a track in the project studio will mean 'integrating several elements at the same time' (Jenkins 2011: 185), such as acquiring and configuring equipment, controlling software, grasping musical features of a style, and learning how to interact productively with others. The order in which these elements will need to be learned might not be knowable before the process is begun but is determined by immediate and emerging needs. Green captures this holistic quality with reference to the 'haphazard, idiosyncratic' ways that music might be approached in 'real-world' contexts, as opposed to linear, cumulative progressions characteristic of music curricula (2008: 10).

While the organic/holistic view is useful for capturing the contingent, emergent nature of learning processes, it disguises the fundamentally sequential nature of the lifespan of a project (see Slater 2015). Projects mature over time and skills develop: skills required in the very early stages of a project are different to those of more seasoned producers taking on more ambitious challenges (such as multi-tracking of large ensembles with multiple microphone arrays). While the planning of curricula (which implies something about intentionality and agency) allows for the differentiation of tasks to match an individual's abilities, the patterning of learning in a context such as the project studio is, in effect, self-differentiating because it is self-ordering in its contingency.

Experience and concept

Experience and concept foreground the intersection between learning through doing versus the development of conceptual knowledge that can take place abstractly. Jenkins describes forms of learning that are 'activity and experience based' (2011: 186), in which experimentation, rehearsal, and performativity provide the basis of an immediate engagement with music and which could be intuitive and perhaps haphazard in nature. The cornerstone of skill acquisition in Green's approach is copying recordings by ear (2008: 10), which recalls Folkestad's predication of learning style on the materials being used – notation versus recording (2006: 141). Cain counterposes these facets with 'conceptual learning' based upon the learning of technical features and terminology to enable informed discussion and analysis (2013: 15).

The relationship between the experiential and the conceptual is, however, dynamic. For example, the refinement of skill in EQing a multi-track drum recording comes through practice, through moving pots with the fingers (either mechanised on the mixing desk or in software with a mouse) and listening to the results. This skill can only be refined in context, by doing, because the effect of those changes on the listener is aesthetic. The concept of equalisation and the psychoacoustic effects of the interaction of frequencies can by learned abstractly wherever the textbook can be opened or the forum accessed but cannot account for the rich and unpredictable diversity of variables along the way (the condition of the snare drum, the temperament of the player, the microphones, the cables, the pre-amp, the plugins, the mixing room, the disposition of the listener).

While the experience/concept duality recalls a body/mind distinction, it is more usefully considered in relation to context-sensitivity (that a skill relates directly to the specific circumstance in which it is required or deployed) and experience-dependence (how one develops skills and knowledge, and draws upon that prior experience as a conceptualised memory to carry out a task; Jenkins 2011: 182).

Socio-architectural dimension

The socio-architectural dimension accounts for the situated nature of learning. While buildings and locations are not determinative of a particular approach to learning (as Folkestad's 'situation' definition would have it [2006: 141]), they do act upon the activities that go on within them by affording certain possibilities (see Gibson 2005). Despite the prevalence of information and communication technologies that undermine the primacy of geographic location, this dimension reminds us that learning is contextual: it is specific to a moment and a social setting. While a project studio might exist in a solitary room with walls on all four sides, the music that is made there is unlikely to exist in isolation from broader cultural artefacts and forces. Moreover, those in the project studio are compelled to learn how to acknowledge and manage their relationship with the broader musical world as well as the practicalities of what it means to have a music studio in a domestic setting.

Learning in the project studio

Learning is context-specific. By capturing something about the project-studio context through the Middlewood Sessions case study, it is easy to convey what the participants said they were learning: how to work with one another, control technology, negotiate with record labels, engage an audience, recognise and distribute roles, balance work and family life, develop effective working processes, understand and value emerging attitudes, configure physical spaces, function within professional studios, get to grips with legalities, translate material from the studio to the live stage (the list goes on). For those working in music-technology education or in the music-production industry, much of this will not be surprising. But in the run of the project, the sequence of events is haphazard and the motivation to learn particular things is driven by immediate concerns: participants had to work out what knowledge and skills they needed as they went along. Participants' discourse suggests four principal categories to describe what they perceived they were learning at the time: technological expertise, technical skill, socio-logistical skills, and idiolect.

The fabric of the studio is populated in accordance with a developing technological expertise. The type and quality of technology is part of a 'knowledge system' (McIntyre 2008: 3) that has to be grasped to facilitate creative action: 'the technology I own has vastly improved in quality. And it is good enough – it just wasn't good enough early enough, and that's part of the learning process really . . . What mics to buy, what computer to buy, what software to use' (Interview 3). Once technologies are suitably in place, the locus of learning shifts to the technical skills required to extend and nuance their application. In the earlier stages, multi-tracking single players in the home provided a low-stakes environment to hone basic microphone techniques, refine approaches to musical arrangement and improve skills in controlling software to maintain a productive workflow. The introduction of larger instrumental groups in the later stages (a seven-piece string orchestra and a nine-piece horn section) brought with it a socio-logistical complexity that had to be understood and controlled.

> In hindsight, we should have started with 'Weightless'. . . . 'Weightless' features long sustained notes and it would've given the ensemble an easy introduction into the recording environment. Instead, the rhythms of 'Morning Star', not particularly easy, presented quite a challenge. The importance of this is that recording sessions need to be organised not only in terms of logistics and precision (notation, equipment) but also in terms of how the session unfolds, what it feels like to be playing and how to maintain a sense of progress and positivity
>
> (Diary, June 2008).

Learning is social as much as it is technical and technological. But all of this supports a more continuous and predominant preoccupation: the development of a musical idiolect that is understood as a subsidiary of the broader notion of style (Moore 2012: 120). To formulate an individual, recognisable sonic identity, the musical features of the formative musical influences and, self-reflexively, the features of the original music being made need to be understood: melody, harmony, rhythm, groove, structure, phrasing, articulation, timbre, texture, lyric topics.

I have derived the four categories of what was being learned from an accumulated list extracted from the data (a fairly straightforward compilation task). To explain how such categories of skills and knowledge were being learned, I propose four processes: encounter, exchange, enculturation, and experimentation. These processes are derived from a theorisation of processes that were spun out over quite some time, spanning a complex set of activities, interactions, doubts, epiphanies, and events.

Encounter

As the project-studio collaboration ages, experiences are accumulated and skills refined. This development is related to the chronological lifespan of the project – people get better at controlling technology through practice, vocabularies of music grow, and the quality of output improves through a mutual interplay of skill development and aspiration. The trajectory of Middlewood Sessions, from amateur pursuit to professional endeavour, traced an expansion of personnel and locations in line with a growing ambition. Expansion has a centre–periphery pattern, with each new layer representing an encounter that has to be navigated. Hennion characterises the (professional) studio as an 'isolation tank' where experiments are carried out by the intermediary producer who, embodying a proxy public, coaxes out, tests, and shapes the musician's talents and individualities before reconstructing these 'bits and pieces' for a 'circle of actual auditors that is gradually widened' (1989: 416). The track – a construction, a representation, a work of art – ripples out to a public that had been imagined and represented in the isolation of the studio. This widening reach, extending from a localised centre, applies to the artefacts of a studio but it also describes a developmental lifespan in which additional actors (people, technologies) and locations are gradually implicated in the constitution of the project studio (Figure 1.1).

At its simplest, a project studio has a central husk consisting of core protagonists (those who instigate and direct the flow of the project) and technology (to capture, store, process, replay, and compare the emergent musical materials). In this case study, family also figured in the core, implicated by the domestic setting and representing the first of the widening circle of auditors. The relationships implied here constitute the initial construct of encounters that has to be navigated: core members need to grasp one another's attitudes and predilections; the capabilities and limitations of technologies need to be mapped out and incorporated into the shared conception for how to encode ideas in sound; and the boundaries of working in the home, with all the repetition and noise that entails, need to be negotiated with family.

As the project stabilises and intentions crystallise, the aspiration towards more polished production invites collaboration with instrumentalists, technicians, and visual artists: social, technical, musical and geographic dimensions grow commensurately. Recording sessions in professional studios, on-location in the drummer's basement studio, or in a converted grain loft are manifestations of the widening circle of encounters whose ripples continue outwards towards an audience – a listening public reached through labels releasing the music, DJs' radio playlists or dance-floor sets and, most directly, during live performance where the once-notional public is present. Each encounter demands learning: the decisiveness required to commit the nascent music to paper, ready for the musicians to play on the day-trip to the professional studio; the legal framework codifying the relationship between artist and label; the logistics of transporting all of the apparatus for performance across the miles between Sheffield and London; the challenges of translating music conceived in the comfort of the spare room to the live stage

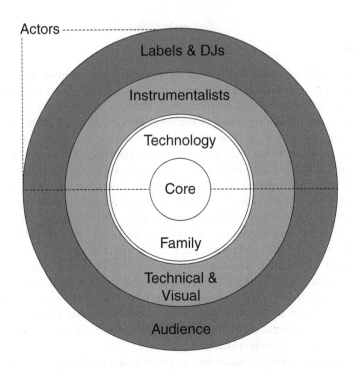

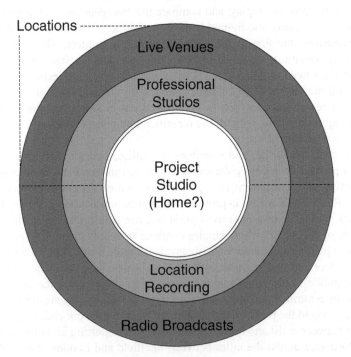

Figure 1.1 Layers of actors and locations

(from imagination to reality); the growing presence of a public with its voice trickling back through snippets of reaction online or captured in the immediacy of a bodily response on the dance floor. This learning is predominantly socio-architectural in nature because encounters tend to involve people or technologies in particular places.

Exchange

The process of demonstrative exchange encapsulates the moment when someone (the agent for learning in that moment) brings a track to a session – either long-cherished or recently discovered – and effuses about structural, rhythmic, melodic, or timbral characteristics of importance to them. The informality of the process should not undermine its potency because it is the means by which a constellation of artefacts coalesces to provide a tangible construct of reference against which the aspirations and achievements of the emerging creative endeavour are measured. It is also the immersive process through which 'the conventions, the knowledges, the system of symbolic codes and techniques' are represented and acquired (McIntyre 2008: 3). In the gestative stages of a project, each track represents a foothold on the path towards establishing a sense of sonic identity in a wider music culture. The ephemeral notions of collective creative identity and aspiration are made tangible because the recordings of works by other artists are just so. Vinyl, CDs, and data files encode musical, cultural, and sonic values, but they also represent finality and fixity – all the stuff of aspiration. Listening to developing material stage-by-stage and side-by-side with existing recordings on the same audio system, spaced apart by fractions of a second, enables a comparison that starkly reveals any disparities in sonic and emotive qualities. Aspiration can be played out and rehearsed in seconds, and the proximity of achievement gauged: as disparity diminishes, achievement approaches.

The constellation of artefacts has to be mirrored by a constellation of skills. The sharing of musical influences proves vital for the early constructions of a shared identity but insufficient to sustain a creative endeavour to maturity much in line with Porcello's observation that 'seasoned engineers and producers in professional settings rarely talk about music in associative terms' (2004: 749). While the emphasis might shift away from exploring musical and sonic patterns towards describing specific instrumental techniques for an arrangement or an explanation of the physics underpinning a microphone array, the notion of exchange remains. While complementarity of musical interests triggers the creative endeavour in the first place, complementarity of skills between all those involved is more vital in the longer term.

Enculturation

Collaboration is a collision of ideas, experiences, and skills. The attraction of collaboration is that encultured histories come into contact. While the process of demonstrative exchange sets up the means by which encultured expertise can be expressed, the organisation of each person's contribution represents a fundamental type of learning. Enculturation describes how people develop expertise according to an engagement with a specific culture (learning corresponds to socio-architectural and experiential/conceptual dimensions in this respect), but here enculturation is understood as a process played out through demonstrative exchanges that mutually affect collaborators. More than simply a resource of knowledge to be shared, enculturated expertise has to be acknowledged and organised.

The participants' discourse in this particular case study reveals a division of roles into two broad categories: creative and technical. Whilst this is a false dichotomy – creativity requires technique, and technical control constitutes an aspect of creativity – the language used to invoke these two states of activity is revealing. The generation of grooves, as a commonly used placeholder for broader notions of creativity (meaning, specifically, spontaneous ideation), is described in naturalistic terms (seeds, germination, water, fluid, flow) while the effort to bring these germs to fruition is couched in mechanistic, menial language (editing, cutting, correcting, tidying, selecting, deciding). In extending this idea, role divisions also resemble an ontological binary reminiscent of the recording and the score, which emerges from the enculturated positions of the two original core members. One has a background rooted in DJ culture, which brought him into contact with particular styles of music based on groove, infusing his engagement with music with notions of immediacy. The other drew on an engagement with experimentalist traditions through formal study that centred around notation and improvisation, which although stylistically disparate, proved complementary to notions of spontaneity implicit in turntablism.

Each history represents a musical ontology that implies a channel of enculturation. One – the recording, understood as the cornerstone of DJ culture – represents a musical culture of shared immediacy; the other – the score, understood as a functional object to facilitate a translation from imagined sound to codified visual representation to audible sound – requires solitary, meticulous attention to written detail. There is no subtext of values here, but there are differences of each type that need to be acknowledged so that the implicit expertise can be deployed as part of a constellation of skills.

Experimentation

Experimentalism forms an indelible genetic imprint on the project studio; it was present as a motivational force in the early 1970s and it persists in the ad hoc experiments in the spare room. Experimentalism is predicated on the availability of time, but it also points to the presence of a permissive and complicit social network whose agency propels learning and discovery in a spirit of collaboration and exploration. Such informality of social relations provides the basis for recursive approaches to musical creativity: isolated blocks of embryonic music can be trialled or the minutiae of technical configurations can be tested in the gradual clarification of the emerging identity as encoded in sound. As the project matures, the location of experimentation shifts from the elucidation of a sonic identity and development of practical skills to a conscious effort to extend knowledge and to test the possibilities of pre-existing skills. The decision to record a seven-piece string section in a grain loft was driven as much by the desire to find out how to do it as the musical opportunities afforded by the ensemble and location – the dynamic nature of intentionality is played out.

Conclusion

In the early stages, the fate of the project was determined by the ability of individuals to develop the skills and knowledge they needed to make their music. As the project grew, new challenges required expanded yet refined knowledge and skills – and new ways to acquire them. Learning in the project studio is most easily situated with the individual, with what they know and can do, but this has its limitations.

> I've learnt that I'm a good arranger, I've learnt that I understand musical structure. . . . I think I've learnt that I should have confidence in my musical instinct, and that's something which is not easy. I've also learnt the technical stuff . . . the software, the mics. I've also learnt what my limitations are. I am quite geeky but there's a point where I can't go any further. So I've learnt, as well, to delegate and that other people's skills and expertise are far more valuable than me trying to acquire those skills in order to maintain control. And it's that relinquishment of needing to do every aspect of a project which has been really good – I'm really pleased that that's what I've learnt. (Interview 3)

Emphasis shifts away from the development of the individual's skills and knowledge towards those of the collective: how to collaborate, how to delegate, how to organise expertise, and how to access and value the skills that others have.

The focus of this chapter has been on emergent learning processes that go on outside formal institutions and curricula as part of a collaborative creative endeavour. While the case study is highly specific (and its specificity is valued here), there are two theoretical structures that have emerged which might have applications in other contexts. The first of these, the five dimensions of learning, has been developed here as a descriptive tool to capture the intentionality, agency, patterning, balance between experience and concept, and socio-architectural situation of particular instances of learning activity. All five dimensions apply to all learning activities. An inversion of this tool, from description to generation, might lead those involved in designing curricula for implementation in institutional settings, whether educational or professional, to consider how to harness the different forces at play in learning activities in a refreshed way. Such an approach would acknowledge the more nuanced view of the possible range of learning styles that is obscured by the over-simplified binary of 'formal' and 'informal' learning. Inflections of each of the five dimensions could lead to an engaging mix of tasks, teaching approaches, and learning activities that, although derived from an exploration of a specific example of creative music making practice, might also be relevant to other subject areas. In this sense, the five dimensions of learning constitute a general pedagogic tool.

The second structure – that of encounter, exchange, enculturation, and experimentation – captures processes specific to collaborative creative activity. While these processes might apply to the design principles of curricula, particularly at task level, there are perhaps most directly relevant for those embarking on a similar creative endeavour: acknowledging and identifying how such processes are playing out (or not) might help participants understand the underlying nature of their collaboration, or might help provide a functional basis upon which a collaboration can be built. Even though these processes are derived from a single case study, they have explanatory power that presents a potent framework for understanding how participants in a collaboration learn what they need know, as they go along, in the pursuit of their shared creative goals.

The primary purpose here was to understand the processes through which knowledge and skills are developed and deployed in the pursuit of a creative end. All of the studies cited in the discussion and formulation of the five dimensions of learning are concerned with the flow from the informal to the formal or the contextualisation of 'formal' education in relation to a much wider range of learning and knowledge-sharing activities. For those working in the project studio, there was no outward flow – they were learning what they needed at that point in time for their own ends. The content and processes of their learning emerged in relation to that particular, immediate context. But while participants had different preoccupations (making their music), the description and theorisation of situated learning processes that I offer here opens up a conduit through which a flow – towards various educational contexts or other creative endeavours (from praxis to practice, or from praxis to praxis) – may potentially begin.

Note

1 Brownswood Recordings (2007) and Wah Wah 45s (2008).

References

Beckett, D., and P. Hager (2002). *Life, Work and Learning: Practice in Postmodernity*. London: Routledge.

Blake, D. (1973). 'Make Your Own Record: At Home'. *Melody Maker*, 20 Jan.: 34.

Born, G. (2005). 'On Musical Mediation: Ontology, Technology and Creativity'. *Twentieth-Century Music*, 2/1: 7–36.

Brock-Nannestad, G. (2012). 'The Lacquer Disc for Immediate Playback: Professional Recording and Home Recording from the 1920s to the 1950s'. In S. Frith and S. Zagorski-Thomas (eds), *The Art of Record Production: An Introductory Reader for a New Academic Field*. Farnham: Ashgate.

Cain, T. (2013). ' "Passing It On": Beyond Formal or Informal Pedagogies'. *Music Education Research*, 15/1: 74–91.

Coombs, P.H. and M. Ahmed (1974). *Attacking Rural Poverty: How Non-Formal Education Can Help*. Baltimore, MA: John Hopkins University Press.

Crowdy, D. (2007). 'Studios at Home in the Solomon Islands: A Case Study of Homesound Studios, Honiara'. *World of Music*, 49/1: 143–54.

Davis, S.G. (2005). ' "That Thing You Do!" Compositional Processes of a Rock Band'. *International Journal of Education and the Arts*, 6/16. Available at <http://www.ijea.org/v6n16> (accessed 2 Apr. 2013).

Feichas, H. (2010). 'Bridging the Gap: Informal Learning Practices as a Pedagogy of Integration'. *British Journal of Music Education*, 27/1: 47–58.

Finney, J., and C. Philpott (2010). 'Informal Learning and Meta-Pedagogy in Initial Teacher Education in England'. *British Journal of Music Education*, 27/1: 7–19.

Folkestad, G. (2006). 'Formal and Informal Learning Situations or Practices vs Formal and Informal Ways of Learning'. *British Journal of Music Education*, 23/2: 135–45.

Fornäs, J., U. Lindberg, and O. Sernhede (1995). *In Garageland: Rock, Youth and Modernity*. London: Routledge.

Gibson, C. (2005). 'Recording Studios: Relational Spaces of Creativity in the City'. *Built Environment*, 31/3: 192–207.

Green, L. (2002). *How Popular Musicians Learn: A Way Ahead for Music Education*. Aldershot: Ashgate.

—— (2008). *Music, Informal Learning and School: A New Classroom Pedagogy*. Farnham: Ashgate.

Greene, P. (2001). 'Mixed Messages: Unsettled Cosmopolitanisms in Nepali Pop'. *Popular Music*, 20/2: 168–87.

Hennion, A. (1989). 'An Intermediary between Production and Consumption: The Producer of Popular Music'. *Science, Technology and Human Values*, 14/4: 400–424.

Horning, S.S. (2004). 'Engineering the Performance: Recording Engineers, Tacit Knowledge and the Art of Controlling Sound'. *Social Studies of Science*, 34/5: 703–31.

Jaffurs, S.E. (2004). 'The Impact of Informal Music Learning Practices in the Classroom, or How I Learned to Teach from a Garage Band'. *International Journal of Music Education*, 22/3: 189–200.

Jenkins, P. (2011). 'Formal and Informal Music Educational Practices'. *Philosophy of Music Education Review*, 19/2: 179–97.

Karlsen, S. (2010). 'BoomTown Music Education and the Need for Authenticity: Informal Learning Put into Practice in Swedish Post-Compulsory Music Education'. *British Journal of Music Education*, 27/1: 35–46.

Leyshon, A. (2009). 'The Software Slump? Digital Music, the Democratisation of Technology, and the Decline of the Recording Studio Sector within the Musical Economy'. *Environment and Planning A*, 41: 1309–31.

McIntyre, P. (2008). 'The Systems Model of Creativity: Analyzing the Distribution of Power in the Studio'. *Journal of the Art of Record Production*, 3. Available at <http://arpjournal.com/686/the-systems-model-of-creativity-analyzing-the-distribution-of-power-in-the-studio> (accessed 30 Sept. 2013).

Moore, A.F. (2012). *Song Means: Analysing and Interpreting Recorded Popular Song*. Farnham: Ashgate.

Partti, H., and S. Karlsen (2010). 'Reconceptualising Musical Learning: New Media, Identity and Community in Music Education'. *Music Education Research*, 12/4: 369–82.

Porcello, T. (2004). 'Speaking of Sound: Language and the Professionalization of Sound-Recording Engineers'. *Social Studies of Science*, 34/5: 733–58.

Robinson, T. (2012). 'Popular Musicians and Instrumental Teachers: The Influence of Informal Learning on Teaching Strategies'. *British Journal of Music Education*, 29/3: 359–70.

Salavuo, M. (2006). 'Open and Informal Online Communities as Forums of Collaborative Musical Activities and Learning'. *British Journal of Music Education*, 23/3: 253–71.

Savage, J. (2005). 'Working Towards a Theory for Music Technologies in the Classroom: How Pupils Engage with and Organise Sounds with New Technologies'. *British Journal of Music Education*, 22/2: 167–80.

Slater, M. (2015). 'Nests, Arcs and Cycles in the Lifespan of a Studio Project'. *Popular Music* 34/1: 67–93.

—— (2016). 'Locating Project Studios and Studio Projects'. *Journal of the Royal Musical Association*, 141/1: 167–202.

—— and A. Martin (2012). 'A Conceptual Foundation for Understanding Musico-Technological Creativity'. *Journal of Music, Technology and Education*, 5/1: 59–76.

Smith, J.A., P. Flowers, and M. Larkin (2009). *Interpretative Phenomenological Analysis: Theory, Method and Research*. London: Sage.

Söderman, J., and G. Folkestad (2004). 'How Hip-hop Musicians Learn: Strategies in Informal Creative Music Making'. *Music Education Research*, 6/3: 313–26.

Spradley, J.P. (1980). *Participant Observation*. Orlando, FL: Holt, Rinehart & Winston.

Théberge, P. (1997). *Any Sound You Can Imagine: Making Music / Consuming Technology*. Middletown, CT: Wesleyan University Press.

—— (2004). 'The Network Studio: Historical and Technological Paths to a New Ideal in Music Making'. *Social Studies of Science*, 34/5: 759–81.

Thompson, P. (2012). 'An Empirical Study into the Learning Practices and Enculturation of DJs, Turntablists, Hip Hop and Dance Music Producers'. *Journal of Music, Technology and Education*, 5/1: 43–58.

Väkevä, L. (2010). 'Garage Band or GarageBand®? Remixing Musical Futures'. *British Journal of Music Education*, 27/1: 59–70.

Wadsworth, P. (2007). 'Strawberry Recording Studios and the Development of Recording Studios in Britain, c.1967–93'. PhD thesis: University of Manchester.

Waldron, J. (2009). 'Exploring a Virtual Music "Community of Practice": Informal Music Learning on the Internet'. *Journal of Music, Technology and Education*, 2/2–3: 97–112.

—— (2013). 'YouTube, Fanvids, Forums, Vlogs and Blogs: Informal Music Learning in a Convergent On- and Offline Music Community'. *International Journal of Music Education*, 31/1: 91–105.

Yin, R.K. (2009). *Case Study Research: Design and Methods*. 4th edn, London: Sage.

2 What has been left unsaid about studio practices

How producers and engineers prepare, manage, and direct recording sessions

Amandine Pras

During recording sessions, record producers and sound engineers play the role of cultural intermediaries between musicians and their future audience. Their role differs from that of artistic leaders, such as film directors, who express their own ideas through a collective creative process. Studio professionals aim to achieve the best possible representation of a given musical project, similarly to photographers, whose goal is to capture the most significant image of their models.

Recently, the delocalisation of well-equipped studios to home studios, combined with the collapse of the traditional business model of record companies, has led musicians to produce their recordings without necessarily hiring studio professionals. And when hired by musicians, producers and engineers often take on both roles at once. This client relationship without the intermediary of record companies modifies the collaborative aspects of the production process. In such a do-it-yourself context, studio professionals need to reinvent their job while musicians need to learn the art of recording and define their expectations when collaborating with studio professionals.

This chapter is based on my professional and teaching experience, as well as five research studies conducted with professional producers, engineers, and musicians. In three sections, it highlights the best practices in conducting recording sessions from the perspectives of musicians and studio professionals coming from different musical backgrounds, countries, and generations. The first section focuses on the preparation of studio sessions to produce successful musical recordings. The second discusses record producers' and sound engineers' skills, as well as the mission and specificities of each profession. The third addresses the myths of artistic direction by making explicit the impact of producers' comments on musical performance.

Introduction

Audio recording has always been about myths. It is common to hear people praising the advantages of analogue versus digital audio or tube versus condenser technology. Some audiophiles aim for vinyl and tapes, others for high-resolution formats. Lately, it has also been trendy to produce lo-fi recordings, which implies the use of cheap gear to record and mix in the box, and then to release MP3 files likely to be played back on earphones or computer speakers. Limitless combinations of these approaches are now possible. Some of my students recorded a performance on a full drum kit to get the rhythmic feel that they wanted and computed a program that changed the drum sounds into simulated 1980s keyboard sounds. They played back these keyboard sounds through a 1970s guitar amplifier and used high-fidelity microphones, pre-amps, and converters to record the sound coming out of the amplifier. This is an exciting time for recording with new and old technology available at different costs, allowing for wild creative ideas in the production process but necessitating important decisions and compromises. While making these decisions, preparation, knowledge, and experience of technology rather than myths or trendiness play a crucial role in ensuring the originality of a production.

The recording industry has encountered major changes during the last 20 years, following the introduction of digital technologies in the 1980s and internet file sharing at the end of the 1990s. Twenty years ago an album would involve a complete production team including a record producer, a recording engineer, a sound editor, a mixer, and a mastering engineer working in studios that were paid for by the record company. At present studio professionals are likely to handle all these roles at once on their own equipment. Musicians, who must finance and manage their recording project themselves without the support of a record company aim for autonomy and thus do not necessarily hire studio professionals from the early stages of their production. In this do-it-yourself context, it is difficult for them to know when it is a good time to call in studio professionals and what to expect from them.

The creative process of recordings is not restricted to sound choices. An artistic approach to capturing good takes also requires preparation and decision-making, such as whether or not the music is going to be recorded in a studio with the full ensemble playing together or separately. Similar to the myths of the audio world, the artistic process of recordings is also subject to many beliefs, such as the first take being the most musical one or the record producers' psychological manipulation being responsible for the transformation of the artists' music. In the same vein, it is common to hear people stating that live recordings are more real than studio recordings or that studio recordings are more authentic without editing. Some free jazz musicians and fans go so far as to state that the process of recording itself kills the music. With the variety of portable equipment that is available at present, recording can occur in any kind of venue and situation with as many tracks as needed and live concerts can be retouched in the studio afterwards. If desired, it is still possible to avoid editing and to capture only one take per piece. It is also possible to choose not to record. But when the decision has been made to capture several takes of a same musical project in a recording studio, an awareness of the impact of the session flow, the producers' comments and the musicians' self-evaluation on the musical performance is necessary.

In this chapter I focus on the preparation, management, and artistic direction of recording sessions. This choice was driven by the tacit characteristic of these practical and social aspects of studio practices that used to be learned on the job.

At present these tacit skills might be taught in school programmes, though students would only have access to a few approaches while in the past a young intern could observe the approach of more than a hundred professionals in a year in a large studio. Therefore there is a pedagogical need for documentation of studio practices from different professional perspectives.

In parallel with the increase in the number of school programmes that offer sound recording courses, the literature on studio practices has increased greatly in the last 15 years. The Art of Record Production was founded in 2005 by researchers and practitioners to discuss studio practices in the context of recent changes of the industry (Frith and Zagorski-Thomas 2012), thus complementing the Audio Engineering Society (AES) and the Tonmeistertagung in Germany who have contributed strongly to the understanding of recording technology for more than 60 years, though with little publication beyond the technology. The academic field of sound studies emerged in the 2000s with a special issue of *Social Studies of Science* (Pinch and Bijsterveld 2004). Studio observations and case studies have been carried on in ethnomusicology in keeping with the democratisation of recording technology (e.g. Greene 2005). Many record producers' manuals and self-reports have been published (e.g. Burgess 2013; Moorefield 2005), as have a collection of famous sound artists' texts (Cox and Warner 2004); the recording technique of Decca producer John Culshaw (Patmore and Clarke 2007), books on the evolution of recording technology (e.g. Chanan 1995; Sterne 2003; Théberge 1997; Zak 2001), and books on the recording process of famous albums that give insight into both sound engineering and session flow (e.g. Ryan and Kehew 2006; Kahn 2001). Although all these sources can be fascinating and have played an important part in my interest in recording, they remain separate case studies that do not follow a systematic research protocol with practitioners.

Hennion (1989) conducted the first ethnographic study into recording studios producing French pop music in the 1980s. He introduced the concept of record producers as cultural intermediaries between the artists and their audience. I extend this concept in this chapter, building on five research studies involving the perspectives of professional record producers, sound engineers, and musicians from different countries, generations, and musical backgrounds. These five studies were conducted between 2008 and 2011 as part of my doctoral thesis at McGill University under the supervision of Catherine Guastavino and in collaboration with musicologist Maryse Lavoie and linguist Caroline Cance. This investigation into different approaches to conducting recording sessions in the current context of production contributes to the research into the analysis of creative processes in music developed by Donin and Thereau (2007) at IRCAM (Paris). Here I report and discuss the five studies' main findings and turn them into practical tools based on my professional and teaching experience.

This work is intended for students, instructors, professionals, and researchers who are interested in musical recording beyond the limitations of musical genre or cultural background. It should be useful for composers and performers who want to learn the art of recording for their own projects and for sound engineers and record producers who question their roles and practices in current music production. In the first section, I present methods to prepare studio sessions according to the aesthetics, constraints, and specificities of a given project in order to provide suitable sound technology and facilitate session flow. In the second section, I describe the roles of record producers and sound engineers at present, with an emphasis on their communication skills. In the third section, I address the impact of record producers' comments on musical performance. The emphasis is on the recording process, not post-production: editing, mixing, and mastering. In conclusion, I propose future directions for research into studio practices as part of the analysis of creative processes in music.

How to prepare for a recording session

Walking into a studio can be a very stressful experience for musicians, who might have spent a significant amount of money for one or two days there, and for sound engineers who are not familiar with the equipment and installation of the venue. I argue that in the current context of recording, appropriate preparation minimises this stress, which goes against the idea that preparation compromises spontaneity and thus the genuine quality of the artistic result. To compare my own preparation to other professionals' practices, I sent an email survey to all the participants of the 2008 Banff International Workshop in Jazz and Creative Music, which included talented young musicians and sound engineers, asking them how they prepared for a recording session (Pras and Guastavino 2011). I also organised a studio experiment during the workshop to test a pre-production method (Pras and Guastavino 2009). The email survey and studio experiment were complemented by interviews with six experienced record producers who had worked throughout the transitional phase of the recording industry (Pras, Cance, and Guastavino 2013; Pras, Lavoie, and Guastavino 2013).[1] Here I comment on the results of these three studies and then present my own preparation approach and teaching ideas.

The perspective of young musicians and sound engineers on session preparation[2]

Fifteen musicians and five sound engineers replied to the question about preparation in the email survey.[3] Musicians mainly expounded on learning the musical material and rehearsing. Their second major concern was how they would prepare physically and warm up to be ready to play. Only two mentioned any need to know about the studio and setup – for example, whether or not there would be acoustic separation or not – and only one would listen to some CDs to get an idea of the type of sound he would be required to produce. Moreover, only one of the musicians raised the question of production factors, while the musicians as a group reported themselves as producing 25 per cent of the sessions they were involved in. On the other hand, sound engineers mainly commented on collecting information about musicians' habits and expectations: how and where they recorded in the past, how they liked to perform, and what their style and aesthetics were. Secondly, they detailed the technical preparation, which included making a list and reservation of microphones, learning how to use the studio equipment, and listening to other recordings in the same genre. They also mentioned planning and administrative troubleshooting. The five sound engineers reported themselves as producing 50 per cent of the sessions they were involved in. These results highlight a discrepancy between musicians, who do not seem to prepare for a recording session any differently than for a concert, and sound engineers, who are very aware of the different parameters beyond technical concerns. While the specific artistic requirements of a recording project are of course well known to the musicians, in the case of self-production the artistic leader needs to think about sound aesthetics before the recording session. Interestingly, sound engineers emphasised the importance of talking with musicians, while musicians did not feel any need to talk with sound engineers.

Evaluation of a preparation method during pre-production meetings[4]

I had engineered several sessions during the 2007 workshop, for which I received the line-up only a few hours beforehand, with no clue about the musical genre and often without the musicians' names. I knew the equipment and the different setup possibilities of the particular studio fairly well, but the organisational limitations did not allow me to get the best out of these sessions, which I felt was a shame since these young musicians were not likely to have access to such a high quality studio very often. This situation gave me the idea of testing my pre-production approach with controlled parameters. A year later 34 musicians from the 2008 workshop – grouped into seven ensembles to be recorded by four sound engineers – participated in pre-production meetings in which I asked them to describe the musical genre of their ensemble and what kind of sound and setup they had in mind for the session. To help them, I provided examples, such as acoustic separation, overdubbing, amount of reverberation, and stereo image. For each criterion, I encouraged them to justify their request. Then, I asked them about their previous recordings as well as other musicians' albums that they would consider as representative of the sound qualities required in their musical genre. Sound engineers could ask any question during these meetings and had to attend a rehearsal or a concert performance of the ensemble before the session. After the workshop, I sent individual emails to all participants to get their feedback on the sound quality.

Only ten musicians replied, but they were all very satisfied with the result. All four sound engineers replied and expressed reservations on the sound quality for five out of the seven sessions and explained how they would have achieved a better result, still in keeping to the musician's requests. They mentioned that the musicians' expectations generated a clear sound quality goal, without forcing them to use specific microphones or techniques. Therefore, the pre-production method succeeded in pleasing the musicians and assisting the sound engineers without them feeling constrained. The meetings included all the sound engineers' descriptions of their preparation from the email survey to provide examples to help the musicians express their ideas and expectations without calling for specific microphones or techniques.

Experienced record producers' perspective on session preparation

In 2009 and 2010, I interviewed six record producers who had more than 20 years of studio experience and were still actively working in music production.[5] All agreed on the need to meet the main artists in the project, the leaders and soloists, in person in order to learn about their personalities, their artistic approaches and influences, and to establish the producer's role and level of artistic involvement in the sessions. They stated how essential it is to go and listen to the musicians live or in rehearsal in order to understand the performers' style, their musical language and sensitivity, and their technical skills and weaknesses, so as to make sure they were ready to record. They also mentioned the importance of analysing the artists' previous records. Moreover, they detailed all the technical and practical parameters that need to be addressed: booking, planning, budgeting, checking the studio acoustics and equipment, hiring a piano tuner, ordering the edition of the score used by the musicians for classical productions, making a microphone list, and so on. However, one particular pop/rock producer reported not preparing anything for the session itself besides having a conceptual discussion with the musicians, especially if he had never worked with them before. This producer has his own professional studio in his house, and he decides on the amount time that he dedicates to each album he produces. Therefore, his working conditions allow him to avoid making decisions before the session and thus to keep as much spontaneity as possible. Classical and contemporary music producers emphasised the need to study the score in order to be able to discuss interpretive choices with the musicians: for example, tempo and incoherencies. Those who wanted to avoid being influenced by previous productions would play the score on the piano; others would opt for listening to earlier versions if they were available. One of the classical producers mentioned two changes in his preparation approach over the years. With experience, he no longer needs to study scores as much as he did 25 years ago. Though, he used to arrive at a session with his only preparation being a knowledge of the score and technical and administrative parameters, at present he meets the musicians in advance to make decisions about the recording setup, session flow, editing, and corrections. Although these producers have different approaches to recording preparation, they all agree on the need to meet the artists before the session, especially nowadays when studio time has become so precious.

My preparation approach and teaching ideas

Similarly to the record producers interviewed, I always meet the musicians before a recording session, or at least the leader of the project. It can be as much as a year in advance for a big project to give them time to work on their ideas and to give me time to come up with propositions before designing a concrete production scenario. Usually, at the time of our first pre-production meeting, I have already seen them live and listened to their previous records. I ask them to tell me about their musical style and influences and the type of sound and production they have in mind by providing examples such as the ones detailed in the preparation method discussed above. Young musicians are likely to find the questions a bit challenging and may often change their minds when they realise that they have answered me just based on previous studio experiences and production trends instead of real creative desires; however, I encourage them to question their answers and keep me informed. I may challenge their suggestions if they seem too distant from their live sound. For example, the first record that I produced was for a French pop band who wanted to sound like U2, although they sounded like a cabaret act in concert. Experienced musicians may want to repeat what they have already done, which will inevitably sound less original: in which case I would challenge them on the purpose of the repetition. I find it important to define my role and artistic involvement during the pre-production meeting: Are they expecting me to work only on the sound? To manage the time of the recording? To provide comments on the takes? Will I do the editing? And so on. If I am expected to be involved in the artistic decisions, I attend rehearsals during which I avoid judging or saying anything about the music, even to myself. Instead I record them to be able to listen to the music at home. I ask the musicians how they feel about their performance, and I write notes to get a better idea of what they are looking for. I attempt to immerse myself the ensemble musical world for this specific recording before doing anything.

I teach a practical course in studio practices at the Steinhardt School of New York University that brings together young composers, performers, and engineers who allow me to understand the needs of the new generation. The course is designed to be as close as possible to a real-life situation. I assign one student per session to be responsible for the setup and microphone list, which must be sent to me at least two days before the session, as well as for the console and software setup during the session, and for the final mix after the session. This student also guides the students who are in charge of instrument and microphone placement during the session. Every class, the students are marked on the process as well as on the result. Different types of ensemble and musical genre are involved throughout the semester, with musicians from the class, from the programme, or external to the university. The line-up with all the musicians' names and a description of their influences and sound expectations must be provided a week before the session, requiring the students to study the musicians' background online, to listen to their previous records and influences, and to propose a studio setup and microphone list according to their sound expectations. All the technical microphone specificities are available in the online course resources so that students can consult them as often as they need. Students are required to explain all their choices for the setup and microphone list and the relation between their sound goals and their technical choices. I then comment on the student's proposition, address any problems, and suggest changes until we agree on a document that is sent to all the students in the class before the session.

The mission and skills of record producers and sound engineers

Record producer and sound engineer used to be distinct roles, but nowadays one professional is likely to handle both during a recording session. This might suggest that these roles have become vague, yet according to the email survey of participants of the 2008 Banff International Workshop in Jazz and Creative Music, young musicians and sound engineers still distinguish between them. Here I present information about the survey methods and the participants, followed by the participants' perceptions of the sound engineers' and record producers' mission and skills and then the record producers perceptions of their own mission and skills. Finally, I discuss both roles according to my own studio experience.

Survey participants and methods[6]

Sixteen musicians and six sound engineers, thirteen males and three females, with an average age of 26 from nine different countries on five continents, replied to the email survey. Twelve out of the sixteen musicians reported playing musical genres other than jazz (pop, rock, R&B, Latin, ska, reggae, classical, contemporary, electro-acoustic), and only two out of the six sound engineers had recorded jazz before. Therefore, our findings are not influenced by a specific musical genre or cultural background. However, the Banff Centre is more likely to attract musicians and sound engineers who have learned their trade in institutions than self-taught professionals. This suggest that the answers will provide interesting insights into the current conceptualisation of studio professionals' roles but should not be generalised to the entire population of young musicians and sound engineers. The 22 participants as a group reported themselves as producing 33 per cent of the sessions they were involved in, while 32.5 per cent of these sessions were produced by a musician in the band or the whole band, 17 per cent were not produced, and 17.5 per cent were produced by a record producer from outside the band. This is in line with the current trend for musicians to produce their own music and for sound engineers to take on the role of producer when there is no producer.

The survey includes two sets of complementary questions regarding sound professionals' roles. In the first set, participants were asked to give their vision of an ideal sound engineer and an ideal record producer. In the second set, participants were asked to describe their positive and negative studio experiences and their own experiences with sound engineers and record producers. These two sets of questions provided two perspectives and highlighted differences in the two groups' conceptualisation of these roles. Roles and perspectives were compared based on the constant comparison method of grounded theory (Corbin and Strauss 2008), which involves classifying all the verbal data into emerging concepts and categories and constantly re-evaluating this classification. Several researchers and professionals with different expertise commented on our classification to ensure its validity. Mission, skills, and interaction emerged as the main categories for the entire study. Skills included the sub-categories of communication, interpersonal, technical, musical, and general skills. Communication skills included creating a good environment, allowing trust and honesty, and uniting all the people involved. This sub-category and concept classification could be compared among questions.

Sound engineers' mission and skills as perceived by young professionals[7]

Participants described the sound engineers' main mission as to create a sound that matched the musicians' requests. Their desired interpersonal skills – being quick, flexible, and transparent – outweighed their desired technical and listening skills. In the first question, musician respondents did not mention any interaction between themselves and the sound engineer, which is consistent with musicians responses to the email survey where the said they felt no need to discuss their sound ideas with studio professionals before a recording session. There is an inconsistency here between the musicians' expectations of a sound suited to their project and their reluctance to interact with the sound engineer, who is supposed to be almost transparent. Some musicians mentioned positive studio experiences in which they appreciated the fact that the sound engineer explained to them what they were doing, and none of them reported negative studio experiences where the sound engineer was too invasive. Furthermore, the sound engineer's technical responsibilities were mentioned mainly when things went wrong (for example, tracks were lost with no backup). This suggests that another important mission of the sound engineer is to free the musicians of technical concerns in the studio. Of course, all other concerns are moot if nothing is recorded or labelled or the files are lost.

Record producers' mission and skills as perceived by young professionals[8]

Participants agreed that the record producer's main mission was to guide the musicians during the recording sessions by taking into consideration the aesthetic context of their project. Similarly to the sound engineer, their desired communication and interpersonal skills – creating a good atmosphere, allowing trust and honesty, uniting all the people involved, keeping people focused, efficiency, patience and compassion, and being open-minded and flexible – outweighed their musical and technical skills. Surprisingly, their listening skills were barely mentioned, although they are described as essential in the literature. Furthermore, there were different perspectives on the producer's interaction with the musicians. On the one hand, they were expected to bring objectivity and constructive ideas, in some cases acting as an artistic director of the project. On the other, some musicians expressed fear of the producer being too intrusive or controlling. They could only see them as providing an extra set of ears on the project. These different perspectives are in keeping with musicians responses to the email survey where they expressed a need to define the level of the producer's artistic involvement before a recording session.

Record producers' missions and skills as described by experienced professionals[9]

Six experienced record producers[10] described their mission as drawing the best musical performance out of the artists. They saw their artistic expertise and their listening, musical, and technical skills as central to their profession. They often referred to their communication and interpersonal skills, as essential to understanding what the project needed during pre-production, to build a trusting relationship with the artists and to keep a constant focus on the artistic result throughout the production process. They stated that they did not want to impose their own aesthetics on the musicians and that they only put forward their own ideas once they understood the project's goals and specificities. Some producers mentioned how challenging recording sessions can be for musicians. They explained that they could smooth difficult moments and conflicts that arose through lack of self-confidence or tiredness by taking decisions and reminding the musicians that they were working toward the same artistic goal.

Five of the record producers could also engineer and all six defined their role as being an interface between music and sound to ensure the coherency of the production. They insisted on the fact that there was no recipes, formulas, or absolute rules in recording and that there are many ways of enjoying a musical performance. However, they tended to seek emotions rather than technicality, this term referring to sound quality as much as musical virtuosity. Two distinct approaches to enhancing musical performances through recording technology were identified from the producer's descriptions: the *Tonmeister* approach, which attempts to create a sound picture based on a mental representation of concert experiences, and the attempt to create a new sonic dimension by using the studio as a musical instrument.[11] It should be noted that the approaches can be combined: one producer referred to the prism on the cover of Pink Floyd's *Dark Side of The Moon* that symbolised the interface between the reality of the white light and the truth of the seven colours that constitute the white light.

Discussion of both roles and different areas of expertise

The last three sections clearly demonstrate how the roles of sound engineer and record producer overlap, though implying a sufficient number of distinct responsibilities that they could be performed by more than one. When one professional is responsible for both roles, technical issues might overshadow the artistic focus or vice versa. The roles differ mainly in the degree of artistic involvement. While sound engineers are expected to gather musical information about the project, they are not supposed to provide comments on the musical performance. There are also different perspectives on the producer's role: experienced record producers affirm that they are in charge of the artistic result, while young musicians and sound engineers express reservations about this. However, all the participants emphasised the importance of communication and interpersonal skills for both record producers and sound engineers.

The most essential skills for both producers and engineers remain their listening skills. These go beyond ear training and imply the ability to listen actively for hours, requiring concentration and experience. Communication skills are very important as well, but they are useless if the interaction with the musicians is not focused on the analysis of music and sound perception. Listening skills allow studio professionals to improve their communication. For instance they can detect when a musician is tired or frustrated or not convinced by a new idea. The art of producing becomes the art of talking only when it is needed and formulating criticisms and suggestions according to what is perceived. Nevertheless, the way criticisms are communicated is crucial. If they are not respectful they end up causing more harm than if they were absent altogether.

Best practices for the artistic direction of recording sessions

According to my own studio experience, defining the level of artistic involvement is the most challenging part of any discussion with musicians, just as commenting on musical performance is the hardest part of the producer's job. These observations inspired me to investigate different levels of artistic involvement based on the verbal descriptions of their own practice by six experienced record producers (Pras, Cance, and Guastavino 2013). Analysis of those interviews provides a model of artistic direction that ranged from light coaching to deep collaboration.[12] I conducted a studio experiment at the Steinhardt School in 2010 involving musicians and record producers to evaluate the impact of producers' comments on musicians' self-evaluation on musical performance (Pras and Guastavino 2013). Here I present the interviewees' background and analysis of their verbal descriptions. Then I discuss four levels of artistic involvement by producers according to the model of artistic direction. Finally, I report the experimental procedure and the main findings of the NYU studio experiment.

Interviewees' background and analysis approach

I interviewed six record producers with outstanding portfolios that included Grammys or other equivalent awards and multiple productions with international artists. They all had more than 20 years of studio experience and were still active in the business. Three were based in Europe and three in North America. Four were mainly involved in classical and contemporary music productions, one primarily in pop/rock, and one primarily in jazz, experimental, and pop/rock. Three had always worked as freelances, one had always worked in a public radio station, and two were house producers for major labels for over 10 years and became freelances after the collapse of record companies. Three of the classical producers received formal *Tonmeister* training, one of the non-classical producers received electrical engineering training and was a self-taught producer, and the other two learned on the job.

The interview guide was based on the email survey findings. The producers were asked to describe their mission, skills, and interaction with musicians. The focus here is on their interaction with musicians and differences in their artistic involvement in the production. To develop the model of artistic direction, two analysis approaches were applied in parallel: the constant comparison method of grounded theory (Corbin and Strauss 2008) used for the email survey and psycho-linguistic analysis (Dubois et al., 2009). The first approach analysed the content of the verbal descriptions, what was being said; the second approach analysed how producers described their interaction with the musicians. A greater amount of verbs implies a more proactive and involved approach, whereas more nouns implies a more passive approach. Greater use of 'I' would suggest more personal experiences, while 'you' and 'we', as well as impersonal formulas such as 'it is' and 'there is', would generally refer to more consensual statements. Linguist Caroline Cance prevented the analysis from being affected by my own bias as a record producer. Finally, the model was presented to the interviewees, who all agreed on it.

From light coaching to deep collaboration with musicians

Producers agreed on the need to observe the situation first in order to adapt their working approach to the aesthetic context and the specificities of the project. The minimum level of artistic involvement consists of playing an intermediary role between the artists and their future audience by providing an extra set of ears on the project. This passive level does not require much verbal communication with the musicians during the recording sessions. It is adopted when the musicians seem resistant to any comment on what they are doing. It does, however, imply that the presence of a professional in the control room has an impact on the musical performance. It is thus close to the sound engineer's level of interaction with the musicians as described by the survey participants. The second level consists of adapting language when providing feedback on technical issues of the performance. Producers explained how they would address specific situations, such as a singer being out of tune to whom they might say 'the B-flat maybe could be a little higher' instead of 'you are flat' (Pras, Cance, and Guastavino 2013: 390). The next level consists of managing the recording session by giving artistic direction between takes. This means producers go beyond the basic performance issues such as rhythmic precision, balance, and intonation, to share their artistic ideas about tempo, musical expression, sound, arrangements, and maybe lyrics. At this level, the producer is likely to take the lead and free the musicians from being too self-conscious when they are playing. Producers reported that second and third levels of interaction were the most common: the second level is appropriate for musicians who know exactly what they are doing and just need somebody in the control room to help keep track of what is happening, the third level is appropriate for musicians who already trust the producer and need their insights. Producers are likely to decide between these two levels after the first take has given them an idea of how ready the musicians are musically. Finally, the highest level of artistic involvement consists of collaborating deeply with the artists to achieve the best possible result. Producers described this level as quite rare and mentioned the need to cope with artists' sensitivities more than at the other levels. Thus, while this level can generate the best results, it also carries a risk of difficult moments or conflicts.

This model can help musicians to define the kind of interaction they want with their record producer. It may also be useful for studio professionals when a session is not going well. It should be noted that the level of interaction could change during the session. For instance, the first one could be an option for a few hours, allowing the musicians to feel that they are in a trustworthy environment. When I feel resistance, I usually wait for the musicians to ask for my opinion on their performance, and then move to the second level, and sometimes to the third on the same day. I love being involved as a collaborator but indeed, it is not very common and I too need to be comfortable enough with the musicians to offer this possibility.

The impact of producers' comments on musicians' self-evaluation on musical performance[13]

Twenty-five musicians in five ensembles participated in a studio experiment at the Steinhardt School. All participants were from the jazz programme as students or faculty. The pianist Andy Milne, the bassist Chris Tordini and the sound engineer Paul Geluso agreed to produce a session each: I produced the last two sessions. The ensembles were asked to prepare four compositions in order to evaluate four different recording conditions: one with no producer and no self-evaluation of the takes, one with a producer but no self-evaluation of the takes, one without a producer but with self-evaluation of the takes, and one with a producer and self-evaluation of the takes. I requested the producers provide comments between each take. Self-evaluation meant that the musicians listened to each take in the control room before recording the next one. For each condition, musicians had to record three complete takes. After each condition, they were asked to select their favourite and explain why. At the end of the recording session, they were asked to comment on the conditions. A few weeks later, all the musicians attended a listening session where they evaluated all their takes again.

Among the four conditions, participants preferred to have a producer and self-evaluation of the takes. Results showed that both types of feedback had a positive impact on musical performance. Specifically, getting comments from an external producer helped musicians focus and improve technically throughout the three takes, while self-evaluation enhanced their creativity and helped them improve from the first take to the second take but not necessarily from the second to the third. Together, these results contradict the common belief that the first take is the best. This is consistent with my own experience that having the musicians listening to the entire first take in the control room usually results in considerable improvements. Often, performers discuss what needs to be changed without the need for the producer to interfere too much. However, in practice, performers often refuse to listen to the first take and wait until the third or fourth to listen, at which point they are already getting tired. If they want to change important parameters such as tempo or arrangements at this point, the first three or four takes cannot be used in the final editing, which wastes time and energy.

The musicians had never worked with the producers before the study and the producers were forced to give feedback between takes. This provided an extreme producing situation and addressed musicians' reservations towards an external producer commenting on their performances as reported in the email survey. While producers remained very respectful in how they phrased their comments, they suggested major changes such as reshaping compositions, arrangements, and tempi: a level of involvement between the second and the third level. None of the musicians complained about the producer being too invasive, though results showed that the producer's comments sometimes made performers too self-conscious and thus negatively impacted on their solos. My hypothesis is that the producers did not yet have enough trust from the musicians to truly succeed in producing at the third level, which requires the musicians to have lost all self-consciousness during the session.

Conclusion

In this chapter, I have analysed the perspectives of young musicians and sound engineers and experienced record producers on the preparation, management, and artistic direction of recording sessions. This analysis has taken into account the current context of recording and the impact of recent technological advances on studio practices. It deals with tacit skills that cannot be learned in internet tutorials and that have not yet been addressed in academic research. I have investigated the contribution of studio professionals to both sound and music quality, thus going beyond sound engineering manuals that focus mainly on recording techniques. A recording aims to convey the musical performance to an audience through technology; thus, sound quality is essential to do justice to the music but cannot fully compensate for a below par musical performance.

I felt fortunate to have the opportunity to interview experienced and successful record producers. The analysis of their descriptions of their practices has allowed me to bring the art of producing to the forefront of musical recording. The subtleties and multidisciplinary characteristics of their profession demonstrate that not all owners of a sound interface and microphones can call themselves studio professionals. The development of the model of artistic direction was the most rewarding part of my doctoral research: I could finally visualise and put into words something that I had experienced in practice for many years. Furthermore, in addition to extending Hennion's finding (1989) that the producer plays an intermediary role between the artists and their audience, this model makes explicit the psychological nature of the profession. One of the interviewees even mentioned that he did not choose it by chance; as a child he had experienced certain family situations that prepared him to do this job (Pras, Cance, and Guastavino 2013: 382). Moreover, the producers identified themselves with 'cleaners, servants, captains of a ship, firemen and midwives' to illustrate their responsibilities and the assistive and intimate aspects of their mission (Pras, Lavoie, and Guastavino

2013: 621). One of them also compared his job to a photographer who aims to capture the most meaningful moments and then bring them together. I attended a photography workshop at the International Photography Center in New York taught by Bobby Lane in 2012, and I was surprised how much decisions on light, pose, camera setup, and frame mirror those on studio setup and recording equipment. Moreover, I observed that the interaction between the photographer and the models is similar to the interaction between the record producer and the musicians in that photographers also needed to free models from self-consciousness. Interestingly, both photographic and sound equipment have become very affordable, leading in some ways to the devaluation of both professions. Although video equipment has also become affordable, the profession of film director have not suffered the same. I assume it is because film directors are artistic leaders while record producers and photographers are responding to the different constraints of an artistic project.

In the following concluding sections, I discuss the process of do-it-yourself productions in the light of the research presented in this chapter. I summarise the reasons to hire studio professionals and what musicians should expect from them in the current context of recording and present ideas for sound recording courses.

Do-it-yourself productions

My research findings demonstrate the benefits of having a sound engineer and a record producer managing the technical and artistic direction of recording sessions to achieve the best possible result. However, musicians who do not want to delegate these responsibilities to a third party could use some of these findings to improve their own productions. For instance, my method of record preparation could be adapted to do-it-yourself productions. I recommend picturing a sound result first, thinking about a studio setup second, and coming up with a microphone list last. The first take should be listened to and discussed by the musicians in order to address eventual changes as soon as possible. The leader of the project may find inspiration from the producers interviewed.

When is it time to call for studio professionals and what to expect from them?

Even when musicians are knowledgeable about the technical aspects of recording, they may prefer to use 100 per cent of their capacity to focus on their musical performance. Likewise, even if they know how to produce a session, they cannot be performing in the studio and listening to the result at the same time, thus they may opt to have another set of ears in the control room to help them with the creative process. In my own experience, it is younger and less experienced musicians who are the most reluctant to get feedback from an outsider, probably because they do not feel confident enough to be confronted by an external professional's opinion. There are also stories about studio professionals who have botched the job, which might lead young musicians to think that they would rather handle all of these responsibilities themselves. Musicians could reduce these negative experiences by ensuring that the sound engineer or the record producer they plan on working with are capable. For this, it is essential – but not sufficient – to feel a good connection with the professional. Musicians should listen to the candidate's portfolio and compare it with their favourite recordings. The role of the professional, their level of artistic involvement, and their remuneration should be defined before the beginning of the production.

Recommendations for sound recording programs

The number of sound recording programmes has increased exponentially all over the world in the last 15 years. These programmes aim to replace studio internships. However, most of them focus on learning how to use recording equipment rather than developing listening skills or learning how to manage recording sessions. At present, how to use recording technology can be self-taught. A young sound engineer with whom I worked in Kolkata, India, had learned how to use all the parameters of the studio equipment on internet tutorials. While he could operate the equipment faster than any of my students or myself, he was primarily following the musicians' requests, without really being able to make such decisions himself or to propose different directions. Therefore, sound recording students would benefit from classes where they could learn from several practitioners and from courses designed to be as close as possible to real-life situations. During recording sessions, I help students to develop their listening skills by asking them to comment on the sound result first, based on their expectations, before providing a technical solution and changing the microphone placement. Again, I grade the process as well as the result to encourage them to experiment with the technology. I hope to have a chance to design producing courses soon that would allow the students to develop their communication skills in interacting with musicians.

Directions for future research

There is a need for more studio observations and experiments in a greater number of cultural contexts and musical genres. I have not investigated the perspective of very experienced musicians on recording sessions, which would be interesting to compare with the perspectives of the very experienced producers I interviewed. Nobody has studied the technical practices of sound engineers with systematic research approaches, such as microphone placement, mixing or mastering, which could provide great documentation for teaching. Finally, there is a need for more studies in the music business that investigated the current recording budgets, production organisation and distribution.

Acknowledgements

This research was funded by the Fonds Québécois de Recherche Société et Culture (FQRSC). I would like to thank Terri Hron and Abigail Kniffin for reviewing the English, Gabriel Gutierrez Arellano for his insights as a former student, as well as Jim Black, Maryse Lavoie, and Caroline Cance for their comments on earlier drafts of this chapter.

Notes

1 On the impact of technological advances on studio practice, see Pras, Lavoie, and Guastavino 2013; on the artistic direction of studio sessions, see Pras, Cance, and Guastavino 2013. These analyses do not include the session preparation that is presented here.
2 For complete findings and analysis, see Pras and Guastavino 2011: 82.
3 Details of the participants' background are given in the following section.
4 For complete findings and analysis, see Pras and Guastavino 2009.
5 Details of the subjects' background are given in the third section.
6 For complete description of participants and questionnaire design, see Pras and Guastavino 2011: 76.
7 For complete findings and analysis, see Pras and Guastavino 2011: 78.
8 For complete findings and analysis, see Pras and Guastavino 2011: 77.
9 For complete findings and analysis of the subjects' approach to recording, see See Pras, Lavoie, Guastavino 2013: 619; for complete findings and analysis of their communication skills, see Pras, Cance, Guastavino 2013.
10 Details of the subjects' background are given in the third section.
11 For the interviewees' attitudes to musical genres, see Pras, Lavoie, and Guastavino 2013: 620; for a review of the literature on aesthetic approaches to musical recordings, see ibid.: 614.
12 For full details, see Pras, Cance, and Guastavino 2013: 387.
13 For complete findings and details, see Pras and Guastavino 2013.

References

Burgess, R. (2013). *The Art of Music Production: The Theory and Practice*. Oxford: Oxford University Press.

Chanan, M. (1995). *Repeated Takes: A Short History of Recording and Its Effects on Music*. London: Verso.

Corbin, J., and A. Strauss (2008). *Basics of Qualitative Research: Techniques and Procedures for Developing Grounded Theory*. Thousand Oaks, CA: Sage.

Cox, C., and D. Warner, eds (2004). *Audio Culture: Readings in Modern Music*. New York: Continuum.

Donin, N., and J. Theureau (2007). 'Theoretical and Methodological Issues Related to Long Term Creative Cognition: The Case of Musical Composition'. *Cognition, Technology and Work*, 9/4: 233–51.

Dubois et al. (2009). *Le Sentir et le dire: Concepts et méthodes en psychologie et linguistique cognitives*. Paris: Editions L'Harmattan.

Frith, S., and S. Zagorski-Thomas (2012). *The Art of Record Production: An Introductory Reader for a New Academic Field*. Farnham: Ashgate.

Greene, P. (2005). *Wired for Sound: Engineering and Technologies in Sonic Cultures*. Middletown, CT: Wesleyan University Press.

Hennion, A. (1989). 'An Intermediary between Production and Consumption: The Producer of Popular Music'. *Science, Technology and Human Values*, 14/4: 400–424.

Kahn, A. (2001). *Kind of Blue: The Making of the Miles Davis Masterpiece*. London: Granta.

Moorefield, V. (2005). *The Producer as Composer: Shaping the Sounds of Popular Music.* Cambridge, MA: MIT Press.

Patmore, D., and E. Clarke (2007). 'Making and Hearing Virtual Worlds: John Culshaw and the Art of Record Production'. *Musicae Scientiae*, 11/2: 269–93.

Pinch, T., and K. Bijsterveld (2004). 'Sound Studies: New Technologies and Music'. *Social Studies of Science*, 34/5: 635–48.

Pras A. and C. Guastavino (2009). 'Improving the Sound Quality of Recordings through Communication between Musicians and Sound Engineers'. Paper presented at the International Computer Music Conference (ICMC), Montreal.

—— and —— (2011). 'The Role of Music Producers and Sound Engineers in the Current Recording Context, as Perceived by Young Professionals'. *Musicae Scientiae*, 15/1: 73–95.

—— and —— (2013). 'The Impact of Producers' Comments and Musicians' Self-Evaluation on Perceived Recording Quality'. *Journal of Music Technology and Education*, 6/1: 81–101.

—— C. Cance, and C. Guastavino (2013). 'Record Producers' Best Practices for Artistic Direction – From Light Coaching to Deeper Collaboration with Musicians'. *Journal of New Music Research*, 42/4: 381–95.

—— M. Lavoie, and C. Guastavino (2013). 'The Impact of Technological Advances on Recording Studio Practices'. *Journal of the American Society for Information Science and Technology*, 64/3: 612–26.

Ryan, B., and K. Kehew (2006) *Recording The Beatles: The Studio Equipment and Techniques Used to Create their Classic Albums.* Houston, TX: Curvebender.

Sterne, J. (2003). *The Audible Past: Cultural Origins of Sound Reproduction.* Durham, NC: Duke University Press.

Théberge, P. (1997). *Any Sound You Can Imagine: Making Music / Consuming Technology.* Middletown, CT: Wesleyan University Press.

Zak, A. (2001). *The Poetics of Rock: Cutting Tracks, Making Records.* Oakland: University of California Press.

3 Studio pedagogy

Perspectives from record producers

Andrew King

Humans always tend to overdo things and we are doing this with technology in the studio today. You don't need 199 tracks to record a three-piece band and that kind of thing never used to happen. It's fascinating that the albums that are still going, that people still talk about, still collect, still love, were all done on 4-, 8- or maybe up to 24-tracks; certainly not 199 or anything like that. We don't need it, we take it too far.

Ken Scott

This chapter considers how educators can develop principles of music production in a digital age. It focuses upon the practices used in the audio industry from both an analogue and digital perspective. Three renowned music producers were interviewed as part of this study. The evaluation of this data involved using interpretative phenomenological analysis and revealed the importance of capturing performance in the studio, the relevance of expertise from a musical and technical perspective, how the affordances of digital technology can affect workflow and decision-making, issues surrounding listening to music and loudness, and the impact of environment and commercial pressures. What is then put forward is a framework for considering designing tasks for students and the foundations for an in-depth environmental study.

The study was focused upon the capture of live performance in the music studio and intentionally did not draw upon expertise within areas such as electronic dance music that have developed significantly through digital technology. In addition, it was necessary for future research to draw upon expertise from producers that have worked (and continue to work) using both analogue and digital technologies in order to understand this phenomenon from an historical perspective.

Technological development is having a profound effect on recording studio practice and more broadly the music industry. The precise nature and point of reference relies upon the user and how they have engaged with the technology. The collaboration between Sony and Philips in the late 1970s and beyond led to the introduction of the first digital consumer playback device, known as the compact disc. It was this device that resulted in a change in consumer habits and the decline in the sale of analogue recording mediums such as the vinyl album, although there is evidence in some parts of the world that the sale of CDs has been in decline during the first decade of the twenty-first century as consumer habits shift to other formats such as digital downloads.

From a pedagogical perspective educators are interested in engaging students with music and igniting a lifelong passion with this art. However, how we engage learners with music especially from a technological perspective has become important in many aspects of music education. The quote that begins this chapter from renowned music producer, manager, and sound engineer Ken Scott highlights an important caveat for both music educators and learners. Attention is drawn to the widely held opinion that a considerable amount of music that is still held in high regard was recorded using technology that was limited by the apparatus that was used to capture these performances: in this instance the number of tracks available to capture the various musicians within an ensemble. Although there is also another important notion put forward here that the technology is being overused in some way. In a similar way to academic texts that present epistemological milestones within a domain, certain albums have been accepted into the canon of recorded works through their longevity, critical appreciation, and sometimes the techniques used in production.

Perhaps a better analogy would be between critically praised works of literature and classic albums. The 1969 novel *Slaughterhouse 5* by Kurt Vonnegut tells the story of time-travelling soldier Billy Pilgrim who believes he has been in an alien zoo. Whilst the 1972 concept album *The Rise and Fall of Ziggy Stardust and the Spiders from Mars* is concerned with David Bowie's alter ego, a rock star who acts as a messenger for extra-terrestrial beings. Both of these artistic endeavours have been accepted by literary and music critics respectively as seminal works within their domains. Although neither of these works would has been produced using a computer with a microprocessor it does not appear to have diminished their artistic value nor effected their longevity. Therefore, the key to the success of these works would appear to rely less upon the technology but perhaps more importantly upon how it was used.

The question that will thus be addressed in this chapter is: what are the key considerations for educators working with young music producers? The aims are to consider the views of industry producers in building a framework for studio practice. In so doing the chapter will focus on the impact the development of technology has had upon recording studio practice and what can be learned about the approaches used in both analogue and digital recording and how these can be considered in educational practice. It is important to consider the placement of technology in music before embarking upon this journey. There are four central themes that emerge from the literature that help establish a context for this work: (1) affordances, agency, and decision-making; (2) environment; (3) approaches to learning with technology in music; and (4) production and consumption.

Contextual issues: Affordances, agency, and decision-making

Taylor sets out two contrasting positions in thinking about technology and agency: technological determinism and voluntarism.[1] The main differences are that 'technological determinism [is] a kind of top-down model and voluntarism its polar opposite' (Taylor 2001: 25). The difference would appear to be that from a technological determinist standpoint the theory attributes agency to technology and therefore has the power to change the lives of human beings. Voluntarism begins with the precept that the technology is neutral and is only good or bad depending upon its use. As suggested by Taylor there are several shades of grey in this dichotomy, but it is not possible to fully engage in a debate of this nature in this chapter. However, when considering the quote at the beginning, it would appear to suggest that digital technologies in the recording studio have influenced workflow and within this decision-making and that has directly affected practice.

The recording studio presents an interesting area for music educators, since it often relies upon complex technology yet there is an artistic use for the technology. When discussing technology more broadly Taylor cites Lewis Mumford and José Ortega y Gasset's view 'that technology, while neutral in and of itself, runs the risk of decreasing our humanity or creating a rift between our creative sides and our scientific sides' (Taylor 2001: 30–31). Although written in 1952 Mumford's *Art and Technics* contains clear considerations regarding the process of music production and therefore would be an interesting area of study in pedagogical recording studio practice. King (2008) has considered collaborative learning in this context when supported by an interface to help support students completing tasks. In addition, using a contingent learning approach (see King 2009) proved an effective way of supporting learners in this environment.

The result of the technological developments would also seem to suggest a change in the number of affordances that are available to those involved in music production. The term 'affordance' refers to an object or an environment in which a learner is able to carry out a number of actions. This was presented from a human–computer interaction perspective by Norman (1998) who suggested an ecological approach that encompasses not only the possible actions but also the experience and desires of the user. In a recording studio the ability to have a far greater number of audio tracks on which to capture the performance of the musicians in the studio represents an increase in the number of affordances and also how the engineer may use these possibilities. For example, when limited to just eight tracks sound engineers would need to make decisions about which guitar performance was going to be put forward for the final mix.

The ability to capture multiple takes of the same performance by an instrumentalist in isolation and making the decision later can be perceived in both a positive and a negative light. Increasing the number of options available does allow for non-destructive editing (see Huber and Runstein 2009: 211) and a large number of takes can be stored for later use. However, the locus of control would seem to pass from the performer to the engineer who is now able to select the performance to be used or piece together different performances for the final mix: albeit often in consultation with the musicians. This needs to be considered alongside the increased ability to edit tracks quite precisely using a range of tools during the post-production stage that alters and elongates the process. It would appear that the range of affordances has enriched the tools at the disposal of the studio team with the possible side effect that it could potentially make the process more time consuming.

The recording studio represents a complex tool-rich environment that, with the digitisation of the technology, presents the learner with a greatly enhanced set of options when compared to the previous analogue technologies. The key to decision-making in this 'dynamic task environment' is that 'it is not enough to know *what* should be done but also *when* should it be done' (Kerstholt and Raaijmakers 1997: 206). A relatively small modern computer with a professional sound card and pre-amplification for instruments can capture a far greater number of recorded tracks than the far larger earlier systems. Within the larger commercial facilities the computer has more commonly taken the place of the multi-track tape recorder, although a certain number of producers and engineers have taken to the computer for the editing and mixing of their work: albeit often through a control surface that is modelled on the layout of an analogue mixing console. Equally as common is the 'analogue front end to a digital system approach', which uses an analogue mixing console in conjunction with audio software such as Pro Tools.

Environment: The 'temple of sound'

In 2010, before Universal took over EMI, Abbey Road Studios were the subject of rumours that it was to be offered for sale by EMI and there were concerns that it might be purchased by property developers.[2] Sony Music Studios in Manhattan had already suffered a similar fate in 2007. Therefore, even though the sale never occurred, it focused minds in the musical world on the risks of closure of these large commercial facilities. In 2009, the world renowned Olympic Studios in London closed its doors after a prestigious history that involved recording albums for bands such as the Rolling Stones and artists such as Jimi Hendrix, although it re-opened in 2013 and now operates in a reduced capacity.

Théberge (2012) described the changing role of the studio in the age of the internet. Census data from the USA demonstrates that between 1997 and 2007 the number of commercially registered studios rose from around 1,230 to 1,700 but this perhaps presents a distorted view. According to Théberge where clearer census data is provided in Canada and a similar increase can be seen in the number of commercially registered facilities, it would appear to be at the expense of larger studio facilities that have declined from around 24 per cent to 10 per cent of the overall commercial studios. This is relevant for music educators involved in teaching sound recording because, as Théberge states, 'during the peak of the analogue multi track studio, every facility had a number of part-time apprentices. . . . With the arrival of digital recording in the 1990s these jobs virtually disappeared' (2012: 87). Since many of the opportunities to learn music production now appear in the education sector there is a responsibility for colleagues to take up this work.

Slater and Martin (2012) described a conceptual foundation for understanding musico-technological creativity, drawing attention to the increased use of technologies from a student or a home enthusiast perspective. The mobilisation of music software has challenged the notion of what exactly a recording studio is, and this is explored through a phenomenological and critical realism lens. Pras, Lavoie, and Guastavino (2013) investigated the impact of technological advances on recording-studio practices, including the delocalisation of studio practice away from the larger commercial facilities and the transition and reinvention undertaken by studio professionals. The socio-economic impact of the advance of digital technologies is cited as the driving force behind this change, although the interviews with industry experts demonstrates that, whilst working across rather than within genres is more commonplace, the aesthetic approach to recording remains unchanged. Both of these views represent how music production has become possible away from the 'temple of sound', yet it also suggests for learners that the approach to recording from an aesthetic point of view remains similar from an industry viewpoint.

Approaches to learning

Many musicians are now able to use computer software to record and edit music in their own homes. There is a need for educators to understand this type of informal learning and put this into the context of an education in sound recording. Green presented the first in-depth evaluation of how pop musicians learn that specifically addresses what some academics call formal and informal approaches[3] to music education largely from the perspective of learning a musical instrument more associated with popular music. Green puts forward the consideration that these approaches: 'are not mutually exclusive, but learners often draw upon or encounter aspects of both' (2002: 59). From the transcripts of interviews with a range of musicians, Green identified listening and copying music using and developing aural skills was the preferred method although some did use notation or guitar tablature.

Of course learning music by listening, copying, and in some cases developing aural skills is not exclusive to the late twentieth century. Katz draws attention to the importance of the introduction of the phonograph in the early twentieth century to the world of jazz. The dissemination of this musical material beyond the music venue brought the genre to the attention of countless musicians who, often isolated, were able to listen and in some cases use aural techniques to learn songs. Katz cites the example of Bix Beiderbecke who used the technology to ignite his passion for musical performance: 'Fascinated by the music, [Beiderbecke] first tried to imitate it on the piano; he soon acquired a cornet and, much to his family's relief, a mute' (Katz 2004: 73).

There are parallels between learning a musical instrument and studio recording. Musicians are embracing the technology that has allowed them access to the world of music production that was once the preserve of the artists fortunate enough to be supported by a record label. Learners can record, mix, and publish certain genres of music using relatively inexpensive hard- and software tools (see King 2012). Théberge (1997) gives a historical account of the rise of the home studio that he suggests is rooted in the desire by some artists in the late 1960s and early 1970s to have more control over the production process. Sometimes this manifested itself as collaborations between sound engineers and artists (for example, Bowie and Scott on *Ziggy Stardust*) in a co-production capacity. Other artists took this to an extreme and opened their own commercial studios, such as Electric Lady (Jimi Hendrix), Ramport (The Who) and Apple Studios (The Beatles). Interestingly, only Electric Lady is still a commercially operating studio in 2014.

Notable musicians who had facilities to rival those found in the commercial world included George Harrison with a facility called FPSHOT[4] in his Friar Park home in Henley. However, it is to the advent of MIDI[5] in the 1980s that many attribute the revolution in home recording technology in the way it allowed users to compose, arrange and mix musical works (see Manning 2013). From a recording perspective Théberge (1997) highlights the introduction of the Alesis ADAT[6] as the first affordable digital multi-track recording device that was aimed at the home or amateur musician market. The difference was that the artists who procured and developed their own facilities typically had experience of recording in one of the commercial facilities and of course could often draw upon a pool of expertise within their professional networks that would include sound engineers and music producers. Computer-based technologies have generally superseded hardware such as the ADAT in the home studio. Audio recording software such as Pro Tools has become an affordable option in home recording and is also used in renowned studios such as Abbey Road and Air Studios, both in London. The question for the educator and the home-studio user is how they then develop their own sound-recording practice without direct access to industry professionals.

The internet can provide a range of forums and guidance, but lack of regulation means the quality of the advice on offer can vary greatly. Groups such as the Audio Engineering Society provide high-quality advice and online databases of recording-specific guidance. However, this and other societies are perhaps designed for the audio professional and often hidden behind a pay wall. There are several high quality magazines such as *Sound on Sound* and *MusicTech*, which, through a combination of physical and online material, provide procedural knowledge and insightful interviews with artists, producers and engineers. In addition, recordproduction.com provides a high number of fascinating interviews with renowned and highly regarded engineers and producers and has the advantage of being free to access.

Although there are a number of good quality resources on offer, some knowledge and the ability to select the appropriate material or advice is necessary. Texts on recording studio practice have developed to include not only analogue approaches to production but also digital. Since *Sound Recording Practice* (Borwick 1996), there have been a number of other notable additions to the literature on such practice, including *Sound and Recording* (Rumsey and McCormick 2009), *Modern Recording Techniques* (Huber and Runstein 2009) *Understanding and Crafting the Mix* (Moylan 2007), and *Practical Recording Techniques* (Bartlett and Bartlett, 2008). In addition, there are handbooks for sound engineers (Ballou, 2002) and to sound system engineering (Davis and Patronis 2006) more generally. These are all excellent and informative texts; however, there has been little empirical evaluation to date of how learners gather theoretical and procedural studio knowledge. This problem could possibly be compounded by the prior knowledge gained by learners before a specialised study of the subject at HE level.

Production and consumption: The loudness wars

An emerging theme in research into sound recording practice that has direct relevance to educators concerns an artistic view of record production. Many of the works cited in the previous section offer insightful procedural and theoretical knowledge of sound recording apparatus and the techniques used in the studio. Frith and Zagorski-Thomas (2012) have produced the first scholarly edited volume that examines in-depth the art of record production. Among other topics, it includes a chapter on the rock record producer, who it describes as the decision-maker in the creative process, and the 'continuous creation' concept that involves the use of both stage and studio for the development of work. The representation of live performance is given a central place. Pras and Guastavino (2013) explore the perspectives of young professionals on the roles of producers and engineers. Communication and interpersonal skills are cited as two of the main requirements of a producer and the idealised sound engineer should have minimal interaction with the artists. Of course, in many smaller commercial facilities a single person can often undertake both producer and engineer roles (Burgess 2008).

Blake describes the multi-faceted view of music producers as 'people managers, whether Svengalis, artist and repertoire developers, or gifted amateur psychologists able to guide temperamental artists through a recording session' (2009: 36). An overview of producers in different contexts is examined through the lens of classical, jazz, rock, pop, and hip-hop. Interestingly the music producer's control over the process seems to increase as new technological developments are introduced. Blake also alludes to the work of Brian Eno and cites the importance of producers as a mediator between artist and listener.

The development of technology has not always proceeded with a desire for a high fidelity sound from a listener perspective. Taylor (2001) cites the example of the 8-track tape that as a playback technology was not as widely adopted as the standard cassette. Despite the supposed superior sound quality of the 8-track tape the flexibility of the cassette tape to store music and its affordability, led to its wider use by the music-listening public. Taylor also draws a parallel with more recent digital downloads: 'as we are seeing once again with the inferior sound of the wildly popular MP3' (Taylor 2001: 23). Rumsey goes further:

> The irony is that now high technical fidelity is possible, few people seem to care very much about it. . . . This lack of consumer concern with the highest fidelity has probably always been a problem for the audio industry, although it is exacerbated by the fact that few people now take the time to sit down in

an ideal listening position and listen to a recorded performance from beginning to end, relishing the 'concert hall experience' in their living rooms.

(Rumsey 2009: 219)

The preferred listening device for many learners could possibly now be the earplugs provided by manufacturers of playback devices including Apple's iPod or the multimedia monitors from the home computer since these are generally the storage mechanisms used for the library of songs that are owned by the user. Bergh and DeNora (2009) highlight the use of MP3 devices by listeners in cultural settings and explore the changing nature of how audiences engage with music. The issue of how music is being consumed is also compounded by what many in the industry refer to as the 'Loudness Wars'. Indeed, music companies, artists, producers, and engineers have been under increased market pressure to produce even louder recordings of musical works. Essentially, the dynamic bandwidth of a musical track has been under increasing pressure and has been restricted in some genres to the upper end of the loudness scale: the lower dynamic levels such as pianissimo, mezzo-piano, or even mezzo-forte are removed and the dynamic level of a song controlled between forte and fortissimo using artificial means.

A database[7] exists that uses an algorithm to calculate the dynamic range of an album and produce a dynamic range score on a 20-point scale: 1–7 'bad', 8–13 'transition', 14–20 'good'. Although from a qualitative perspective the labels of the scale may seem crude it does highlight the issue being discussed here. Thousands of tracks and albums have been analysed by industry professionals and uploaded to this database. An informed survey actively demonstrates that music within certain genres is of a more restricted dynamic range and this has been increasing over time: rap music and heavy metal are genres that standout. Interestingly, previous and current classical music recordings have retained their broad dynamic ranges as noted when comparing earlier vinyl reproductions to compact disc and digital downloads. What is particularly interesting is that albums in genres such as rock music that have been reissued in a digital format can often fair less favourably in terms of dynamic range compared with earlier releases on vinyl. A detailed analysis of the entire database would be required to paint a more significant picture of the patterns that have emerged but even a preliminary review of the data suggests there is an issue with dynamic range and music. More detailed information about this topic can be found in the work of Vickers (2010) and web descriptions (e.g. Lamere 2009).

The literature that informs this study places into context how technology is viewed from a social perspective and highlights the number of affordances that digital technology provides for the learner. It demonstrates the way the music industry has changed and shows how young musicians are able to engage with music production. Approaches to learning in similar contexts are discussed and key texts are outlined. Attention is also drawn to the production and consumption of recorded music and the relevance of the artistic approach alongside a need to understanding loudness in music. These areas provide a foundation for investigating the key considerations for educators working with young music producers.

Interview study: Perspectives from three leading producers

The research design for this study was qualitative in nature and involved in-depth interviews with record producers concerning the use of both analogue and digital technologies in the recording studio. The aims of the study were:

- to understand the phenomenological perspective in the changes between analogue and digital recording methods from an industry perspective; and
- to explore how these changes could potentially impact upon learners engaged with using technology in music production.

It is anticipated by investigating an industry perspective a greater understanding can be developed for educators working with technology. A suggested framework for developing an approach towards understanding studio pedagogy will then be put forward.

For the purposes of this study it was necessary to approach industry professionals with both a wide knowledge of the recording industry and who had worked during the transition from analogue to digital machinery in the studio. Three renowned experts in the areas of music production, sound engineering, composition and music management were recruited as part of this study:

- Chris Kimsey (CK): production credits include the Rolling Stones, Peter Frampton, Marillion, the Cult, Emerson, Lake and Palmer, the Chieftains, New Model Army, Duran Duran, Yes, Elton John, and Paul McCartney.
- Craig Leon (CL): production credits include the Ramones, Blondie, Talking Heads, Méav, Luciano Pavarotti, Andreas Scholl, Sir James Galway, the Pogues, Jesus Jones, the Fall, the Bangles, and Joshua Bell.
- Ken Scott (KS): production credits include the Beatles, Elton John, Pink Floyd, Procol Harum, Mahavishnu Orchestra, Duran Duran, Jeff Beck Group, Supertramp, Devo, Level 42, and David Bowie.

All three experts have won industry awards and were still active in the music industry in 2014. They have recorded a wide range of different genres in various capacities and from a quantitative perspective are responsible for a considerable number of platinum and gold albums.

A semi-structured interview of approximately one hour took place with each expert, consisting of a set of 10 prepared questions that led to further dialogue that explored the use of digital and analogue technologies in the recording studio. Each interviewee was made aware of the nature of the study and gave ethical consent for the research to take place using standard procedures such as those outlined in Gillham (2005). Each interview was dual-coded verbatim and interpretative phenomenological analysis (Smith, Flowers, and Larkin 2009) was used to explore the transcriptions and develop the emergent themes.

Analysis

Two superordinate themes emerged in the data concerning pedagogical recording studio practice: (1) knowledge and skills and (2) human perspective. Table 3.1

Table 3.1 Superordinate themes and subthemes from interviews with record producers

Superordinate themes	Subthemes
Knowledge and skills	• Capture of performance • Expertise • Studio tools • Workflow
Human perspective	• Decision making • Artistic touches • Environment • Commercial

shows both of these themes and the subthemes within them. The ensuing discussion provides examples of each of the themes within the two main areas with extracts taken from the transcripts.

Knowledge and skills

The first of the superordinate themes identifies some of the knowledge and skills necessary for producers. The capture of performance within certain genres of music is cited as an important consideration, as is the expertise to make sense of the affordances of digital recording technology. The tools in the studio and an in-depth understanding of how to use them within the workflow of the production chain are also highlighted.

Capture of performance

The affordances that digital technology provide to the engineer or producer suggest that in some instances digital technology is being used to piece together elements of audio tracks rather than capture the performance of a well-rehearsed musician(s).

KS: You got the whole thing of not getting performance in the studio, the copy and pasting of edits together, as opposed to play, and play well.

KS: I co-produced four albums with David Bowie and 95 per cent of the vocals used on those albums were first take from beginning to end and each one was just a complete performance.

Chris Kimsey reinforces this point:

CK: There is a real need for students to understand that the important thing in the first instance of a recording is the source. To get that performance as good as it can be without just putting it down and then getting the best bits and sticking it all together.

He goes further to relate this practice to studio musicianship:

CK: Grabbing from all those bits [audio tracks] of the takes all over the place and compiling them into one. I think that makes for very lazy musicianship and also it steers the engineer into the direction that 'well actually, we only need a good bit here and we can put that everywhere' and that's not good.

It is even suggested later that the locus of control when capturing performance in the studio has shifted in some instances from the artist to the engineer or producer:

CK: I think digital [recording] has promoted the egos of some engineers and producers in that . . . they feel they have more control over the artist and really it should be the other way around. The producer/engineer should be encouraging the artist to give their best performance.

Craig Leon has a similar view regarding recording using digital technologies:

CL: Some people in pop recording tend to do lazy things like a lot of digital programming and straightening things out, quantising, grabbing sections of songs and repeating them which tends to make more boring flat recordings that aren't a result of the digital technologies but a result of operator error or operator laziness, should I say?

However, it would seem to suggest the affordances at the disposal of those responsible for the recording are at fault and not the technology per se. It would also seem that this issue is not restricted to the capture of popular music:

CL: What I have noticed a lot with classical musicians these days is that they are quite savvy with sequencing and punching in and moving things about in the digital domain, and actually some are quite lazy players these days as a result.

Another interesting point concerning how the performance was captured across different genres of music is also made:

CL: For me it has always been pretty much the same and in the case of these two folk albums it was very much 'routinening' the material with the players and working everything out with the artist. . . . The studio setup amongst all of that is pretty much the same, the setup doesn't change from a classical recording or say something like the Ramones, it is all about trying to capture something live.

Expertise

The issue of expertise in a studio context is contentious in modern recording practice. The proliferation of affordances provided by computers and software in the production chain can be a positive development if used in a certain way:

CK: I think the plusses of [digital recording] are that if you're knowledgeable and you have the imagination to shape and edit music responsibly you can be a little more constructive than analogue in terms of editing.

This comment would appear to go beyond the knowledge of how to use the tools from a procedural context and places the focus on expert knowledge concerning the concepts of recording practice. Musical expertise is also seen as a potential issue:

CL: An old [vinyl] album of mine was an electronic album done in a very classical way . . . and it is coming out again. . . . [They] divided the work up into sections when it was meant to be two through-composed pieces for different sides. They had put big gaps between the sections of the movements.

The album was re-released in a digital format and because of a lack of expertise (or care) on the part of those leading the project the work was divided into artificial sections that would spoil the flow of the music.[8]

Studio tools

The use of studio tools such as reverbs and an understanding of their purpose was also a matter of interest:

KS: Nowadays plugins are so available that the engineer . . . has got a different reverb on every instrument and it pulls everything apart. We used to use reverb to bring everything together. . . . Now it is just separating everything.

Having so many options with reverb that would have not been available before has distorted how this tool is used. In addition, how both computer software tools and other outboard equipment is of interest:

INTERVIEWER: For the processes in the studio do you use computer-based, outboard or a combination?

KS: Generally a combination. . . . I use very little in effects . . . a little compression, limiting at times one maybe two reverbs. But then there is the odd occasion that you want a special effect, you want a phasing or a flange or something like that on [the audio track] which these days is a hell of a lot easier to use a [digital] plugin.

This is a useful example of how a music producer can adopt new practices and how tasks are carried out.

How the technical apparatus is used in the studio has also changed. The ability to use automation to control aspects such as stereo positioning and loudness have taken the performance aspect from mixing a song:

CK: I still do a live performance on the console because I found that as soon as computers started coming in mixes become pretty linear and not moving enough for me dynamically and sonically.

It is interesting that the digitisation of studio tools has largely removed a performance aspect during the mixing of a track. While automation may offer more precision, it is important for educators to encourage students to capture automation in a live context and then use the digital editing tools to alter it where necessary. The affordances that digital technology gives to the user in terms of the number of tracks to record instruments can also have an effect on the sound:

CK: I see people using thirty microphones on a drum kit and you learned not to do that because you have extreme phase problems because the more microphones you put on anything you have phase related problems, which will change and weaken and make thinner the sound even though you correct the phase on each microphone.

The choices undertaken by students involved in digital recording can have negative consequences and it is important that leaners understand the basic principles such as phase cancellation. The digital technology has allowed musicians to have tools away from commercial facilities that allow them to work remotely:

CL: I did one track, it wasn't a classical track, it was a film track with Luciano Pavarotti [in 2002] where he basically sang the entire track a cappella, he was doing it as an overdub at his house. . . . [We] would record the basic track and then he would overdub. . . . In this case he didn't like the arrangement so he sang the track a cappella and said 'I know you can now record the orchestra with a click track and sync to me', which I had to do.

It would seem even renowned artists whose careers began in the analogue age recognised the affordances of digital technology and would use them to simplify their own involvement in how a performance was captured.

Workflow

How music is edited in the digital domain has changed from the analogue workflow process. The introduction of the computer as a production tool has added a visual element (the waveform) with a number of other affordances such as tempo maps that show bars and beats:

CK: Because [some young engineers] are relying upon beats and bars to do their editing rather than their ears they are just looking at the waveform and this becomes a mathematical rather than a musical edit. We are listening to music so it is paramount that the edit works musically. Even when editing is done on a strict bar resolution you may still have to move it a little so you still have to use your ears.

This point is reinforced by Ken Scott:

KS: The typical digital mind will look at the screen and just do it to the grid which is not the way a human will play. . . . I've seen second engineers: on the earliest part of the edit [the drummer] hits the bass drum fractionally early, the second part of the edit he hits the bass drum fractionally late, but they do [the edit] on the grid and the bass drum ends up falling in the incorrect place and it just sounds wrong; it's that looking as opposed to hearing.

Listening is an important skill for educators to develop in learners by presenting opportunities for them to use aural skills alongside visual representations. The number of affordances now available to the trainee engineer has changed:

CL: We have the ability to do things that we had no idea could even exist . . . were just fantasy in the old days of analogue recording and the digital domain has opened us up into a whole new world of recording

It is important to consider how to harness the potential that digital recording provides to students whilst still understanding production values. How tracks can be edited has also changed and can have benefits for certain types of recordings:

CL: I think technology makes a lot of things easier, editing for one thing is much easier, very precise tuning is possible and this is abused in a lot of ways. . . . When I am mixing something in digital – which is mostly orchestral these days – it is actually easier for me to get a more uniform sound because I can mix the whole album in . . . one timeline and I can go back and forwards and reference it much quicker than doing individual songs.

Although there are important considerations with this greater level of editing control for musicians:

CL: The younger artists tend to want to create a blander performance . . . because they know that digital technology exists and they know how they can edit. So they will over edit and over think themselves. For example by shaving slight parts of a bow sound or taking a note from one edit and placing it in another edit which can make the performance less good, and this is one example of how to abuse the technology because people are familiar with what they can do.

Therefore the conundrum for the young music producer is to understand whether any advantaged gained with precision editing can in some work negate the artistic nature of the performance they are trying to capture. The post-production time in the studio may have increased as the number of audio tracks recorded has resulted in more options to consider at this stage:

KS: The person that gets it to mix is all of a sudden going to get 100 guitar solos to edit and he has to decide which one it's going to be.

All of the considerations put forward within this superordinate theme highlight the potential of digital recording whilst also stressing the importance of understanding the processes and production values that should take place in the studio. If educators can develop knowledge and skills alongside the importance of effective working in the studio with the necessary expertise then the opportunities of digital recording can be more fully realised.

Human perspective

The second of the superordinate themes reveals some of the possible human perspectives for the young music producer to consider. The timing and ability to make decisions are seen as a core skill alongside the artistic touches necessary for music production. The environment is also an important consideration in some musical contexts alongside the commercial pressures that are evident in modern recording practice.

Decision-making

The affordances of digital recording as opposed to analogue have affected the decision-making process in the recording studio. When the number of audio tracks limited engineers it was possible to make decisions that have a direct effect on the mixing stage:

KS: The earliest was four track [analogue recording] and you had to make decisions up front. . . . You were probably recording bass, drums, rhythm guitar, and maybe a keyboard on the same track and had to make decisions about what it was going to sound like there and then.

This is further emphasised for students engaged with using digital technology:

KS: What they should learn first off is how to make a decision and how to listen as opposed to look, do a mix with the computer screen covered and don't overdo everything.

Not making the decisions too early can have an impact upon capturing performance:

CK: That created an internal balance which in turn meant what went to tape was far more cohesive than what's happening with digital. It seems to be in digital people just throw down a track, throw down a track and then sort it out later. Whilst actually you would sort it out at source as you do it. It also keeps the integrity of the performance at a higher level.

However, not all the older analogue technologies were less capable in all respects, and similar decisions had to be made:

CL: Just because an old analogue desk may have 120 channels and equalisers you didn't have to use them all. You have to be judicious in your choice of what you are doing with the equipment.

The important consideration in this section appears to be when and how decisions are made and how this can affect the sound that is being captured. How educators develop these key decision-making skills is of the upmost importance.

Artistic touches

The affordances offered by digital technology can aid in achieving a good recording if those involved in the production are capable of realising this:

CL: It is very easy to get a good sound these days compared to the work that you had to do before.

Although the possibilities of digital suggest young engineers have greater opportunities to produce good recordings, how these artistic touches are applied is a point for debate:

KS: Let's use another analogy with . . . EQ [equalisation]. A lot of people these days go microphone, pre[-amp] and into Pro Tools and they record everything flat and sort it out later. For me that never works because if everything is just flat, you don't know what frequencies the whole thing is to create a full scale frequency map . . . so that Guitar 2 is in a slightly different frequency range from Guitar 1, so you can tell the difference.

Although this was initially the case with monophonic recording, it is still important in stereo (and digital) to have a different timbre for instruments of similar design:

KS: Let's use the Beatles as an example, we had to get a different sound between John and George, to make sure you could hear the two parts because it was all coming out of one speaker. . . . I still think you should make them sound different as well so if they ever do come together you can tell the difference and you try and build this full spectrum of sound. If you are leaving everything flat you don't know what it's going to sound like in the end so how can you record the next bit to get it to match in. If everything is blue you don't know how the red is going to fit in a picture.

The artistic approach is not only limited to equalisation but also the number of tracks recorded. When recording music it is important to not lose sight of the sonic attributes of the whole work:

CK: As you're progressing through the production you're not really listening to the total sound or the instruments that are in the arrangement so you will be adding things sonically or performance wise that aren't related to everything else that has been recorded. . . . When you come to mix it all you realise parts don't work together.

Digital technology in some instances has taken the artistry away from the performer and into the hands of the production team:

CL: I have had younger sopranos . . . who think 'I don't have to hit that high note' and doing it a couple of tones lower and then asking for it to be tuned up or you can punch in the high C a number of times . . . but for me it doesn't always flow properly. . . . Technology has actually hampered the live feel of the recordings.

Environment

The environment used to capture the recording can be an important element for a considerable amount of recorded music:

CK: Microphone choice first, then the size and acoustic sound of the recording room . . . as long as the room I put the musicians in is the sound I want to capture for me. . . . I am less concerned about what's in the control room.

The room used to record is an important consideration for young engineers for certain styles of music. It is reasonable to suggest that a considerable amount of electronic dance music could feasibly do without this requirement apart from the capture of some vocal parts. This is different for other genres, such as classical:

CL: I don't use too many digital reverbs because I tend to use the sound of the hall.

It is also suggested that the history of the environment can also have an impact upon the production:

KS: EMI [Abbey Road] Number 2 . . . the most magical studio in the world. . . . It is do with the sound of the room but also every time I go there I will stand at the top of the stairs and the hair will stand up at the back of my neck, there is so much history in there you feel it in the walls . . . it's amazing.

Commercial

There is a perception that analogue approaches to music production are more expensive than digital. In addition, budgets have decreased for this type of activity:

KS: In so many places it is not even offered to [bands] and because of expense a lot of record companies say you have to do it a certain way and these days it is more expensive to do it analogue [recording].

The lack of availability of analogue tape makes this a superfluous consideration in modern recording practice. However, the number of affordances that digital technologies offer can sometimes extend the time taken to mix an album, and these additional costs in labour need to also be considered:

KS: When we recorded *Honky Château* with Elton [John] the whole album was recorded in two weeks and quickly into the charts after completion. Some albums produced using digital means are spending six months in the post-production stage.

The perception of music producers and the pragmatics of the situation have translated into how experts are being influenced to work:

CL: I partly think this is to do with the economics: we just don't have the budgets these days for going into commercial studios rather than home studios.

Alongside the changes that influence the time spent at the mixing stage there are also pressures from artists to produce recordings of increased loudness:

CK: So the Loudness Wars become an interesting factor because it has taken the dynamics out of modern recording and most young users/musicians want their music to be louder than anyone else's.

Although this is a well-known phenomenon within modern recorded music, industry experts can put pressure on producers to follow current trends:

CK: The mastering engineer says it sounds fantastic, I don't have to do much to it, but I've really got to raise the level because if I just put it onto CD at your level its going to sound really quiet because of the Loudness Wars.

Towards a framework for considering audio recording principles

It seems clear from the superordinate themes identified in this research that knowledge, skills, and a human perspective are useful starting points for educators engaged with using technology in music production. The capture of performance and the preparation of musicians entering the studio can help alleviate the locus of control shifting from artists to engineer. The Eighth Annual Art of Record Production Conference in Quebec had a special interest group that explored this particular theme. At the time of writing this chapter the outcome of this symposium is being brought together into an edited volume.

Expertise and studio tools are also important considerations and a deeper understanding of how tools are used needs to be developed alongside when this apparatus is used (Figure 3.1). There is a wealth of information concerning the theory and use of the technology but perhaps less has been achieved in understanding the nature of the production itself. An understanding of musical form is also integral to the skills necessary for young music producers to develop the requisite musical understanding alongside the technical know-how. How recorded sound is critically evaluated also requires attention with more subjective artistic interpretation being as important as the mathematical view of editing.

The number of new affordances that digital technology adds to the production chain can serve to distract the learner from what is important in the production: the music. One of the key ingredients from a human perspective is how decisions are made and the timing of those judgements. Perhaps by providing the necessary scaffolding educators can use specific criteria in order to develop an

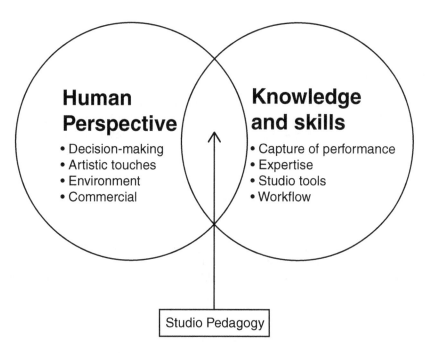

Figure 3.1 Framework for recording-studio pedagogy

understanding of the processes involved. This could subsequently lead to forming views about how processes are applied in the studio and consideration of the importance of these tools from an artistic perspective.

The environment can have an impact, yet access to large-scale commercial facilities will be beyond the reach of many music educators. Many of the albums by artists such as the Beatles were recorded in a large room that allowed interaction between performers and the real-time capture of a considerable amount of the recording, and there are important differences between this approach and subsequent studio albums that relied upon overdubbing additional parts but the very essence of the recording remained the same. All of this was achieved before scientific evaluation of the acoustics had taken place.

Commercial restrictions have put pressure on budgets for recordings. Disruptive technology (see Christensen 1997) such as MP3s altered the recording industry and caused a radical rethink of the relationship between production companies and consumers, and many people cited file-sharing as the main contributing factor to shrinking budgets. The pressure applied to sound engineers and artists to increase the loudness of recorded work in some genres is a matter for concern for educators. Artistic realisation could be restricted through a limited dynamic bandwidth and the fatigue caused by listening to sound at high amplitude levels has implication for how humans engage with music. In a 2013 interview, renowned mastering engineer Bob Katz talked about technologies that are beginning to be put in place to negate the need for industry specialists to keep increasing loudness. The full impact of this is yet to be fully realised in the music industry in 2014.

Conclusion

The access and affordances that digital technology offers to young musicians is without doubt a significant enabler for musical creation. Yet how these technologies are harnessed has become an increasingly important consideration for educators. If technology is viewed as a tool for the production of music, then an approach that makes the technology more transparent would appear to be fundamental. It would seem the locus of control in some musical genres too often unnecessarily rest with the technology and those who operate it rather than the artist. Mumford discusses the perspective of technology in relation to the phonograph:

> For that final purposeful act, the whole apparatus, physical and neural, is indispensable: yet the most minute analysis of the brain tissue, along with the phonograph's mechanical paraphernalia, would still throw no light upon the emotional stimulation, the aesthetic form, and the purpose and meaning of music.
>
> (Mumford 1967: 27)

This brings to the foreground the important question of whether the digital technology used to capture human performance has, in the hands of some users and in some genres, changed our perception of music. Although, this research acknowledges a more in-depth environmental study into different genres of recorded music, including producers who have worked exclusively in the digital domain, is now necessary, what will hopefully be of use to researchers is access to the perspectives of producers who have experienced the industry across many decades.

Acknowledgements

I wish to acknowledge the contribution of Chris Kimsey, Craig Leon, and Ken Scott: three legendary music producers.

Notes

1   There is a further position, technological somnambulism, that views technology as a tool, but it is not relevant to this discussion.
2   Fortunately, several artists and producers connected with the studio quickly made efforts to save it with composers such as Sir Andrew Lloyd Webber offering to purchase it. The UK government granted it Grade II listed status and removed any possibility that it would be developed into housing.
3   Formal and informal music learning in certain contexts refers to aspects of music learning that occur both within and outside the classroom respectively.
4   Friar Park Studio, Henley-on-Thames.
5   Musical Instrument Digital Interface.
6   An 8-track digital recorder that could be daisy-chained with other units to increase the capacity of tracks.
7   See <http://dr.loudness-war.info>.
8   All of the interviewees indicated that it was rare for the initial producers or engineers of an album to be consulted if it was remastered for digital release.

References

Ballou, G.M., ed. (2002). *The Handbook for Sound Engineers*. Oxford: Focal Press.

Bartlett, B., and J. Bartlett (2008). *Practical Recording Techniques.* Oxford: Focal Press.

Bergh, A., and T. DeNora (2009). 'From Wind-Up to iPod: Techno-Cultures of Listening'. In N. Cook et al., *The Cambridge Companion to Recorded Music.* New York: Cambridge University Press.

Blake, A. (2009). 'Recording Practices and the Role of the Producer'. In N. Cook et al., *The Cambridge Companion to Recorded Music.* New York: Cambridge University Press.

Borwick, J. (1996). *Sound Recording Practice.* Oxford: Oxford University Press.

Burgess, R.J. (2008). 'Producer Compensation: Challenges and Options in the New Music Business'. *Journal on the Art of Record Production*, 3: 1–9.

Christensen,. (1997). *The Innovators Dilemma: When New Technologies Cause Great Firms to Fail.* Boston, MA: Harvard Business School Press.

Davis, D., and E. Patronis (2006). *Sound System Engineering.* Oxford: Focal Press.

Frith, S., and S. Zagorski-Thomas, eds (2012). *The Art of Record Production.* Farnham: Ashgate.

Gillham, B. (2005). *Research Interviewing: The Range of Techniques.* Maidenhead, Berks.: Open University Press.

Green, L. (2002). *How Popular Musicians Learn: A Way Ahead for Music Education.* Aldershot: Ashgate.

Huber, D.M., and R.E. Runstein (2009). *Modern Recording Techniques.* Oxford: Focal Press.

Katz, M. (2004). *Capturing Sound: How Technology has Changed Music.* Berkeley: University of California Press.

King, A. (2008). 'Collaborative Learning in the Music Studio'. *Music Education Research,* 10/3: 423–43.

—— (2009). 'Contingent Learning for Creative Music Technologists'. *Technology, Pedagogy and Education,* 18/2: 137–53.

—— (2012). 'The Student Prince: Music-Making with Technology'. In G. McPherson and G. Welch (eds). *The Oxford Handbook of Music Education,* vol. 2. New York: Oxford University Press.

Kersholt, J.H., and J.G.W. Raaijmakers (1997). 'Decision Making in Dynamic Task Environments'. In R. Ranyard, W.R. Crozier, and O. Svenson (eds), *Decision Making: Cognitive Models and Explanations.* London: Routledge.

Lamere, P. (2009). 'The Loudness War Analyzed', *Music Machinery* [blog]. Available at <http://musicmachinery.com/2009/03/23/the-loudness-war> (accessed 30 Oct 2015).

Manning, P. (2013). *Electronic and Computer Music.* Oxford: Oxford University Press.

Moylan, W. (2007). *Understanding and Crafting the Mix.* Oxford: Focal Press.

Mumford, L. (1952). *Art and Technics.* London: Oxford University Press.

—— (1967). *The Myth of the Machine.* London: Martin Secker & Warburg.

Norman, D. (1998). *The Design of Everyday Things.* New York: Basic Books.

Pras, A., and Guastavino, C. (2013). 'The Impact of Producers' Comments and Musicians' Self-Evaluation on Perceived Recording Quality'. *Journal of Music, Technology and Education,* 6/1: 81–101.

—— M. Lavoie, and C. Guastavino (2013). 'The Impact of Technological Advances on Recording Studio Practices'. *Journal of the American Society for Information Science and Technology,* 64/3: 612–26.

Rumsey, F. (2009). 'Faithful to His Masters Voice? Questions of Fidelity and Infidelity in Music Recording'. In M. Doğantan-Dack, *Recorded Music: Philosophical and Critical Reflections.* London: Middlesex University Press.

—— and T. McCormick (2009). *Sound and Recording.* Oxford: Focal Press.

Slater, M., and A. Martin (2012). 'A Conceptual Foundation for Understanding Musico-Technological Creativity'. *Journal of Music, Technology and Education,* 5/1: 59–76.

Smith, J.A., P. Flowers, and M. Larkin (2009). *Interpretative Phenomenological Analysis.* London: Sage.

Taylor, T.D. (2001). *Strange Sounds: Music, Technology and Culture.* New York: Routledge.

Théberge, P. (1997). *Any Sound You Can Imagine: Making Music / Consuming Technology.* Hanover, NH: Wesleyan University Press.

—— (2012). 'The End of the World as We Know It: The Changing Role of the Studio in the Age of the Internet'. In S. Frith and S. Zagorski-Thomas (eds), *The Art of Record Production.* Farnham: Ashgate.

Vickers, E. (2010). 'The Loudness War: Background Speculation and Recommendations'. In *The Proceedings of the Audio Engineering Society 129th Convention,* vol. 1. AES: San Francisco.

4 How is theoretical research meeting the challenges of pedagogy in the field of record production?

Simon Zagorski-Thomas

Introduction

My experience in the academic field of record production has involved keeping a finger in many disciplinary pies: music technology / recording arts,[1] popular music studies, ethnomusicology, performance studies, and the analysis of music without recourse to scores. In the decade that I have been involved in running the Art of Record Production conference, journal, and academic association, contributions have come from academics in all of these disciplines and more. In 2009 and 2010, the conferences included sessions on music technology and education and one of the key divisions that was evident in those discussions and elsewhere has been between, on the one hand, researchers interested in a theoretical understanding of the production process and the recorded output and, on the other, practitioners and educators interested in the history and current practices of 'how to'. Of course there were people with feet in both camps and there were many points of intersection and overlap in the subject matter and approaches. Over the years and in a variety of publications (e.g. Zagorski-Thomas 2007, 2010a, 2010b, 2012, forthcoming; Zagorski-Thomas and Frith 2012), I have attempted to find ways to build connections between these two camps and, indeed, that is a vital feature of the various Art of Record Production projects. My research has focused in particular on the ecological approach to perception (Gibson 1979) and embodied cognition (Lakoff and Johnson 2003), and I will be using examples from this later, but my point is about the bridging of the gap more generally between theory and practice. Of course, I am far from alone in this aspiration, but, as with virtually any vocational academic subject, there is a gap of understanding between the theoreticians and the practitioners that needs continuous attention if it is not to become too wide. An additional issue in this field is that the higher education agenda has been led by practitioners rather than theoreticians but in a more recent turn, at least in the UK, many of these practitioner/educators are now taking doctorates and a younger generation of academics with doctorates are starting to move into academic teaching posts. Little by little then, the pedagogy is becoming more research informed and even research led. How though, as my title asks, is the theoretical research meeting the challenges of pedagogy?

Defining the question

Before I can attempt any answers to this question, there are two definitions that need to be attempted. What type of theoretical research am I talking about and what do I mean by the phrase 'the challenges of pedagogy in the field of record production'? I'm going to address the latter before the former and, as part of that, should also address the sub-question of what I mean by the field of record production. While it should obviously include the education of sound engineers, record producers, and the contemporary forms of composition that include the processing and production techniques of modern studio practice, I contend that it should also include performers, arrangers, and the more 'traditional' score-based modes of composition.

We draw a much cleaner line between theatre-based and screen-based forms of drama than we do between the live stage and the recording studio in music. The theatre and the concert hall provide a one-time-only, real-time performance experienced from a fixed and relatively distant perspective. The cinema and recorded music are non-linear constructions where the audience can be placed in almost any spatial relationship with the performers: near or far. When actors and writers of drama are being educated they are taught about the different skills required on the stage and for screen, and yet this hardly ever happens when educating musicians about the concert stage in comparison to the recording studio. In addition to my recent efforts on the master's courses at the London College of Music,[2] I have encountered only a few examples where the education of musicians recognises the different skills required in these two areas. Bhupinder Chaggar at Leeds College of Music taught a module on studio musicianship that was discontinued in the 2011/12 academic year and Amy Blier-Carruthers teaches a module on studio experience to postgraduates at the Royal College of Music. Many popular music courses such as the commercial music degree at Bath Spa and the popular music performance pathways at the London College of Music include modules on production that teach performers how to use recording technology, but that is not the same thing. In addition, many performance courses require students to make recordings that are included in portfolio assessments. It seems very rare though for performance students to be taught, for example, about the way that their engagement with recording technology can alter the resulting sound, what kinds of options they may have in terms of monitoring and how it may affect their performance or the different approaches or strategies they may adopt in relation to 'take selection'[3] and editing. All in all, in a world where a large proportion of a musician's working life may be spent in studios and where recordings are routinely used to assess and select musicians for work, the educational system should be doing its utmost to make students alive to the creative possibilities and technical requirements of the recording process.

The flipside to this is that, in my experience, music technology and recording arts courses tend to be focused on teaching students how to use the technology with less recourse to questions of how to work with musicians in the studio or how the technical practicalities of production might affect musical meaning. Based on my experience as an external examiner in the UK and of discussion and observation through conferences and visits to other universities around the world, I see a mismatch, or at the very least a pronounced imbalance, between the theoretical content and the practical aims in these types of higher education courses. The theoretical content relating to technology tends to be science focused – concerned with the way it works rather than its musical effect – and the musicology/cultural theory tends to be from the reception-based approach of the sociology of popular music audiences, genres, and subcultures. Neither of these bodies of knowledge has a strong and intuitive link to informing and underpinning the conventions of professional practice that constitutes much of the rest of course content.

Part of the reason for this, and for the parallel gaps in performance and composition pedagogy, is down to intransigence in the university and conservatoire system and part is down to the virtual absence of pedagogical resources in these aspects of the subject area. This scarcity stems from the lack of a substantive body of theoretical analysis and understanding of this area which, in turn, flows from the fact that it is only very recently that there has been any research in this area. It is, therefore, important to point out that, while I am discussing these issues in the context of a book geared towards music technology and recording arts in education, the bigger issue is that of achieving the wider recognition within music pedagogy in general that the experience of listening to and creating recorded music is substantially different to the live stage. With this bigger issue in mind though, the challenges that are faced by pedagogy in the field of record production are twofold:

1   to engage with the complexities of studying the recorded artefact and how they differ from the concert stage; and
2   to use that knowledge, along with the existing body of knowledge about the uses of audio technology, to delve more meaningfully into the nature of the recording process.

The study of music as a recorded artefact has only really been engaged with in popular music studies and, in a more tangential way, in ethnomusicology. The question of how recorded music differs from live performance is largely ignored though – even in performance studies and popular music studies. In the mainstream of music pedagogy, little or no analytical distinctions are made between examining a 'work' as a score, a live performance, or a recording. At the same time, the pedagogy that involves listening skills in recording arts courses is mainly about learning to recognise what kinds of techniques and processing were used to make the recording sound as it does.[4] The question of how the manipulation, distortion, and schematic representation of performances that is inherent in the nature of recorded music influences a listener's interpretation is seldom or never broached. And if this kind of knowledge is never explored in music pedagogy that relates to interpretation and ontology, then it cannot be applied to the task of examining its implications on the production process. Although the small amount of pedagogy relating to performance in the studio can and does discuss the practicalities of the process and the teaching of production engages with the way technology alters sound, without a theoretical substrate that seeks to explain how these factors can affect a recorded performance and the interpretations they are likely to induce, it remains a very 'thin' subject area for higher education.

The other aspect of defining this question is the nature of the theoretical research. As I have discussed, one of the crucial questions is; how do recordings create meaning? Answers to this question will facilitate the development of educational strategies that not only allow analysis to move beyond the restrictions of the score but will also allow the education of performers, composers, producers, and sound engineers to meet the challenges of the workplace and the norms of contemporary musical practice. The challenge resides in expanding the pedagogy from ideas such as 'if this parameter, then this sound' into 'this form of interpretation stems from this sonic characteristic (and these technical parameters)'. This expands the whole role of the practitioner from someone who learns the current 'right' ways of doing things to someone who has a theoretical understanding of the consequences of their creative decisions and can thus construct a more nuanced form of practice that is more based around the creative requirements of a particular project. And that, of course, is the aim of higher education.

One way in which this challenge is being met is through the application of the ecological approach to perception, embodied cognition, and conceptual blending to musical analysis (see e.g. Clarke 2005, 2007; Moore 2012; Zagorski-Thomas 2012; 2014a). Another is through a range of strands in performance research that are examining the forms of interaction and the social relationships and dynamics that are played out in all forms of musical activity (see e.g. Bayley 2011; Blier-Caruthers 2010; Kaastra 2008; Rink 2002). There are, of course, other approaches being taken in research that will inform this kind of pedagogy: for example, McIntyre (2011) on musical creative systems, Danielsen (2006, 2010) on the analysis of rhythm in recorded performance, Stobart (2008) on new approaches in ethnomusicology, and Clarke and Cook (2004) on new developments in empirical musicology. Rather than attempt a definitive survey of the research area, I am going to use three examples of which I have first hand knowledge and experience to illustrate some of the ways in which I believe music technology pedagogy and research need to progress.

Example one: Performance in the studio

The first example is performance in the studio. I recently organised a research network on this topic in which eight core researchers and several invited guests from a variety of backgrounds came together to discuss the issues and to explore the potential fruitfulness of interdisciplinary collaboration. The network studied a staged recording session which was documented through multiple-camera video, screen capture of the recording software, all of the audio session files and details of the editing process, and interviews with all the participants. This has allowed the theoretical links between the differing analytical approaches that the researchers engaged in to be examined. Some preliminary findings were published as part of the on-line conference on the website and this will be explored further in an edited collection to be published in 2015.[5] An interesting additional aspect of this project is that the Grammy-winning producer of the session, Mike Howlett, works part-time as an academic at the Queensland University of Technology. As part of the network's discussions, he and the other participants have provided a very insightful narrative of explanation and analysis that blurs the boundaries between a case study by observer/researchers and auto-ethnography/practice as research. Indeed, Howlett (2009) looks at several case studies from his own creative practice as a producer to explore the issues of encouraging and facilitating performances in the studio.

Another project that obviously feeds into this area of research is the broader look at performance studies in music spearheaded by the Centre for Musical Performance as Creative Practice (CMPCP) involving a collaboration between the universities of Oxford and Cambridge, King's College London, and Royal Holloway College.[6] The associated Performance Studies Network (PSN) conference at the University of Cambridge in April 2013 showcased the wide range of work currently being undertaken in this field. While there was not a great deal of work that dealt with the differences between the recording studio and the concert stage, many of the approaches provide valuable theoretical frameworks for developing research informed pedagogy on performance in the studio.

I had also been working on a parallel project as a visiting fellow at the CMPCP in conjunction with Amy Blier-Carruthers from the Royal College of Music on student attitudes to performance in the studio, some of the findings of which were presented at the PSN conference. This involved studies with students from the London College of Music, Leeds College of Music, the Royal College of Music, Guildhall School of Music and Drama and tech music schools. The students had a range of musical backgrounds from hip-hop and rock to jazz and classical and a range of techniques including interviews, filmed recording sessions, video recall, and written statements were used. The aim was to examine students' attitudes to and knowledge about the recording process and to use this knowledge to develop pedagogical strategies for giving them a better understanding of the creative possibilities of recorded music.

Both instrumental and vocal students and music-production students would benefit greatly from a more nuanced understanding of the possibilities and requirements of performing in the studio. One of the key findings of the research, however, is more about the requirements of the research itself than the nature of the results. While the theoretical knowledge is crucial for framing the research, the importance of practice-as-research and auto-ethnography in this process has also illustrated that practical knowledge, the experience of 'doing', is equally crucial. Of course, vocational pedagogy is no stranger to the idea that important knowledge can come through practical experience. However, vocational pedagogy and practice-as-research both suffer from their lowly position in the traditional hierarchy of academic subjects and research methodologies in the university system. While that may discourage some and prevent others through a lack of funding, this does seem to be the way forward. The important thing is to develop rigorous approaches to the representation and dissemination of these types of experiential knowledge. A written exegesis is unlikely to be sufficient. Multimedia presentations that allow a 'reader' to see, hear, and possibly otherwise engage with a researcher's practice can also be 'annotated' to help to impart this experience of doing-as-knowing through descriptive or analytical voice-over commentary or illustrative practical experiments or demonstrations that the reader can engage in. Indeed, these kinds of annotation are not only useful for dissemination, they also force the researcher to develop a richer cognitive model of this doing as knowing (see e.g. Ingold 2013), and to find more concrete and explicit links between this practical knowledge and their theoretical framework.

Example two: Record production in musicology

The second example relates to research that seeks to bring record production into the mainstream of musical analysis. While, as mentioned in the discussion of the Art of Record Production conference, this seems to have attracted researchers from a wide range of disciplines, there is a much more firmly entrenched system of thought in music analysis than there is in the relatively new subject areas of music technology and performance studies. Musical notation and the score as a cipher for the work still have a firm stranglehold on analytical pedagogy in music departments. I am certainly not suggesting that the study of scores is not a useful activity, but it is a distorting one. The visual representation of music that it provides, privileges certain aspects of the musical experience above others and encourages the analysis of, for example, harmony and form above timbral shaping and expressive timing. One of the perhaps ironic side effects of recorded music is that it encouraged the development of performance studies as a discipline by providing an alternative form of representation of musical works to notation. Drawing on the analogy of theatre and film/television/video as parallel to live and recorded music, the irony lies in the fact that performance studies has tended to use recordings to develop theories about live performance practice.

At the same time, music-technology / recording-arts courses seem resistant to incorporating discussions of musical meaning into their examination of technical mediation and audio quality. The majority of the pedagogic literature in this area either has recourse to empirical estimations of space and distance in recorded music or relates to subjective yet descriptive terms such as 'punchy' or 'thin' when it makes an attempt to explain the effect of a particular technique or technology.[7] Notions such as the persona of the recorded performer(s) (Frith 1998: 183–202; Moore 2012: 179–214), the staging of the recorded performance (Moylan 1992; Lacasse 2005; Zagorski-Thomas 2014a) and the communicative nature of musical performance (Monson 1997: 73–96) are important theoretical contributions to our understanding of how we interpret recorded music and yet they are rarely used in production pedagogy. Similarly, research on groove (Danielsen 2006) and the perception of rhythm (London 2004) or subjective terminology such as heaviness (Mynett 2013) or authenticity (Moore 2012) are equally unlikely to appear in curricula.

My experience with both undergraduate and postgraduate students interested in the practicalities of production is that this type of research is the hardest to get them to engage with because the connections between theory and practice are the least clear. They can see how the theoretical approaches may relate to an academic analysis of the music but not how that might make them a better producer. I am not suggesting that should be the yardstick for assessing research such as this or, indeed, for curriculum design, just that students tend to apply it, and it is one of the primary motivations for most students of recording. There are, however, two clear ways in which this type of analysis can be related to practice: the development of an incisive musical ear and an understanding of how processing affects interpretation. I am going to deal with the second of these more fully in relation to the third example in the next section, but the basic premise is that our perceptual and cognitive system works in a particular way and an understanding of that allows recordists to manipulate the sonic output to suggest particular forms of interpretation.

The development of an incisive musical ear is such a basic and key skill in the world of production that it almost seems too obvious to mention: like saying that a good footballer needs good ball skills. The challenge for both research and pedagogy is to define what an incisive musical ear is and to break that definition down into a series of features that would allow us to build strategies to enable their acquisition. Existing literature for recording pedagogy in this area focuses on technical ear training (e.g. Corey 2010) or relating particular techniques to general or instrument-specific characteristics such as 'clang', 'power', 'string noise', and so on (e.g. Case 2007; Izhaki 2008). These are vital skills for sound recorders in the same way that an ability to recognise intervals, rhythms, and chord progressions are vital skills for musicians. However, both types of students also need the skills that will provide them with an ability to 'see' the bigger musical picture: the ways in which these details combine to suggest or encourage a particular form of interpretation. Of course, the problem in the past has been that the theoretical basis for this kind of bigger musical picture has been couched in terms derived from a musicology based on notation. As the musicology of recorded music and record production progresses in conjunction with other analytical approaches based on the sound of music rather than the instructions for how to create the sound, there is ever increasing scope to incorporate this into pedagogy.

How though, can concepts such as persona, staging, heaviness, or authenticity help with the practicalities of learning how to produce recorded music? I would argue that they help with an understanding of the bigger musical picture, but that, in itself, is another rather broad and bland statement that needs unpicking and examining in detail before it will be of any practical use. The key feature of all of these concepts is that they are attempts to identify some invariant properties of the process of interpretation among particular groups of listeners. Discussion of persona is concerned with various aspects of the perceived character of a performer, staging is concerned with the perceived environment in which the performance occurs, heaviness is a gestural and attitudinal term, and authenticity is a concept that seeks to explore and explain the subjective notion of the perceived validity of a performer or performance and the ways in which that may be assessed. In the past, a good producer had to learn how to manipulate these factors in the appropriate manner through the acquisition of tacit knowledge (Polanyi 1966) and without a common professional vocabulary through which to explore them. Production was not (and, for the most part, still is not) discussed in these terms but the ideas behind them were and are implicit in their practice. As this type of research filters through into pedagogy and the industry becomes increasingly populated with university educated practitioners, these representational and explanatory models will become ubiquitous in the professional world. Producers will understand that features like these are phenomena that can be affected by the complex interaction of factors such as gesture, narrative, position, and environment which, in turn, are affected by the complex interaction of performing, arranging, recording, and mixing techniques.

If higher education pedagogy in vocational subjects like this is to justify its continued existence then it needs to demonstrate that it offers a substantive and qualitative 'step up' from the wide range of practical equipment and software training that is available in the hobbyist literature[8] and private diplomas and certificates.[9] At the same time, it also needs to be grounded in a richer soil than the narrow confines of traditional academic models of knowledge and understanding. There is no point in merely trying to transplant the educational model of the apprentice system from the studios to the universities while grafting on some additional theory about how the technology works. There is also no point in universities acting as training centres for particular software or hardware platforms. There are two directions that this could go in. The first is in the direction of software development and the nature of musical sound, and the second is in the direction of musicology and providing the bigger musical picture so that students can get a real understanding of how the technology they use affects and creates musical meaning. As the first direction takes me outside the normal scope of music education and into computing and physics, I will focus on the second.

This step up beyond the hobbyist 'how-to' agenda to include the bigger musical picture by engaging with ideas from current musicology that seek to explain how we interpret recorded music needs to be elaborated a little further. As mentioned in the introduction, the experience of recorded music is fundamentally different to the experience of live music in the same way that theatre is different to cinema. Just as film makers can determine our perspective on a scene, can put us in an intimate or distant relationship with an actor at any given moment, can stitch together multiple different performances to create a single narrative and so forth, so too can the makers of recorded music. Some of this is to do with getting film actors to behave differently to stage actors, some is to do with getting screen writers to produce different types of scripts to playwrights, and some is to do with the use of the technology. Each of these has parallels with live and recorded music. In addition to these differences there is the common ground – for example, the sense of narrative and character in drama and of form and dynamics in music. If music-technology / recording-arts pedagogy is to rise to the challenge of demonstrating its categorical difference to product training and the online hints and tips of industry veterans, then it needs to show that it is providing students with the conceptual tools to think about how music is put together. There is a new wave of research that has been, over the past decade, developing ways of thinking about how musical sound suggests meaning and this could provide those conceptual tools. It is then up to educators to build research informed curricula that encourage students to make the connections between the practical techniques and their musical vision. For example, if they start to think of heaviness in terms of perceived gesture and attitude, they might decide to look for audio processing techniques that encourage a conceptual fusion of the activity of several separate musicians into a large and powerful single agency. This might be combined with timbral and spatial processing that is suggestive of high energy activity happening close to the listener in a confined space – or alternatively, something that is more distant, public, and stadium-like. A great deal of this research in musicology on the interpretation of musical sound (rather than notation) is based on recent work in neuroscience, perceptual theory, and cognition, and that is where I will turn for my third example.

Example three: Cognition versus psychoacoustics

The third example is concerned with research that seeks to introduce a more complex 'higher level' element into the psychoacoustics of the recording process. Current academic texts on psychoacoustics seem to focus on the physiology of hearing and make it hard for students to make meaningful connections between the theoretical work and processes such as dynamic compression and frequency equalisation (see e.g. Howard and Angus 1996; Rossing, Moore, and Wheeler 2001). Recent work on the cognitive basis of musical (and sonic) interpretation can provide these sorts of connections and allow students a much richer engagement with the musical effect these processes can elicit from listeners.

Once again, I am going to draw upon research of which I have first-hand knowledge and experience but that should not be taken to imply that there is not a lot of other work in this area. The background is Gibson's (1979) ecological approach to perception, work on embodied cognition, and cross-domain mapping particularly from the field of cognitive linguistics (see e.g. Fauconnier and Turner 2003; Feldman 2008; Lakoff and Johnson 2003; and) and work from neuroscience on how perception and action are physiologically are linked in some very significant ways (e.g. Damasio 2000; Rohrer 2005). This work from other disciplines has informed the work of Clarke (2005) and Moore (2012) as well as my own and forms the basis for a range of different approaches to musical analysis (e.g. Windsor and De Bézenac 2012; Zbikowski 2004). One of the key features of the ecological approach to perception is the way in which invariant properties, features which recur frequently in the perceptual input, become associated with the affordance of specific activity[10] through repeated experience rather than cognition and interpretation (Zagorski-Thomas 2014b). Frequent experience establishes pathways through the brain connecting the perception of invariant properties to affordances. Through this mechanism a child may, for example, learn that when they hit something with their hand it makes a noise, they get a sensation of pressure on their hand, and there are particular visual invariant properties to do with seeing their hand moving and stopping. They will also learn that harder physical effort makes sounds richer in high frequency harmonics. The neuroscience supporting embodied cognition (see e.g. Feldman 2008: 163–71) suggests that the same parts of the brain that are active in the performance of certain actions are also active when we see someone else perform those actions. Theories of embodied cognition extend this notion to not only suggest that my understanding of seeing (or hearing) someone hit an object is based on this kind of empathic brain activity – that is, I understand it by partially experiencing the action of hitting something myself – but also that all of our understanding is based on cross-domain mapping from what we perceive to some previous bodily experience. Cross-domain mapping (see Fauconnier and Turner 2003) is the process of making connections from some established pathways to others. Thus, in a very simple example, the sound of an electronic snare drum, something that involves no hitting and only electronics and speaker-cone movement, would create cross-domain mapping with the sound of a real drum because it shares certain sonic invariant properties. This mapping then causes me to associate other features of a real drum hit – perhaps to do with energy and gesture – with the electronic sound. This energy and gesture information may also engender further cross-domain mapping to emotional responses such as aggression or excitement.

This perceptual and cognitive model of how we interpret musical sound can be broadened to explain specific phenomena such as the schematic nature of recordings. For example, some recordings use cartoon-like sonic representations of spatial audio and their artificiality is easily recognisable, as is the 'real'[11] spatial environment that they represent (Zagorski-Thomas, forthcoming). Thus, a realistic representation of a rock band playing in a large hall would involve a long reverberation time where the low-frequency sounds would sustain for longer than the high-frequency ones. This would create a louder and more sustained bass end to the frequency spectrum but the reverberation tails would blur the start of new sounds making the rhythm of the music less clear and the pitches of the notes would fade into one another making the melody and harmony sound muddy and discordant. A frequently used schematic representation of a large hall in recorded popular music involves the addition of long reverberation tails only to high frequency sounds and the dynamic compression of the bass sound so that the tail end of the note doesn't fade away so quickly. This creates some of the features of real hall ambience without the muddiness and loss of rhythmic clarity. In the parlance of the theoretical model, it uses some of the invariant properties of spatial sound to trigger, through cross-domain mapping, the impression of the real thing.

When psychoacoustics are involved in recording education, the approach taken is usually at the physiological level of factors such as inter-ear timing differences and head-related transfer functions. The notion of how the basic cognition of the auditory stream occurs, the recognition of different sonic 'objects', is not generally seen in the literature or the course structures in this area. It might seem obvious that recording and mixing is all about influencing how a listener interprets a complex musical structure: which instruments should be grouped together, which should stand out more and what kind of space this is all happening in. However, the process through which, for example, dynamic compression of a single musical element within an ensemble recording might affect our interpretation of its expressive content, rhythmic impetus, spatial relationship, or any other musical meaning is not at all obvious (see e.g. Walther-Hansen 2012).

This again is a place where exploring the nature of embodied cognition and its part in the interpretation of musical sound may be aided by the types of practice-as-research and doing-as-knowing that were discussed earlier. Be that as it may, it is certainly one of the areas in which higher education pedagogy can differentiate itself from the hobbyist training approach.

Conclusions

Ken Robinson (2006), a former advisor to the British government on creative and cultural education, spoke in his talk on creativity at the Technology Entertainment and Design conference about the problems with the current hierarchy of academic subjects and forms of thought in the education system. His particular bugbear was the way that schools focus on these academic forms of thought and actively discourage other forms of creative thinking (including doing-as-thinking) as offering no future. Indeed, he characterised schooling as an extended admissions process for universities. Working in a post-1992 UK university that focuses on vocational courses[12] affords me a view of both how the engrained hierarchy of subjects and universities is making the acceptance of alternative ideas about knowledge difficult and slow and how the legacy of vocational training courses and the scarcity of research in some of these areas makes it hard to undermine that hierarchy through research informed teaching excellence. There is an intransigence that is built into the entire higher education and research funding system that means that change is only ever likely to come at a glacial pace.

That said, the desire to create a vibrant research community within this supposedly research-unfriendly sector of higher education has been made abundantly clear to me over the past decade through my work on the Art of Record Production project. In addition, that desire is also inflected with an ethos of 'keeping it real' by maintaining strong connections with practitioners and industry professionals. The challenge, therefore, is to create a research culture that maintains a firm grounding in practice without compromising the rigour of the research. The examples presented in this chapter have suggested two clear strategies in this regard. The first is to develop an approach to practice-as-research that recognises and embraces work such as Ingold's *Making* (2013) and doing-as-thinking but which, nonetheless, requires stringent criteria about testability and communicability. In this regard, I believe that there is a lot of mileage in the presentation of practice through annotated multimedia formats. The schematic representational capabilities of video and audio that I have discussed in relation to the research subject matter also lend themselves to highlighting and examining particular features of practical experience. This may take the form of close-ups, slow motion, multiple camera angles, repeated viewing, and other forms of non-linear presentation. It may also involve the extrapolation of particular features or factors for further analysis and practical experimentation and interviews or commentaries that can be superimposed post facto onto video documentation of practice. This also involves placing this kind of practice-as-research within the context of theoretical research. Clear connections that demonstrate the linkage and compatibility between these forms of research are essential.

The second strategy that my examples suggested was to use the emerging research in musicology, music psychology, and sociology to put some clear theoretical water between university pedagogy in this area and the hobbyist hints and tips and product training agenda that can be found in the trade literature, the internet, and some areas of private education provision. One of the cornerstones of that rather unpleasant management-speak term, 'graduateness' is the capacity for critical thinking and independent problem-solving. That requires the ability to apply theoretical thinking to a practical problem and is one of the biggest challenges facing vocational courses which are under pressure to also deliver training for industry-standard tools and platforms. As discussed, this challenge is characterised by a twin need to motivate students to engage with the theory by demonstrating the advantages it brings in terms of practical skills and to demonstrate the desirability of this type of approach over straightforward training so that the students choose to enrol. I have pointed to a specific strand of current musicology and the perceptual and cognitive theoretical substrate that underpins it, because I believe that is a particularly fruitful avenue of study, but the more general point about vocational university courses differentiating themselves from training is not tied to that area of research.

Returning to the specifics of the question in the title, I would suggest that research in music is on the cusp of a radical shift in direction and that shift is reflected in the two strategies discussed. Studying the interpretation of music through the prism of perceptual theory and cognitive science should not, as demonstrated in my third example, mean that musicologists all have to become psychologists or sociologists. Just as the theory of relativity, psychoanalysis, and Marxism helped to set the agenda for thought in the humanities for most of the twentieth century, the new approach to knowledge engendered by the internet and computers, neuroscience, and embodied cognition from linguistics appear to be setting a different agenda for the twenty-first century. These new directions in research and their influence on the cultural and philosophical zeitgeist appear, to me, to be set to enable some very exciting new directions in pedagogy. I see that in the relative backwater that is the academic field of record production, but also in the wider world of musicology and the humanities in general.

Notes

1 The conventions of nomenclature seem to have evolved such that broadly, the types of courses that in the UK come under the banner of 'music technology' are more usually categorised as 'recording arts' in the USA. There is a good deal of ambiguity everywhere about the differentiation between desktop electronic popular music composition

and computer-based recording and mixing; not least because there is a great deal of overlap between the two areas. The term 'record production' certainly is not a solution to this problem, but it does allow the inclusion of both of these topics whilst eschewing electronic popular music composition and sound engineering for the concert stage: that is, it allows me to make an important distinction between live and recorded music.

2 The students on my master's in record production work with MMus performance and popular music performance students in a level 7 module on performance in the studio.

3 By 'take selection' I mean the choice between different recorded performances or sections of performances.

4 See e.g. Corey 2010; see also: 'In no time you will develop a frequency memory which will allow you to connect the sound you imagine in your head with the needed parameters you have to dial to get it, more quickly and easily than ever' (*Train Your Ears*, <http://TrainYourEars.com> [accessed 30 Oct. 2015]).

5 See <http://www.artofrecordproduction.com/index.php/ahrc-performance-in-the-studio> (accessed 5 Oct. 2013).

6 This project is funded by the UK Arts and Humanities Research Council (see <http://www.cmpcp.ac.uk/index.html> [accessed 5 Oct. 2013])

7 For an interesting discussion of the nature of this kind of language and the way that it influences practice, see Porcello 2004.

8 e.g. *Sound On Sound*, <http://www.soundonsound.com/> (accessed 31 Oct. 2015); *Pensado's Place*, YouTube, <https://www.youtube.com/user/PensadosPlace>.

9 e.g. School of Audio Engineering (see <http://www.sae.edu/gbr/> [accessed 31 Oct. 2015]); SSR (see <http://www.s-s-r.com/> [accessed 31 Oct. 2015]).

10 This activity may be mental or muscular and, as such, may be a bodily action by the individual concerned or may be the perception of some activity occurring outside their body.

11 I use the term 'real' in inverted commas because, of course, stereo-recorded sound is a schematic representation of spatial sound in its own right. The illusion of the spatial representation is dependent on the listener being in the correct relationship to the two sound sources of the stereo playback so that they are 'fooled' by it. The same is true visually of film and photographs. They may be a less schematic representation than a cartoon but we do not mistake them for reality.

12 Aside from music, music technology, and the performing arts in the London College of Music, the rest of the University of West London includes art, design, media, computing, nursing, business, hospitality, and tourism with no departments for 'traditional' university academic subjects such as English, history, economics, politics, philosophy, mathematics, physics, chemistry, or biology.

References

Bayley, A. (2011). 'Ethnographic Research into Contemporary String Quartet Rehearsal'. *Ethnomusicology Forum*, 20/3: 385–411.

Blier-Caruthers, A. (2010). 'Live Performance – Studio Recording: An Ethnographic and Analytical Study of Sir Charles Mackerras'. PhD thesis, Kings College London.

Case, A.U. (2007). *Sound FX: Unlocking the Creative Potential of Recording Studio Effects*. Burlington, MA: Focal Press.

Clarke, E.F. (2005). *Ways of Listening: An Ecological Approach to the Perception of Musical Meaning*. New York: Oxford University Press.

—— (2007). 'The Impact of Recording on Listening'. *Twentieth Century Music*, 4/1: 47–70.

—— and N. Cook, eds (2004). *Empirical Musicology: Aims, Methods, Prospects*. Oxford: Oxford University Press.

Corey, J. (2010). *Audio Production and Critical Listening: Technical Ear Training*. Waltham, MA: Focal Press.

Damasio, A. (2000). *The Feeling of What Happens: Body, Emotion and the Making of Consciousness*, new edn. London: Vintage.

Danielsen, A. (2006). *Presence and Pleasure: The Funk Grooves of James Brown and Parliament*. Middletown, CT: Wesleyan University Press.

—— (2010). *Musical Rhythm in the Age of Digital Reproduction*. Farnham: Ashgate.

Fauconnier, G., and M. Turner (2003). *The Way We Think: Conceptual Blending and the Mind's Hidden Complexities*. New York: Basic Books.

Feldman, J.A. (2008). *From Molecule to Metaphor: A Neural Theory of Language*. Cambridge, MA: MIT Press.

Frith, S. (1998). *Performing Rites: Evaluating Popular Music*, new edn. Oxford: Oxford Paperbacks.

Gibson, J.J. (1979). *The Ecological Approach to Visual Perception*. Hillsdale, NJ: Lawrence Erlbaum Associates.

Howard, D.M., and J. Angus (1996). *Acoustics and Psychoacoustics*. Oxford: Focal Press.

Howlett, M. (2009). 'The Record Producer as Nexus: Creative Inspiration, Technology and the Recording Industry'. PhD thesis: University Of Glamorgan.

Ingold, T. (2013). *Making: Anthropology, Archaeology, Art and Architecture*. London and New York: Routledge.

Izhaki, R. (2008). *Mixing Audio: Concepts, Practices and Tools*, Burlington, MA: Focal Press.

Kaastra, L.T. (2008). 'Systematic Approaches to the Study of Cognition in Western Art Music Performance'. PhD thesis: University of British Columbia.

Lacasse, S. (2005). 'Persona, Emotions and Technology: The Phonographic Staging of the Popular Music Voice'. Paper presented at the Art of Record Production conference, London. Available at <http://www.artofrecordproduction.com/content/view/143/> (accessed 30 June 2011).

Lakoff, G., and M. Johnson (2003). *Metaphors We Live By*, 2nd edn. Chicago: University of Chicago Press.

London, J. (2004). *Hearing in Time: Psychological Aspects of Musical Meter.* New York: Oxford University Press.

McIntyre, P. (2011). *Creativity and Cultural Production: Issues for Media Practice*. Basingstoke: Palgrave Macmillan.

Monson, I. (1997). *Saying Something: Jazz Improvisation and Interaction*. Chicago: University of Chicago Press.

Moore, A.F. (2012). *Song Means: Analysing and Interpreting Recorded Popular Song*. Farnham: Ashgate.

Moylan, W. (1992). *The Art of Recording: Understanding and Crafting the Mix*. Burlington, MA: Focal Press.

Mynett, M. (2013). 'Contemporary Metal Music Production'. PhD thesis, University of Huddersfield.

Polanyi, M. (1966). *The Tacit Dimension*. Chicago: University of Chicago Press.

Porcello, T. (2004). 'Speaking of Sound: Language and the Professionalization of Sound-Recording Engineers'. *Social Studies of Science*, 34/5: 733–58.

Rink, J. (2002). *Musical Performance: A Guide to Understanding*. Cambridge: Cambridge University Press.

Robinson, K. (2006). 'Do Schools Kill Creativity?' Speech at Technology, Entertainment and Design conference, Monterey, California [video], <http://www.ted.com/talks/ken_robinson_says_schools_kill_creativity.html> (accessed 5 Oct. 2013).

Rohrer, T. (2005). 'Image Schemata in the Brain'. In B. Hampe and J. Grady (eds), *From Perception to Meaning: Image Schemas in Cognitive Linguistics*. Berlin: De Gruyter.

Rossing, T.D., R.F. Moore, and P.A. Wheeler (2001). *The Science of Sound*, 3rd edn. Harlow: Addison Wesley.

Stobart, H., ed. (2008). *The New (Ethno) Musicologies*. Plymouth: Scarecrow Press.

Walther-Hansen, M. (2012). 'The Perception of Sounds in Phonographic Space'. PhD thesis, University of Copenhagen.

Windsor, W.L. and C. De Bézenac (2012). 'Music and Affordances'. *Musicae Scientiae*, 16/1: 102–20.

Zagorski-Thomas, S. (2007). 'The Musicology of Record Production'. *Twentieth Century Music*, 4/2: 189–207.

—— (2010a). 'Real and Unreal Performances'. In A. Danielsen (ed.), *Rhythm in the Age of Digital Reproduction*. Farnham: Ashgate.

—— (2010b). 'The Stadium in Your Bedroom: Functional Staging, Authenticity and the Audience-Led Aesthetic in Record Production'. *Popular Music*, 29/2: 251–66.

—— (2012). 'Musical Meaning and the Musicology of Record Production'. *Beitraege zur Popularmusikforschung*, 38: 135–48.

—— (2014a). *The Musicology of Record Production*. Cambridge: Cambridge University Press.

—— (2014b). 'The Spectromorphology of Recorded Popular Music: The Shaping of Sonic Cartoons through Record Production'. In R. Fink, M.L. O'Brien, and Z. Wallmark (eds), *The Relentless Pursuit of Tone: Timbre in Popular Music*. New York: Oxford University Press.

—— (forthcoming). 'Sonic Cartoons'. In H. Schulze and J. Papenburg (eds), *Sound As Popular Culture: A Research Companion*, Cambridge MA: MIT Press.

—— and S. Frith, eds (2012). *The Art of Record Production: An Introductory Reader to a New Academic Field*. Farnham: Ashgate.

Zbikowski, L.M. (2004). 'Modelling the Groove: Conceptual Structure and Popular Music'. *Journal of the Royal Musical Association*, 129/2: 272–97.

Part II
Game technology

5 Impact of music on game play and communication of emotional intent

Don Knox, Gianna Cassidy and Anna Paisley

Music is a fundamental channel of communication in games, with the potential to effect player performance and experience greatly. However, the nature of the relationship between player and music and the process of communication, in particular from composer to player, has been relatively neglected. This chapter presents a two-part study investigating the processes and outcomes of musical communication from composer intent to player perception, performance, and experience. Emphasis is placed on communication of emotion and the role of music attributes in this process. The results shed light on the processes applied by the composer in order to communicate emotion, which have a resultant impact on the game-play experience and performance, communication of context, navigation, and functional reference in the game.

Introduction

Music is a fundamental channel of informational and affective communication in the video-game medium, long recognised by the industry and those who play games (see Collins 2008; Whalen 2004; Zehnder and Lipscomb 2006). Music assists the player in navigating the 'play space', directing the player through the sequence of game play, and providing functional reference and feedback (Whalen 2004). Music has also been employed to establish, enrich, and manipulate the nature of player performance and experience. Research indicates that soundtrack and player-selected music can influence parameters including accuracy, speed, retrospective estimation, and enjoyment (see Cassidy and MacDonald 2008, 2009, 2010; Zehnder and Lipscomb 2006). However, the nature of the relationship between player and music and the process of communication from composer to player have been relatively ignored. There is a need to investigate the processes and outcomes of music composition for games, subsequent musical communication during game play, and the impact of music on the player experience. This chapter describes research which focused on musical communication between the game-music composer and the player.

A common focus of research into the effects of music on the listener is emotion. Although there remains some disagreement in the literature over the precise mechanisms (Konecni 2008), there is a consensus that music evokes emotions in the listener (Juslin and Västfjäll 2008). There are several affective components of the listener's emotional response. For example, emotions are relatively intense and short-lived reactions to some event or stimulus, whereas moods are less acute and can last for hours or days (Juslin and Västfjäll 2008). Emotional engagement with music has been shown to be central to music use in everyday life, and self-regulation of mood is a common reason given for listening to music (Sloboda and O'Neill 2001; North, Hargreaves, and Hargreaves 2004). Research into the use of music for mood regulation in adolescents has shed light on key mechanisms centred around the satisfaction of personal mood-related goals – such as mood improvement, distraction from stress and worries, and promotion of self-reflection (Saarikallio and Erkkila 2007).

Although external factors play a key role in the meaning of music – personal meaning and memories affect our emotional connection with music (Miell, MacDonald, and Hargreaves 2005) – there is marked agreement between listeners about the emotion being expressed by music (Krumhansl 2002). Listeners display a common emotional response to a wide range of stimuli (Ekman and Friesen 1998), and much research has focused on music attributes and their role in causing emotional reactions: for example, tempo, timbre, articulation, and brightness (Chapin et al. 2008; Gabrielsson and Lindström 2001; Juslin 2000; Meyer 1956; Scherer and Zentner 2001; Schoonderwaldt et al. 2002). Higher-level musical structure is the focus of theories about musical expectation (Meyer 1956). This assumes the listener forms expectancies about the continuation of a particular musical performance and that violation of these assumptions results in an associated emotional reaction (Narmour 1990). Frameworks for studying this relationship have been proposed. Juslin and Timmers (2010) suggest a modification of the lens model of Brunswik (1956). The model encompasses measures of performance and music structure and how they influence perceived emotion. Studies examining communication of music emotion typically create bespoke stimuli where music attributes are manipulated experimentally. This raises a question about the ecological validity of studying the composer's creative intent. It is important that the composer is given specific directions regarding the emotion to be evoked by their music. Equally they should have free rein to create music and manipulate any musical parameters, cues, or features they see fit, and this should be a natural part of their normal creative process. The problem is finding a context where these conflicting requirements are met, and the game context has potential in this regard. Game-music composers are accustomed to being instructed by the game director on the nature of the music they must create. The music is required to fit an emotional theme allied to a specific segment of the game narrative. It is therefore a natural context in which to study the composition of music to communicate emotion, where the function of the music is very different, and the resulting effects upon the listener (the player) can be observed in terms of their reactions, feelings, and game performance parameters.

A common method of measuring listeners' emotional responses to music is the two-dimensional circumplex model (Thayer 1989), an adaptation of Russell's circumplex model of affect (Russell 1980), designed specifically around music emotion. Feeltrace is a software tool designed to measure emotion in real time (Cowie et al. 2000; see Figure 5.1). The horizontal axis represents valence (negative to positive from left to right), and the vertical axis represents arousal (low to high), with four quadrants equating to exuberance, contentment, anxiety and depression. It is common to overlay mood adjectives relating to points in the four mood quadrants (Hevner, 1935; Juslin 2000; Picard 1997).

This model has also been used in music emotion classification research which aims to identify expressed emotion through analysis of the digital music file (Eerola and Vuoskoski 2010; Knox et al. 2008; Knox et al. 2011; Lu, Liu, and Zhang 2006). The aim is to extract those features which correspond to the musical attributes important to the expression of emotion, typically separated into categories of intensity, timbre, and rhythm. Attributes are selected by reference to empirical research which has identified key musical features in the communication of music emotion (Juslin 2000, 2001; Meyer 1956). Subsequent stages involve statistical analysis and modelling of the extracted feature set in reference

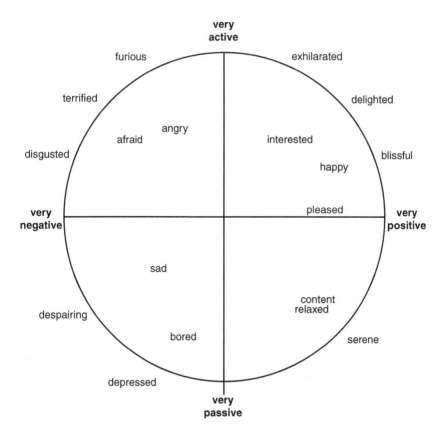

Figure 5.1 The circumplex model of affect

to the circumplex model. A typical hierarchical classification approach uses intensity features to determine the analysed music's position on the arousal axis of the circumplex model, whereas timbre and rhythm features are used to determine position on the valence axis (Lu, Liu, and Zhang 2006; Knox et al. 2008; Knox et al. 2011). The relative weighting of rhythm and timbre features are altered during valence classification. For example, classical music may be classified as low arousal if it has a slower tempo and less prominent rhythm. Music expressing contentment tends toward brightness and is more harmonic than depressed music. Thus, timbre features are important in disambiguating these two mood clusters (Juslin 2000). Recent research suggests this technique may be genre-dependent. In popular music some acoustical features become less useful in disambiguating mood than in the case of classical music, as tracks may have similar acoustical properties regardless of the emotion the music expresses (Beveridge and Knox 2012a). Timbre has been shown to be strongly correlated with how a piece of popular music is placed in both the valence and arousal dimensions of the circumplex model (Beveridge and Knox 2012b) and music intensity is much less important in dictating which mood cluster the listener will identify a piece of music as belonging to.

In summary, game music has been shown to have a significant role in affecting the game-play experience and the player's performance (Cassidy and MacDonald 2008, 2009, 2010; Zehnder and Lipscomb, 2006). The nature of the relationship between player and music and how the composer communicates meaning to the player is relatively ignored in the literature, and there is a need for more empirical investigation. This can be approached by adopting techniques developed in previous research into evoking emotion in the listener: specifically those examining how music attributes are manipulated for emotional effect and measuring both composer intent and player experience in reference to the circumplex model. This approach has potential to shed light on music attributes deemed important by the composer for emotional expression and the relative importance of timbral, rhythmic, and intensity parameters for disambiguating mood. The context of game music also has potential to contribute to research into the communication of music emotion. It is arguably ecologically valid in that it is a natural context for a composer to be given direction on the emotion to be communicated by their music, and there is an explicit goal of evoking an emotional reaction from the listener (player). It is also suited to observing the functional effects of music emotion on the listener in terms of range of player performance and experience parameters.

The first part of the study focuses on the game-music composer as they create the music for a game, with emphasis on the intended effect upon the player, musical attributes deemed important for emotional expression, and the relative importance of timbral, rhythmic, and intensity parameters for disambiguating emotion. The second part of the study focuses on the player's perceived emotion during the game and the effect of the composed music on a range of player performance and experience parameters.

The game-music composer

Methodology

A game-music composer was given an industry brief requiring 10 minutes of music for a custom mod of the game Angry Bots, consisting of four levels of play. He was given a montage of screen shots and shown a video clip of game play to gain a feel for the game genre. He was then given a description of the game narrative and mood associated with each game level. The descriptions given in the brief made reference to the circumplex model (Figure 5.1).

- Level 1:   30-second cut scene and narrative. The player is preparing to enter the game world and receives a brief narrative setting up an atmosphere of calmness and security for the upcoming activity. The emotional tone is in line with the low arousal, positive valence quadrant of the circumplex: calm, relaxed.
- Level 2:   First game-play area, lasting 2 to 5 minutes. The confidence and security of the cut scene is contradicted in this tense section. Emotional tone is high arousal, negative valence, specifically fear and anxiety.
- Level 3:   Lasting around 2 to 5 minutes, the Boss is encountered here. As in level 2, the emotional tone is high arousal, negative valence but specifically anger and aggression.
- Level 4:   Final 30-second cut scene. The player has achieved the goal of defeating the Boss, and is rewarded with a cut scene representing victory and accomplishment. Emotional tone is high arousal, positive valence: happy, excited.

The study was designed to examine the composer's intent regarding communication of emotion, and the functions and processes he applied to achieve this goal. He kept a video diary to record his progress as he created the music for the game, supplemented by a written log where key thoughts and actions were recorded. An advantage of this process is that the composer is studied in his usual creative context, helping him maintain focus on his activity (Laterza, Carmichael, and Procter 2007). After completing the composition process, a face-to-face semi-structured interview was carried out with the composer in order to generate qualitative descriptions of his approach to creating music for emotional effect. Initial prompts were developed as a basis for qualitative exploration (Weiss 1995), designed to encouraged the composer to talk about the emotional effect he intended for the music, the specific musical parameters manipulated for emotional effect, and how he disambiguated mood for each level of the game. The interview and video-diary transcripts and written logs were analysed in order to identify emerging themes around the ideas expressed by the composer. Finally a questionnaire was administered, consisting of forced-response questions designed to generate quantitative data on musical attributes used by the composer. The list of attributes was informed by research on music attributes important to expression of music emotion (see Gabrielsson and Lindstrom, 2001; Juslin, 2000; Meyer 1956) and attributes used to characterise music in the music genome project.[1] The attributes encompass rhythm, timbre, melody, sound level, and high-level music structure, including tempo, rhythm, pitch variation, timbre, and sound-level variation. This parameter set has been used in previous research due to its relatively concise nature and the fact that the attributes are objective descriptions of the music content (Reed and Lee 2007).

Results

The composer described writing music to evoke an emotional reaction. He spoke of putting himself in the player's position, thinking about how they would feel or react when hearing the music. He described trying to influence the player's arousal levels, specifically making them excited and raising their heart rate, inducing a state of relaxed calm by making the music predictable and consistent and then taking them 'out of their comfort zone' by making the music more unsettling and less predictable. He described in detail the manipulation of music attributes to achieve the desired emotional tone for each level in the game. Throughout his descriptions he emphasised his use of tempo, rhythm, and timbral/tonal aspects of the music in order to distinguish different moods.

Game-level 1 music

For the relaxed, calm level the composer described creating a soft, bright timbre and the use of instruments in a higher register such as xylophone or bell-like sounds to distinguish relaxed music from the other mood quadrants. The track is in a major key, with a prominent, simple melody with narrow pitch variation. A simple and regular rhythm was created by synthesisers and delay effects rather than percussive instruments. A predictable, repetitive structure and sparse instrumentation distinguished it from the fear and anger tracks. The tempo is around 90–100bpm, lower than the anger and excited mood quadrants (around 130bpm), but similar to fear and anxiety. Synthesiser sounds had slow attack characteristics.

Game-level 2 music

The fear and anxiety music of level 2 was in a minor key. The composer used harsh, dissonant sounds, where timbre was key to distinguishing between this track and the relaxed/calm segment. A low, sustained bass part and an atonal melody with wide melodic pitch range were intended to create a feeling of unease in the player and to sharply focus their attention on the game by introducing unsettling musical sounds. Sounds in general were pitched lower than the relaxed/calm segment. Rhythm was introduced in the form of a regular, low-tempo, sparse drum arrangement. Articulation was faster than the relaxed track and more staccato sound elements are introduced. The track is less repetitive than the relaxed and happy track. The composer considered the main difference between this track and the anger/frustration track to be tempo and the prominence of rhythm and percussive attributes:

COMPOSER: If you took out the drums from the anger track and reduced the tempo a bit you'd have a fairly decent fear and anxiety sort of thing happening.

Game-level 3 music

Anger and frustration are emphasised with harsh timbre and dissonant sounds. In combination with the minor mode and melody, this aimed to unsettle the listener. Synthesiser sounds are bright, and phrasing is rhythmic. The composer described his aim as increasing the player's arousal levels by increasing tempo, using a regular emphatic beat interspersed with prominent aggressive drum patterns and percussion. The composer describes it as being louder and more dynamic (in terms of sound level) than the relaxed/calm track. The track is similar in tempo to excited/happy but less regular in structure and rhythm.

Game-level 4 music

For the excited/happy tone of level 4, the composer described introducing a major key, bright, soft timbre, consonant harmony and major melody to distinguish this track from the two negatively valenced levels. Synthesiser sounds were less unreal or abstract than other levels. A prominent, melodic bass line was introduced which complimented a distinct melody. The composer described the importance of melody to the expressed emotion of this track:

C: A distinct melody to it. I think that's really important for this kind of feeling.

He stated that his aim was to create an uplifting or joyous feeling in the listener. Drum parts were prominent, regular and simple, and tempo did not change appreciably from level 3. Overall the track has little variation in structure or dynamics. Tempo and prominence of rhythm separates this track from relaxed/calm.

Overall in disambiguating emotion for each game level the composer describes his emphasis of tonal/timbral attributes and rhythm and tempo.

C: It's the notes, scales used, the difference between major and minor . . . the use of discordant sounds for the middle two tracks [fear/anxiety; anger/frustration]. Rhythm as well – a giant difference, using drums as a means of switching between emotions

In general, the picture that emerges is one of a composer who emphasises timbral/tonal attributes along with tempo and rhythm in order to both express and differentiate between different music emotions. In comparison, overall sound level, intensity or dynamic variations in level are mentioned rarely. A word-frequency analysis of the interview transcript was carried out in which phrases used by the composer to describe his music and the composition process were sorted into categories commonly used to describe music attributes for music emotion: intensity, timbre, rhythm (see Table 5.1). Phrases related to intensity include level, loudness, and dynamics; rhythm includes phrases such as tempo, percussion, beat, and drums; timbre includes mode, spectrum, melody, bass. The 'other' category relates to attributes that fall into neither of the previous categories and encompasses attributes like arrangement and repetition.

Table 5.1 Music attribute categories

Attribute category	Count	Percentage
Intensity	10	7.4
Timbre	70	52.2
Rhythm	47	35
Other	7	5.2

Corroborating questionnaire

The composer's questionnaire responses are summarised in Figure 5.2. The responses are overlaid on the circumplex model in order to illustrate how the attributes correlate with the emotional tone the composer was aiming for. The high activity/negative

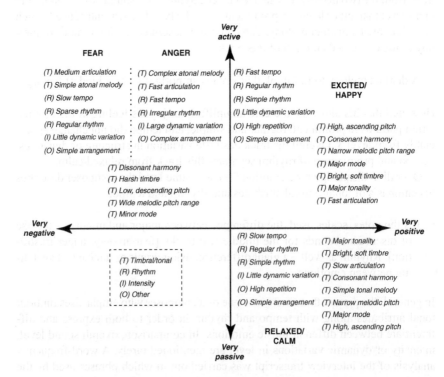

Figure 5.2 Attributes of the music for each emotion in the game

valence quadrant shows the attributes which are shared by fear and anger and also those which the composer used to distinguish them.

This figure underlines the approach adopted by the composer. For example the use of bright or harsh timbre and major or minor mode to distinguish between positive and negative moods on the valence axis is clear, as is the variation of melodic pitch range. Tempo and rhythm are used to disambiguate fear and anger. There is little mention of intensity or loudness besides loudness variations used to emphasise anger. In general, his approach is in keeping with findings from previous research, where timbre and rhythm attributes are key to communicating valence (Juslin 2000, 2001) and also results from emotion classification of popular music (Beveridge and Knox 2012b), where dynamics and intensity have little effect in disambiguating mood in terms of either arousal or valence.

The player

Part 2 of the study was designed to examine the relationship between the music, the player's perceived emotion in game, and the effect of the music on player performance and experience. The following section reports on a selected in-depth case study taken from the wider experiment employing 70 participants, with the aim of providing insight into the player experience.

Methodology

The participant was a 32-year-old male who engaged with both music and video games regularly and primarily for recreational purposes, recruited voluntarily, and unremunerated. A post-test questionnaire measuring musical and video-game experience indicated high perceived self-musicality, a high level of engagement with and importance of music, video-game play at least 'once a month', and preference for first-person-shooter games. Employing a repeated-measures design within a sequential mixed-methods framework, the participant was required to complete a 10 minute (maximum) session with the game described in part 1 in three conditions: (1) with game sounds only, (2) music and game sounds, and (3) silence. All testing took place within a usability facility complete with a replica living-room area to enhance ecological validity of the obtained results. Two discrete video cameras controlled remotely from the observation room situated behind a 2-way mirror recorded the participant's face and bodily movements (see Figure 5.3).

The participant then completed a face-to-face semi-structured interview addressing play experience; a 'cognitive walkthrough' session; a circumplex model to account for both induced (felt) and perceived emotion at each stage of the game; and a post-test background questionnaire, completion of which marked the end of the testing session at approximately 90 minutes. A chief aim of the post-test interview was to address the importance of music in game play and the participant's perception of the game music with regard to composer intentions and the resultant impact on the overall game experience. Of particular interest was whether the participant recognised the shift in the emotive content

Figure 5.3 The eMotion Lab at Glasgow Caledonian University: participant (top) and screen
capture of game play (bottom)

of the music relative to each of the four levels of the game and the impact this
had upon game play. A series of open-ended questions were administered with
further probes in instances where the participant mentioned anything of significance to the overarching aims of the study (see Braun and Clarke 2006). The
cognitive walkthrough session required him to observe a visual recording of his
participation (self and game play) in condition 2 (music and game sounds). Specifically the participant was asked to recall how he was feeling during each phase
of the game. To draw a direct comparison between the intended versus evoked
emotion of the music, the participant was asked to annotate a circumplex model
to indicate his affective state throughout each of the four phases of the game.

Results

Post-test interview

Semantic thematic analysis resulted in the identification of an initial set ($n = 4$) of recurrent themes. Clustering and further latent thematic analysis was used to organise the themes at the semantic level. What follows is an overview of each theme.

THEME 1: INCREASED FOCUS AND ENGAGEMENT

The first theme draws direct parallels with the literature on the experience of 'flow' in game play (Cowley et al. 2008) and in particular to the dimension of 'cognitive efficiency'. Discourse surrounding the participant's perceived level of increased focus and engagement made apparent the impact of music upon his perceived arousal levels and subsequent behaviour. Music was implicated as a catalyst for increased attentiveness and higher levels of engagement with the game:

PLAYER: The second time [music and game sounds] . . . erm . . . I felt quite focused.
P: Physically I felt a bit tenser. . . . I felt as if I was kind of sitting a bit straighter or sitting a bit closer to the screen . . . but I think that's all part of the focus.

Furthermore, the participant explicitly cited the addition of music as a causal contributor to his greater apparent level of focus and engagement within the game:

P: The second time I felt focused because of the music.

THEME 2: INCREASED ENJOYMENT

The second theme pertains to the recreational value of the game. This appeared to be enhanced by the inclusion of music, with recourse to the palpable enjoyment of the experience in contrast to the other conditions:

INTERVIEWER: Just in talking about your 'enjoyment' . . . erm . . . did you enjoy playing the game overall?
P: Mmm-hmm [*nods*] . . . mostly on the second occasion . . . I felt as if I was enjoying it better.
P: The third time [no sound] . . . probably quite bored I would say.

Direct references to music as a key factor in the participant's feelings of enjoyment permeated the transcript, in comparisons between game play across all three conditions.

I: Why on the second occasion [music and game sounds] in particular?

P: [*long pause*] Without having the . . . the contrast of the [other] two occasions I probably couldn't have answered it, but . . . looking at it them . . . next to the first occasion [game sounds only] and the third occasion [no sound] it . . . it was definitely because of the music that was in it.

THEME 3: INCREASED INTERACTION AND PERSONAL IMPORTANCE

The music facilitated a more enjoyable and engaging experience for the user, with many references to increased interaction with the game as a result of the music. Importantly this appeared to foster a deeper sense of subjective, personal relevance and importance of his experience and performance:

P: The last time [no sound] . . . because it was silent . . . erm, I felt quite detached from it . . . as if it wasn't important.

I: Can you explain to me what you mean by that?"

P: Erm, I just felt as if it wasn't very [*long pause*] important it was quite . . . two-dimensional . . . to me . . . em . . . you're involved and you're moving a character about the screen and you're . . . you're dictating what happens but . . . there wasn't really any depth to it . . . and I felt myself . . . probably paying a little bit less attention to it than I probably should have.

I: Okay . . . And can I ask what you mean by there wasn't 'any depth to it'? Why do you think that might be and what you mean by that exactly?

P: [*long pause*] erm . . . you're, you're still getting interaction, you're still interacting with the character on the screen and you're still determining the movements . . . but . . . I feel as if that's you engaging with the game . . . I didn't feel very . . . engaged . . . because it was silent.

In line with previous research and theory (see Cassidy and MacDonald 2008), the verbal account provides a clear example of the power of music as a tool to create a more positive game-play experience and to enhance one's performance through increasing affinity with the game and thus the intrinsic value of the overall experience to the individual. This tangible augmentation of game play through music quite often manifested itself in a motivational desire to perform better:

P: I kind of felt as if [*long pause*] at that time anyway [music and game sounds] I felt as if I was enjoying it better. . . . . I wanted to do better at it. . . . I felt as if . . . I was part of it and that made me want to do better at it.

THEME 4: MUSICAL FUNCTION

The final theme stems from the abundance of instances throughout the interview in which the participant made reference to the functional properties of the music within the game. These mechanisms characterised each of the levels within the game and appeared frequently to distinguish a safety/danger binary:

P: There's a definite staging in the, the music . . . as you move from one level to the next.

I: What do you mean by that?

P: Well, in the first part of the game when they [*long pause*] collect the orb things . . . there's erm. . . . The music's a bit calmer . . . but . . . I didn't really feel as if I was under any threat . . . at the beginning. . . . When you manage to open that first door [entry to level 2] . . . there's a change in the music which to me kind of . . . it's like a kind of switch to me . . . so it's time to kind of focus. . . . When you hear a kind of . . . an increase in the tempo or there's something that's a little bit more kind of urgent about the music that's being played so . . . and that kind of thing helps me,

Music appeared to assist the semantic operations of the videogame through the provision of additional audio cues. Expanding upon this reception of musical cues within the context of game play, the participant made direct comparisons between his experience and performance across all three conditions, alluding to the ability of music to enhance the narrative of the game as well as to bestow an innate sense of what to expect at each stage:

P: It was kind of telling as well. . . . You can kind of tell when something is going to happen as well because of the change.

I: Okay . . . And just in talking about the music . . . that's in the game . . . how would you describe the music . . . contained in the game?

P: Erm [*long pause*], on the second occasion I would probably say that it was quite atmospheric to begin with . . . erm . . . and ambient [*long pause*]. The minute you move through the first section, erm . . . it got . . . quite [*long pause*] up-tempo. . . . No [not] up-tempo, 'up-tempo' is the wrong phrase . . . . It got kind of . . . 'immediate' is probably the. . . . It was quite, erm. . . . 'Intimidating' is not the right word, but it was quite. . . . It's obviously there to . . . to create a sense of . . . urgency . . . and it makes you. . . . It kind of draws you in, it makes, it makes the game feel urgent . . . erm . . . and again you get that kind of change of pace going into the third section as well . . . where it's maybe not as urgent as the second bit, but . . . erm . . . the change of music kind of lets you know what's going to happen.

This retrieval of information from the participant's awareness of musical cues in turn appeared to enhance subsequent performance. In particular the participant routinely spoke of instances in which the music appeared to incite a subsequently affirmed need to increase his focus and concentration levels:

I: You talked about . . . sort of a change between . . . 'atmospheric' to a more sort of 'immediate'.

P: Mmm-hmm.

I: Erm . . . 'up-tempo' change in the music . . . erm . . . did that have any impact on your experience at all?

P: Immediately, yes, as soon as I heard the change in music.

I: In what way?

P: Erm . . . well it was a kind of clue that something was . . . was going to hap-
     pen . . . erm and again . . . that made me kind of focus a bit more . . . than
     I had been.

I: Okay . . . erm . . . You spoke about the music, erm. . . . You said it was 'obvi-
     ously' there to 'create a sense of urgency'. . . . Can I ask why you think that?

P: [*long pause*] Well, putting it in context of the first time that I'd played the game
     [game sounds only] . . . erm, without that change . . . you, you've only really got
     the visual clues . . . of what's going to happen so when . . . you're faced with . . .
     that flying thing . . . you don't really know that's going to come up until you
     see it, but . . . knowing that, that was going to come . . . the second time when
     I played it [music and game sounds] . . . without assuming that the game was
     going to be the same, you hear the change in the music and right away that kind
     of triggers the fact . . . although you remember having been there the last time.

The latter theme in particular has clear implications for the wider aims of the
study, exposing both the processes and outcomes of musical communication from
composer to player and the resultant impact of this music on a range of player
(performance, experience) and game (communication of context, navigation,
functional reference) parameters. Furthermore, the participant's explicit recognition of the functional value of the music and concordant vocalisation of 'definitive
staging of the music' provides a gateway to the exploration of intended versus
perceived emotive content of the music.

Cognitive walkthrough

The participant had previously identified 'stages' of music and this initial feedback was used to form the basis of the cognitive walkthrough.

GAME-LEVEL 1 MUSIC

As indicated by a direct comparison of the two completed circumplex models,
the intended emotive content of the first phase of music aligned with that of the
perceived emotion felt by the participant (see Figure 5.4). Throughout this stage
the participant stated that the music made him feel 'relaxed' and that that he felt
that this was largely the intention of the piece:

P: I think it's supposed to . . . kind of. . . . It's supposed to relax you right away . . .
     but, erm . . . kind of gives you the impression that there's nothing immediate
     going to happen. . . . Whereas you get the change here [*P looks at I as the
     game enters level 2*].

GAME-LEVEL 2 MUSIC

The participant was also cognisant of the composer's intentional shift from level
1 of the game to level 2. Rather than fear or anxiety, however, the participant
indicated that he felt both alert and interested, as well as excited and furthermore
believed that the chief intention of the music at this stage was to make the listener

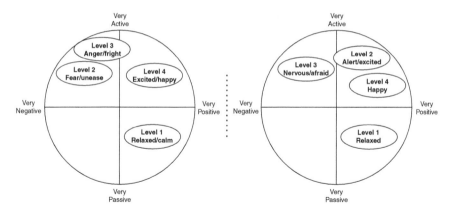

Figure 5.4 Composer (left) and participant (right) circumplex model annotations for the
game music

feel alert. Yet, while the composer's intention to communicate a more negative
sense of arousal was not matched with that of the participant's actual, felt emotion,
the intended and perceived emotions were nonetheless matched in terms of arousal.

GAME-LEVEL 3 MUSIC

Again the participant was immediately aware of the intended shift in music as the
game progressed from level 2 to level 3:

P: That change there made me feel a little bit nervous . . . when [level 2] changes
    to [level 3] it's not quite the same . . . as the first section . . . erm . . . it's. . . .
    The music's quite sinister there I think.
P: It was . . . intended to have some kind of change on you . . . whether it's nerves
    or not, I don't know . . . erm. . . . I think it's supposed to unsettle you.

As implied in the preceding extract, the participant suggested a sinister undertone
to the music, which led to subjective feelings of nervousness:

P: Nervous is probably the . . . easiest way to put it . . . well if it had to be some-
    where it would be afraid.

GAME-LEVEL 4 MUSIC

With regard to the final cut-scene of the game, both the composer and participant
described the music as 'happy', with the participant indicating a further intention
of the music to be celebratory:

P: It's probably quite celebratory.
I: And how did that make you feel?
P: [*long pause*] Well, happy that I'd finished the game.

In summary, it appears that the intended emotive content of the music did not differ greatly from that of the subjective emotion felt by the participant content. With the exception of the second track, the participant's responses fell into the mood quadrant the composer intended. The participant immediately recognised the distinct phases of the music created by the composer.

Discussion

Results from part 1 highlight the composer's intention to evoke an emotional reaction from the player. He describes a desire to influence arousal levels, increase heart rate, to induce a state of relaxation and calm and then upset this through introducing unexpected elements in the music. A range of musical attributes were manipulated to communicate each emotion, and these are detailed in Figure 5.2. To a large extent they correlate with previous research on performance and music content features associated with expressed emotion (Gabrielsson and Lindstrom 2001; Juslin and Timmers 2010). Timbre, mode, and tonality are used to distinguish between positive and negative moods on the valence axis, as is variation of melodic pitch range. However his use of these attributes to disambiguate high-arousal emotions is in contrast to classical music research which suggests timbral features are less important than rhythm in this regard (Juslin 2000; Lu, Liu, and Zhang 2006). Loudness and intensity attributes are used only to emphasise anger and are not used to modulate arousal. Although specific to one composer and one genre (electronic music), these result support recent research focusing on popular music, where communication of emotion relies on spectrally derived features rather than intensity features (Beveridge and Knox 2012b).

Results from part 2 highlight enhanced player experience and performance in the presence of music, with reference in particular to increased arousal, attention, and engagement with the game; increased enjoyment; a more positive experience, better performance, greater engagement, and affinity with the game. All of which were reported to be a direct result of the musical accompaniment. Moreover, the participant cited the facilitative role of the music with regard to game performance aspects, making explicit reference to the 'staging' of the music and the impact this had on his underlying affect, overall experience and performance.

An initial state of calm is successfully conveyed to the player in game level 1. In level 2, the player perceived a transition in the urgency of the music, with resultant effects upon his levels of focus, interest, and arousal. In this regard the composer was successful in his goal of increasing the player's levels of arousal and focus. However the player perceived the positive valence emotion of excitement rather than the fear intended by the composer. The composer aimed to create a feeling of unease primarily through harsh timbre and dissonant sounds to emphasise fear, and also fast staccato articulation and regular, low-tempo rhythm. Staccato articulation and slow tempo have been found to be successful in communicating fear (Juslin 2000), as has dull timbre, in contrast to the composer's use of harsh timbre. Bright timbre is generally associated with positive valence, and it is conceivable that this played a role in the player's perception of positive emotion. In game level 3, the player felt nervous and afraid, unsettled by the perceived sinister mood of the music. In this regard the composer is successful in communicating high arousal and negative valence. He does not convey the anger he intended through use of harsh timbre, dynamic level variations, faster tempo, and prominent rhythm patterns. The happy/excited feel of level 4 is successfully communicated by the composer using major mode and tonality, fast tempo, and simple and regular rhythm.

Overall, the composer successfully conveys positive emotions to the player. However the results for game levels 2 and 3 highlight a disconnect between the composer and the player when communicating negative emotions. The main differences between the music for fear (level 2) and anger (level 3) were tempo, rhythm regularity, melodic complexity, and variation in level dynamics, otherwise these levels share similar attributes. From the player's perspective it seems that tempo, rhythm, and intensity were instrumental in communicating positive or negative valence, and the composer's use of timbre, pitch, and mode have been less influential. The player's perception in this regard aligns with previous research which indicates rhythm attributes are more important in disambiguating high arousal emotions (Juslin 2000; Lu, Liu, and Zhang 2006).

This research examined musical communication between composer and player in a comprehensive game context. The results add to a growing body of evidence supporting the effects of music on game play, specifically increased focus and engagement, enjoyment, and interaction. The game-play context has potential in that it is an ecologically valid context for composers to be given direction as regards the emotional content of their music. Adopting the perspective of both the composer and player has shed light on the processes applied by the composer in order to communicate emotion and the resultant impact on the game-play experience and performance, communication of context, navigation, and functional reference in the game. Specifically this highlighted the composer's manipulation of musical attributes to convey emotion and the degree to which this has been successful from the player's point of view. The game-music context is very different to previous experimental approaches to the communication of emotion through modulation of music attributes (cf. Juslin and Timmers 2010) and involves the composition of electronic music. Thus the research focuses on a very different type and function of music. The results indicate some variation between attributes used by this composer and those identified in the literature to being key to expressing certain emotions. There is also miscommunication of negative emotions. Further research is required to explore whether these issues are specific to the musical genre or communication of emotion in a game music context.

The study is limited in that only one composer participated in the study, working in one genre of music (electronic music), and this may be extended to involve multiple composers music genres in order to explore the process of composition for emotional effect more widely. This initial step in investigating musical communication in the game context has subsequently been extended to a mixed method design employing 70 participants, quantitatively investigating the impact of the composed music upon a range of player performance and experience measures, including flow experience using a GameFlow questionnaire (Cowley et al.

2008); emotional state using the positive and negative affect schedule PANAS (Watson, Clark, and Tellegen 1988), and performance measures including avatar behaviour (e.g. number of shots fired, accuracy, and duration).

Note

1 See <www.pandora.com>.

References

Beveridge, S., and D. Knox (2012a). 'Emotion Recognition in Western Popular Music: The Role of Melodic Structure'. Paper presented at the Twelfth International Conference on Music Perception and Cognition, Thessaloniki.
—— and —— (2012b). 'A Feature Survey for Emotion Classification of Western Popular Music'. Oral session at the Ninth International Symposium on Computer Music Modeling and Retrieval (CMMR), Music and Emotions, Queen Mary University of London. <http://www.cmmr2012.eecs.qmul.ac.uk/sites/cmmr2012.eecs.qmul.ac.uk/files/pdf/papers/cmmr2012_submission_44.pdf> (accessed 9 Nov. 2015).
Braun, V., and V. Clarke (2006). 'Using Thematic Analysis in Psychology'. *Qualitative Research in Psychology*, 3/2: 77–101.
Brunswik, E. (1956). *Perception and the Representative Design of Experiments*. Berkeley: University of California Press.
Cassidy, G.G., and R.A.R. MacDonald (2008). 'The Role of Music in Videogames: The Effects of Self-Selected and Experimenter-Selected Music on Driving Game Performance and Experience'. Paper presented at the Tenth International Conference on Music Perception and Cognition, Sapporo, Japan.
—— and —— (2009). 'The Effects of Music Choice on Task Performance: A Study of the Impact of Self-Selected and Experimenter-Selected Music on Driving Game Performance and Experience'. *Musicae Scientiae*, 13/2: 357–86.
—— and —— (2010). 'The Effects of Music on Time Perception and Performance of a Driving Game'. *Scandinavian Journal of Psychology*, 51/6: 455–64.
Chapin, H., E. Large, K. Jantzen, J.A.S. Kelso, and F. Steinberg (2008). 'Dynamics of Emotional Communication in Performed Music'. *Journal of the Acoustical Society of America*, 124: 2432.
Collins, K., ed. (2008). *From Pac-Man to Pop Music: Interactive Audio in Games and New Media*. Aldershot: Ashgate.
Cowie, R., E. Douglas-Cowie, S. Savvidou, E. McMahon, M. Sawey, and M. Schroder (2000). Feeltrace: An Instrument for Recording Perceived Emotion in Real Time'. In *Proceedings of the ISCA Workshop on Speech and Emotion*. <http://www.isca-speech.org/archive_open/speech_emotion/spem.pdf>.
Cowley, B., D. Charles, M. Black and R. Hickey (2008). 'Towards an Understanding of Flow in Video Games'. *Computers in Entertainment*, 6/2: 1–27.
Eerola, T., and J.K. Vuoskoski (2010). 'A Comparison of the Discrete and Dimensional Models of Emotion in Music'. *Psychology of Music*, 39/1: 18–49.
Ekman, P., and W.V. Friesen (1998). 'Constants Across Culture in the Face and Emotion'. In J. Jenkins, K. Oatley, and N. Stein (eds), *Human Emotions: A Reader*. Malden, MA: Blackwell.
Gabrielsson, A., and E. Lindström (2001). 'The Influence of Musical Structure on Emotional Expression'. In P.N. Juslin and J. Sloboda (eds), *Music and Emotion: Theory and Research*. Oxford: Oxford University Press.

Hevner, K. (1935). 'Expression in Music: A Discussion of Experimental Studies and Theories'. *Psychology Review*, 42: 186–204.

Juslin, P.N. (2000). 'Cue Utilization in Communication of Emotion in Music Performance: Relating Performance to Perception'. *Journal of Experimental Psychology: Human Perception and Performance*, 26/6: 1797–1813.

—— (2001). 'Communicating Emotion in Music Performance'. In P.N. Juslin and J.A. Sloboda (eds), *Music and Emotion: Theory and Research*. Oxford: Oxford University Press.

—— and R. Timmers (2010). 'Expression and Communication of Emotion in Music Performance'. In P.N. Juslin and J.A. Sloboda (eds), *Handbook of Music and Emotion: Theory, Research, and Applications*. Oxford: Oxford University Press.

—— and D. Västfjäll (2008). 'Emotional Responses to Music: The Need to Consider Underlying Mechanisms'. *Behavioural and Brain Sciences*, 31: 559–75.

Knox, D., G.G., Cassidy, S. Beveridge, and R. MacDonald (2008). 'Music Emotion Classification by Audio Signal Analysis: Analysis of Self-Selected Music during Game Play'. Paper presented at the Tenth International Conference on Music Perception and Cognition, Sapporo, Japan.

—— L. Mitchell, S. Beveridge, and R. MacDonald (2011). 'Acoustic Analysis and Mood Classification of Pain-Relieving Music'. *Journal of the Acoustical Society of America*, 130/3: 1673–82.

Konecni, V.J. (2008). 'Does Music Induce Emotion? A Theoretical and Methodological Analysis'. *Psychology of Aesthetics, Creativity, and the Arts*, 2/2: 115–29.

Krumhansl, C. (2002). 'Music: A Link Between Cognition and Emotion'. *Current Directions in Psychological Science*, 11/2: 45–50.

Laterza, V., P. Carmichael, and R. Procter (2007). 'Using Video Diaries to Explore the Nature of Education Research. Paper presented at 'Developing and Researching a Virtual Research Environment for Education' symposium at British Education Research Association Conference, London.

Lu, L., D. Liu, and H.J. Zhang (2006). 'Automatic Mood Detection and Tracking of Music Audio Signals'. *IEEE Transactions on Audio, Speech and Language Processing*, 14/1: 5–18.

Meyer, L.B. (1956). *Emotion and Meaning in Music*. Chicago: University of Chicago Press.

Miell D., R.A.R. MacDonald, and D.J. Hargreaves, eds (2005). *Musical Communication*. Oxford: Oxford University Press.

Narmour, E. (1990). *The Analysis and Cognition of Basic Melodic Structures: The Implication-Realization Model*. Chicago: University of Chicago Press.

North, A.C., D.J. Hargreaves, and J.J. Hargreaves (2004). 'Uses of Music in Everyday Life'. *Music Perception*, 22/1: 41.

Picard, R.W. (1997). *Affective Computing*. Cambridge, MA: MIT Press.

Reed, J., and C.H. Lee (2007). 'A Study on Attribute-Based Taxonomy for Music Information Retrieval'. In *Proceedings of the 8th International Conference on Music Information Retrieval, Vienna*. Available at <http://ismir2007.ismir.net/proceedings/ISMIR2007_p485_reed.pdf> (accessed 15 Nov. 2015).

Russell, J.A. (1980). 'A Circumplex Model of Affect'. *Journal of Personality and Social Psychology*, 39: 1161–78.

Saarikallio, S., and J. Erkkila. (2007). 'The Role of Music in Adolescents' Mood Regulation'. *Psychology of Music*, 35/1: 88–109.

Scherer, K.R., and M.R. Zentner (2001). 'Emotional Effects of Music: Production Rules'. In P.N. Juslin and J. Sloboda (eds), *Music and Emotion: Theory and Research*. Oxford: Oxford University Press.

Schoonderwaldt, E., A. Friberg, R. Bresin, and P.N. Juslin (2002). 'A System for Improving the Communication of Emotion in Music Performance by Feedback Learning'. *Journal of the Acoustical Society of America*, 111/5: 2471.

Sloboda, J.A., and S.A. O'Neill (2001). 'Emotions in Everyday Listening to Music'. In P.N Juslin and J.A. Sloboda (eds), *Music and Emotion: Theory and Research.* New York: Oxford University Press.

Thayer, R.E. (1989). *The Biopsychology of Mood and Arousal.* Oxford: Oxford University Press.

Watson, D., L.A. Clark, and A. Tellegen (1988). 'Development and Validation of Brief Measures of Positive and Negative Affect: The PANAS Scales'. *Journal of Personality and Social Psychology*, 54/6: 1063–70.

Weiss, R.S. (1995). *Learning from Strangers: The Art and Method of Qualitative Interview Studies*. New York: Free Press.

Whalen, Z. (2004). 'Play Along: An Approach to Videogame Music'. *Game Studies*, 4/1. <http://gamestudies.org/0401/whalen/?ref=SeksDE.Com> (accessed 15 Nov. 2015).

Zehnder, S., and S.D. Lipscomb (2006). 'The Role of Music in Video Games'. In P. Vorderer and J. Bryant (eds), *Playing Video Games: Motives, Responses, and Consequences.* Mahwah, NJ: Lawrence Erlbaum Associates.

6 Redesigning the familiar

How effective are directional control pads in developing musicianship in 8- to 12-year-old children?

Matthew C. Applegate

This chapter addresses the interactions between users of directional video-game control pads that have been modified to act as musical instruments, how they are used, and whether this owes anything to their original context. Video games and game play with their continued use create a by-product of generic skills and muscle memory. This research proposes an additional use for these learnt skills and one that is transferable outside of purely video-game play. Building on previous research that used a Nintendo DS and players' hand–eye coordination to perform music, specially designed software was created to mimic the performance of a musical instrument with eight outcomes for use in a workshop setting. The new software relies on groups of four learners interacting together to perform music beyond that of simple experimentation and to teach basic musical skills. Additionally the software with its leap from its previous incarnation with one musical outcome per participant to eight had to be considerably redesigned and renegotiated to remain easy to use and allow for a low entry point into the world of musical performance. The design of the software was continually re-assessed throughout the research to find the most consistent and useful instrument and notation layout. Once completed the software was used in a workshop setting to test its effectiveness. For the research, multiple questionnaires and musical aptitude tests were conducted before and after the workshop. Audio and video recordings of the workshops were also made to ascertain the effectiveness of the design in relation to the amount of musical information that had been communicated in the use of the software and retained by the participants.

Introduction

Computers have, over the last 30 years, become more ubiquitous and accessible to the general public. Originally existing primarily for universities or large businesses, computer technology has now expanded into the home and entertainment sector and has grown to include video-game technology. With processing power and mobility increasing computers are now embedded in everyday life. This abrupt consumer-led evolution often renders technology obsolete. One remnant of this continued planned and perceived obsolescence is the cognitive and physical impacts left on users by its continued use of a directional control pad: a control interface that has arguably become generic across most systems with only moderate adaptation and addition during its evolution through seven generations of games consoles.

Krakauer and Shadmehr (2006) argue that everyday real-world tasks require muscle memory, which improves with practice and becomes automatic. However the muscle memory used in interacting with video games is arguably not often representative of the outcome of a character or situation in a video game and is not often directly transferable to the real world. However, this is not to say that this learnt behaviour is simply a waste of cognitive and physical skills, quite the opposite, it could be argued to offer an opportunity. For example, videos games could help improve real-world cognitive musical skills and muscle memory learnt in video games could help improve musical performance. Previous research by Applegate (2010, 2011) investigated how a Nintendo DS was altered into a simple drum part for an electronic samba band that used visual cues similar to that of musical simulation games such as *Guitar Hero*.

The prior research, albeit on a limited scale in terms of depth and number of participants, helped illustrate that participants could be engaged musically through the use of the re-purposed video-game technology. However, the previous research was limited to single note lengths and each performer only produced one sound each in turn, achieving a very limited musical vocabulary. The research relied on the use of a touch screen as a drum and on the participants' hand–eye coordination instead of any prior knowledge of the generic layout of the directional control pad.

This research aims to extend this concept with the addition of melody and harmony which in turn necessitated the eight inputs provided by the generic control pad layout. By introducing these additional elements it includes 'the three basic elements of music' – rhythm, melody, and harmony (Harris and Crozier 2000: 37), and it is intended to provide the participants with a much more comprehensive music-learning experience. Although these additional elements were introduced and used, only rhythm was assessed in relation to the effectiveness of the software design. An assessment of the participants' understanding of melody and harmony and whether the software had any impact on this understanding would require a more in-depth study with the participants and lies outside the scope of this research.

The use of music notation

Learning musical notation is a common stumbling block for new students attempting to learn music. An abstract notational system coupled with the physical demands of learning an entirely new interface can often lead to failure:

> One of the paradoxes of music learning in the Western classical tradition is that the abilities required for performing and functioning in the aural art of music often rests on skills developed through decoding visual notation.
>
> (Heuser 2007: 385)

Previous research into this issue ranges from simplifications of the standard musical notation system (George 2008; Underwood 2008), to hand symbols to reinforce the notation (Cousins and Persellin 1999), to colour-coded notation systems (Rogers 1991). All of these systems have their respective strengths and weaknesses; however, all rely on the use of semiotics and subsequently require the learning of an entirely new abstract framework prior to musical performance taking place.

What this research proposes is a musical system with notation based around the generic interface of a re-purposed video-game system. The system is intended to allow for an immediate experience and one that is beyond that of the users' current musical abilities. By utilising previous physical interactions with a video-game system, this research aims to assess the potential of lowering the cognitive and physical entry point in which novices can begin to experience musical performance.

Musical instruments

Musical instruments have been used for approximately 35,000 years (Ghosh 2009). Their original design and layout were limited and governed by the physics of the pitches and timbres they were required to produce. To perform on these 'new' instruments an entirely new system of physical interaction needed to be learnt: an interaction that would be otherwise alien to everyday life. However, the use of a pre-existing and familiar physical layout could potentially allow for a greater speed of adoption and acquisition of new musical skills. This research does not claim that the adoption of a video-game system as a musical instrument would be without a period of learning: learning a new instrument or a new song would be analogous to the experience of changing from one video game or system to another with its different rules and button layouts, and skill-sets require time to learn. Both a car-driving game and a platform game can use the same video-game system, but they rely on different skill-sets and software layout within the hardware's' physical constraints and in turn require time to learn. Nor does the research intend to suggest that a device is so embedded into everyday life that everyone who encounters it is immediately familiar and competent enough with it to create and perform music on it, but to suggest that, because of its availability and familiarity amongst the age group concerned, the device may be adaptable for such purposes more readily.

Game technology and education

Using video-game technology as an educational tool has yet to be fully explored. However, it is of increasing interest to researchers and government policy-makers, with a proportion of larger scale research taking place in recent years (McFarlane, Sparrowhawk, and Heald 2003; Schuler 2009). Nintendo's *Dr. Kawashima's Brain Training* is arguably aimed at either promoting this concept of learning or implying it, although its educational themes were widely publicised in the press through the research carried out by the LTS (Learning and Teaching Scotland) national adviser for emerging technologies and learning, Derek Robertson (cited in MacDonald 2008; see also *BBC News* 2008), only to be criticised a year later (*BBC News* 2009; Sage 2009).

It could also be argued that the current experience of playing a video game is so dissimilar to that of playing one from the 1980s until perhaps early 2000 that the experience and its potential has to be constantly re-evaluated, and educational research conducted in that early period (Bowman 1982; Driskell and Dwyer 1984) although informative can only cover a part of what is now a much more complex and immersive experience. Prior research has been conducted using pre-existing commercial software to highlight specific areas of the educational curriculum (Sandford et al. 2006), and Moshirnia examined 'the effectiveness of a modified video game, *Civilization IV*, in improving the comprehension and retention of historical knowledge of 10th, 11th, and 12th grade students' (2007: 511). Interestingly these research projects seek to assess the cognitive impact that video games can have on the children who use them or highlight certain acquired mental and physical abilities gained from the experiences as Griffiths describes in his previous research:

> Research dating right back to the early 1980s has consistently shown that playing computer games (irrespective of genre) produces reductions in reaction times, improved hand-eye co-ordination and raises players' self-esteem. What's more, curiosity, fun and the nature of the challenge also appear to add to a game's educational potential.
>
> (Griffiths 2002: 47; cf. Griffiths and Hunt 1995)

Additionally, Greenfield reviews neuroscientist Daphne Bavelier's research in which she 'observed that video gamers possess increased visual attention, and can handle more complex visual attention switching tasks' (Greenfield 2008: 173; cf. Achtman, Green, and Bavelier 2008; Green and Bavelier 2006a, 2006b) highlighting a visual physical remnant of game playing. This research is primarily concerned with the physical remnant of previous game play itself and seeks to address a potential use for these abilities both inside and outside the video-game playing world. The subject of this research should be seen in contrast to 'edutainment' or games with educational features (Leyland 1996), which often separate the educational information from the game-playing element, often but not exclusively offering the game-play sections as rewards for completing the educational components. The software for this research is closely modelled on existing video games and existing modes of game play. In the software there is no separation between educational features and game play as the software is merely an amalgamation of the two concepts. This research seeks to assess what children can learn through physically playing video games in contrast to what they can learn through playing games with educational features.

It should also be noted that existing musical games or more specifically what are termed 'rhythm games' such as *Guitar Hero* (2005) and *Rock Band* (2007) arguably do offer a limited amount of potential for transferable skill in terms of timing and hand–eye coordination. However, the interactions are loosely based on the music they intend to recreate and often do not offer a one-to-one, note-for-note interactive recreation of the music. Denis and Jouvelot found a similar issue with existing systems: 'The main educational by-product of such systems is dexterity and memory, but players are mere reproducers and have no musical control' (2004: 3–4). This is one of the key areas that this investigation intends to expand upon to offer a more realistic musical experience. By creating new, albeit similar, software, it allows it to be customised instead of relying on existing software that may only in part illustrate areas necessary for this study.

Summary

The purpose of this chapter is to describe and assess the effectiveness of software designed for teaching a transferable skill on a device that is becoming more-and-more ubiquitous and embedded in everyday life: a generic directional video-game control pad. The research is designed to take advantages of the users' previous cultural perceptions and physical interactions with technological device to develop new skills which are potentially transferable beyond its original purpose. A crude analogy of this would be: although a video game can teach a person to jump over a great chasm or dodge a bullet in a video-game world, these skills are not in any way transferable to the real world, whereas the timing and hand–eye coordination could potentially be transferred to real-world experiences, including playing musical instruments.

The presence of a gaming device possibly induced the participants to view the sessions and software as fun, such that 'the fun element of activities enabled them to forget the therapeutic nature of the experiences' (Tam et al. 2007: 110), which may otherwise have detracted from the learning and concentration required for acquiring a new skill. It should be noted that this research was not concerned with the software and workshops' effectiveness in relation to other existing software and teaching methods available. Nor is it the aim of the software to teach traditional music theory or concepts such as standard notation. The study is focused on its own effectiveness in conveying basic musical ideas and musicianship such as:

- How effective is the software's design in teaching basic musical skills such as rhythm?
- Can the design of the software be enhanced through an understanding of its use?

It was presumed, based on previous research, that participants familiar with a directional control pad would be able to retain basic musical information such as rhythm, but the question of how much and how accurately remains open. For this reason qualitative action research, employing in-depth interview techniques and continually re-assessing the effectiveness of the design was used, allowing for self-reflexivity to achieve the most effective means of teaching musical skills with the tools created.

Method

This study used a qualitative research method designed using elements of action research such as in-depth interview techniques and also a quasi-cascade style evaluation of the software during the study that informed how the work developed. The age range of the participants was 8 to 12 years for the following reasons:

• Cooper has indicated that the ability to hear and distinguish different frequencies has fully matured by the age of 8 (1994; cited in Stalinski, Schellenberg, and Trehub 2008).
• It begins after Piaget's 'concrete operation stage' in children's thinking processes (Smith Cowie, and Blades 2003).

Software design

The first version of the *Super Chip Tune Samba Band* player software (Applegate 2010) was designed with limited outcomes: the production of a simple drum sounds for use in musical performances. The simplicity of design allowed for ease of use and rapid assimilation of a new means of music performance. Denis and Jouvelot describe and prescribe a similar approach to a new means of music performance in a gaming environment:

> In traditional music education, *ludus* is overemphasised over *paidia*, since mastering musical instruments or notation are very time-consuming processes that delay the spontaneity and sharing between musicians. Designing music environments with no entry boundaries due to instrumental dexterity or abstract knowledge would get us closer to a genuine game setting, thus increasing students' pleasure and motivation.
>
> (Denis and Jouvelot 2004: 4)

This statement must be borne in mind as the player software is adapted to produce more than one outcome. Additional musical information needed to be included, providing up to eight outcomes, whilst maintaining simplicity and accessibility. The new software allowed the participant to access eight notes of a diatonic scale. The diatonic scale is the most frequently employed in western music and according to Mithen, 'this relatively small number might, it has been suggested, relate to cognitive constraints on human memory' (2005: 52) and informed the range of notes accessible through the new software.

   Gladwell discusses Miller's research into 'channel capacity', the number of pieces of information that can be retained in the immediate human memory and be distinguishable from other pieces of information (2000: 175–6; see Miller 1956). This number is suggested to be about seven which is another reason for constraining the amount of musical tones available. The eight different sounds or notes combined with up to four performers afforded the opportunity to perform musical pieces designed for four parts. Combining both the rhythmic and group performance properties of the *Super Chip Tune Samba Band* software with eight different sounds per participant allowed for both a greater musical vocabulary as well as a greater level of musicianship.

The re-designed instrument is based on an existing design familiar to participants aged 8 to 12 (mobile phone, hand-held video-game controller, toy):

- the device itself was designed to use a vast array of software, not limited to one set outcome;
- the hardware is capable of producing a wide range of audio output;
- the hardware has eight buttons, either physical or software-based.

Several pilot designs of potential systems were undertaken to assess the efficiency of the proposed devices (see Schuler 2009: 6). Although restricted text entry, small screen size, and limited battery life are unlikely to affect this specific research, several possibilities for the end device were considered. Doing so allowed for a better design and more self-reflexivity throughout the research. It is also paramount that where possible the design did not restrict learning in any way and assessing more than one device may highlight design issues. According to McFarlane, Sparrowhawk, and Heald:

> In terms of operating the software it is better if the user interface is obvious and no written instructions are needed, especially for young children. Where help is needed, or important information is conveyed through text, it is vital that the reading age of the text matches the target age of the audience.
> (McFarlane, Sparrowhawk, and Heald 2003: 6)

They also highlight the problem of sound:

> Noisy games are distracting to non-users, so where games are played in the classroom while other children are doing other work it is important to have headphones. In primary schools children often work in pairs at the back of the classroom, and the disadvantage of headphones is that it makes discussion much more difficult. Headphones are much more widely used in secondary school environments.
> (McFarlane, Sparrowhawk, and Heald 2003: 11)

Therefore, another consideration in the design of the software was how the participants would perform and communicate and how this could be achieved in a classroom setting. There were five separate designs and builds for the player software pilots featuring fully functioning software running natively on the Apple iPhone 3GS, Motorola DEXT, Leapfrog's Leap Pad, Nintendo DS, and finally a generic USB controller. Two of those are discussed here to highlight the reflexivity of the study to find the most suitable outcome.

Testing the software

Although previous research used the Nintendo DS (Figure 6.1), a pilot study of the effectiveness of using an Apple iPhone/iPod Touch was conducted, as the device itself has arguably become more widespread and familiar among 8 to 12 year olds. The now widely available Apple iPhone was programmed to mimic eight inputs of a generic game controller. Using the iPhone touch screen, eight uniquely coloured buttons were provided for the player.

Despite having the buttons of the same size and laid out in a similar pattern to the Nintendo DS and other controllers, the pilot group found that pressing the buttons correctly was considerably difficult. One respondent aged 8 had fingers that were larger than the buttons which masked the other buttons from view. There were also technical issues from the device itself: if a button was pressed with the finger half on the button and half off, the device ignored the attempt, only direct and touches enclosed in the button area were accepted.

Factors such as masking the button layout with one's own hand, suggested that performance which required the participant to play specific notes, even at slower speeds could be difficult. Additionally as they were to read musical notation from another device it would divide the participant's attention even further if the button required visually locating before pressing. In this case it was decided that because of the iPhone's lack of discernible buttons, it was not a suitable candidate for the final player software.

Although this pilot study was largely observational and ad hoc, it raised an interesting point. Even though the interface was laid out in a similar pattern to a generic control pad it was found difficult to use by the participants, suggesting familiarity with the device relies much more on its physical shape than its appearance. In the case of the iPhone, the absence of any physical difference across the device's touch screen surface made it difficult to use. In the absence of physical buttons, the fingers had no resting point or home key to situate themselves on and return to, and the need for visual confirmation slowed the process down. The participants' ability to feel the control pad under their fingers even when inactive plays an important role.

The fifth and final design ran separate software on a hand-held device and on a standard Windows PC or Apple Mac. This change allowed for additional information to be obtained as the devices could be synced with the computer notation software directly. The inputs could be recorded against the notation software to assess the accuracy of the performers in real time. Although this combining of notation and player software meant only one piece of software needed to be developed, the software itself was considerably more complicated.

The widely used USB control pad based on the Sony Playstation 3 control pad and its predecessors offer a suitable physical match for the notation software.

Figure 6.1 Player software on Nintendo DS

The U, D, L, R and 1, 2, 3, 4 physical buttons correspond to those in the notation software, in addition the L1, L2, R1, R2 could be used for additional musical expression such as piano or forte.

The resulting layout could be expressed as standard notation as shown (Figure 6.2), however this system was not used in the software or the sessions and is just a means of conveying the musical information. Additionally, using a generic controller rather than any specific device and its associations, allowed a more succinct reading of the participants' interactions with the device.

Notational aspects

The second aspect of the software is the animated notation which is run on either a standard PC or Mac and is based on the *Super Chip Tune Samba Band* used in previous research. The adaptation had to take into account that instead of asking each player to only produce a single type of sound, they would now have to produce up to eight different sounds each. The notation (Figure 6.3) represents parts for four players and each can have one of the eight different performance blocks at a time: the performance blocks simply illustrate what button or direction is to be pressed as the performance bar passes over it.

Previous research by Macrae and Dixon, used similar scrolling musical notation in an attempt to convey musical information beyond just musical expression

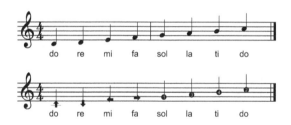

Figure 6.2 Example of possible notation

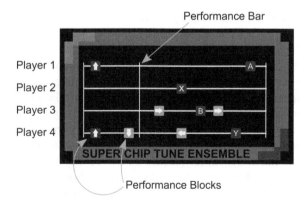

Figure 6.3 Original musical-notation screen layout

Figure 6.4 Original set of buttons

as found in games such as *Guitar Hero*. In a project entitled 'Note-Scroller', the notation software featured a projected image of the scrolling notes flowing towards the physical musical keyboard in a vertical manner. This allowed for an approach which is more 'intuitive to non-music literate users than standard music notation [thus removing one of] the typical barriers that deter people from learning to play instruments such as the cost of tuition, availability and the requirement of reading standard music notation' (Macrae and Dixon 2008: 1).

An example of this decoding barrier is illustrated in standard notation. Simply asking the performer to play an A above middle C. Without prior knowledge of what this symbol means or where A is located, the performer cannot perform the music correctly. The symbol needs to be decoded into a pitch and then into its location on the instrument. Whereas in the notation proposed in this research the symbol has a direct connection with the location of the note to be performed. The symbol is the location of the note.

The performance blocks were named after the buttons that were to be played (Figure 6.4), ↑ simply equates to pressing the ↑-button, B equates to pressing the B-button. This system is considerably simpler than standard musical notation. Although every attempt was made to lower the entry point into music performance, this research does not suggest that there would not be some period of learning, but it is hoped that users' previous experience with the generic layout of the new musical instrument will help speed adoption of it.

Notation software design pilots

The final approach taken was to divide the controller in to two areas: left (↑, ↓, ←, →) and right (A, B, X, Y). Assigning the left side of the controller the colour red and the right side of the controller the colour blue allowed the software to use the familiarity of up, down, left, right and still access eight different outcomes, thus creating a red ↑ and a blue ↑, a red ↓ and a blue ↓, and so on (Figure 6.5), which simplified the visual layout (Figure 6.6). The horizontal length of the performance blocks corresponded to the actual length of the note to be played.

This had an immediate impact on the frequency of correct notes and was deemed to be a better design and layout for the final notation software. The fewer different symbols reduced the cognitive load on the participant, but this still required them to scan until the end of the bar for the next note and then jump back to the beginning, much in line with standard musical notation. Although this was considered to be effective for *Super Chip Tune Samba Band*, which had only required each participant to perform one action, this software allows eight possible outcomes.

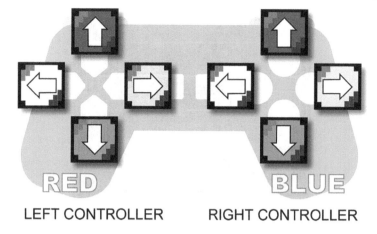

Figure 6.5 Second set of buttons divided into red and blue

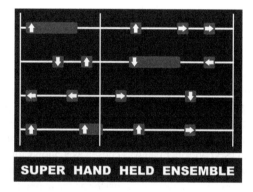

Figure 6.6 Second musical-notation screen layout

This was solved by moving the performance blocks instead of the performance bar: the notes to be performed move from right to left and are to be performed whilst between the two performance bars, in the 'performance area'. This lowered the area of the screen that needed to be focused on (Figure 6.7) and the need to continually scan the entire screen, as the notes to be performed appear gradually nearer the performance area in the peripheral vision.

According to Gladwell, 'when we, read, we are capable of taking in only about one key word and then four characters to the left and fifteen characters to the right at any one time' (2000: 108). Although this applies to reading text, the concept of perceptual span is equally applicable to using the software. What is to the left of the performance bar is less important than what is approaching from the right: the bars to the left have already been performed, those to the right have yet to be

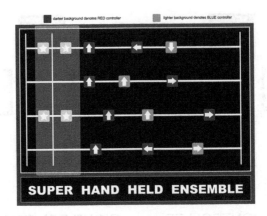

Figure 6.7 Third musical-notation screen layout with performance area

performed and more focus is dedicated towards that area. Additionally the background colour was changed from black to a lighter grey to allow for more definition of the performance blocks, which increased the accuracy of the performance.

Design summary

The primary goal of the software was to allow for the lowest cognitive and physical strain on the participants, allowing them to concentrate on engaging with and assimilating the musical information presented. Multiple pilot tests allowed for unforeseen design and software problems to be corrected prior to the full-scale test being conducted. The generic USB controller pad was chosen as it allows four players access to eight physically discernible inputs, and, as the control pads are directly linked to the notation system, it allows for analysis of the performance in real time and afterwards.

Workshops and musical aptitude tests

The workshop was designed for twenty participants in five groups of four. Technology-for-play needs to be provided in a 'natural setting' (Lichtman 2006: 137) rather than a controlled environment, so the children were taught and observed in either their school or their home. Prior to the workshops each of the participants was given a musical aptitude test, similar to those outlined by Edwards and colleagues (2000), involving pitch, harmony, and dynamics, with an emphasis given to rhythm. Rhythm was assessed in two separate tests, with a total of 20 questions:

1   The participant was played a repeating rhythm and was asked to join in when they felt confident in clapping or tapping along with it. This helps assess both aural skills in following the music as well as muscle coordination in reproducing it. This was done with ten different rhythms, some of which are also used in the workshops themselves.

2   The second test had the participant listen to rhythms and repeat them by clapping or tapping them without the aid of the original being present. This test helps highlight the additional element of remembering musical rhythms and tempo. This was done with ten different rhythms some of which are also used in the workshops themselves.

These were recorded with video and audio for analysis after the event. The tests were repeated after the workshops to assess their impact.

Assessment of the workshops

Assessment of the workshop involved analysing data from both the control pad and the sound and video recordings. The control-pad data shows every note played and scores them in relation to the on-screen notation, and the audio-visual recordings allow for greater scrutiny of this data. For example, the control-pad data could show a note was played incorrectly; however, there may have been external influence on this, such as another child interfering with the control pad. The video evidence would help assess if the child had been allowed the full opportunity to focus on the performance or not.

Discussion

This research built on my own earlier work (Applegate 2011). Children from three different socio-economic and educational backgrounds – primary school, faith-based secondary school, and home schooled – were observed, and a control group at each school did not take part in the workshop. This made the results more widely applicable. Assessing the children's aptitude and organising them into groups with a similar level of musicianship helped to create a level starting point for all of the groups and in turn provided an additional level of reliability to the data. Questionnaires before and after the workshops were designed to collect information on music and video game habits to see if there was a correlation between them and ability in the workshops. The research employed several different data collection methods such as audio as well as video to ensure a reliable record as possible. Despite all these efforts the small sample size of this research should be noted for the conclusions drawn from it. Additionally this research in no way attempts to imply that the research is applicable to all 8-to-12-year-old children but to those specific children who took part in the workshops.

Conclusion

Jane McGonigal in her TED (Technology, Entertainment, Design) Talk discussed how much time people were playing games and posed the question: 'What exactly are gamers getting so good at?'

It was recently published by a researcher at Carnegie Mellon University [Jesse Schell]. The average young person today in a country with a strong gamer culture will have spent 10,000 hours playing online games, by the age of 21. Now 10,000 hours is a really interesting number for two reasons. First of all, for children in the United States 10,080 hours is the exact amount of time you will spend in school from fifth grade to high school graduation if you have perfect attendance. So, the big question is, 'What exactly are gamers getting so good at?'

(McGonigal 2010)

In conclusion this research proposes that one of the things gamers are getting good at is muscle memory, hand–eye coordination, and familiarity with a directional control pad, all of which are learnt from continued exposure to video games and all of which are transferable to the real world. Additionally, these skills can have (as in the case of this research) musical information superimposed on to them, allowing the participants to learn in the game world and recall in the real world.

It should be noted that the workshop and the software were primarily concerned with the reproduction of existing music. The software aligns itself with Pichlmair and Kayali's definition of a rhythm game like *Guitar Hero* or *Rock Band*: 'rhythm games offer little freedom of expression apart from the prerogative to perform while playing. They strictly force rules on the player, on how she has to react to a specific stimulus displayed on screen or communicated by sound' (2007: 426).

However, this learnt muscle memory, hand–eye coordination, and familiarity with a directional control pad could be employed for purely creative purposes and the software could be adapted and used as a simple instrument and compositional tool with its alternative notation system. This alternative musical system may encourage participants who had been discouraged by traditional notation and instruments to attempt the creation of music.

Limitations and future directions

Further research could include alterations to the software to give real-time feedback to the players on their accuracy to see if this has any impact on learning and concentration. As Egenfeldt-Nielsen observes, edutainment often has 'little intrinsic motivation' and 'relies more on extrinsic motivation through rewards, rather than intrinsic motivation. Extrinsic motivation is not really related to the game but consists of arbitrary rewards, for example getting points for completing a level' (2008: 2). Although this research did not use extrinsic rewards and lies outside Egenfeldt-Nielsen's definition of 'edutainment', a graphical extrinsic reward system may be something to consider for future research.

One of the performers in each group could be replaced by a parent or teacher as suggested by Sandford and colleagues:

The teachers and students in the case studies generally reported that using games in lessons was motivating. However, the study suggests that student motivation might be more likely to arise 1) when students were using games familiar from their home environment, and 2) when students were able to have some degree of autonomy in playing the game.

(Sandford et al. 2006: 2)

It could be suggested that the generic layout of the software would have helped alleviate the problems raised in point 1. Point 2 affords the opportunity to assess this issue by having a researcher, teacher, or parent as an active participant, while allowing another group more autonomy. Different visual styles and different control-pad colours could even be used to assess their impact on learning and engagement. A comparison of software such as *Guitar Hero* with *Super Hand Held Ensemble* could also be worth investigation.

Finally, the small number of participants could be seen as a problem, and a longer research project which also assessed melody and harmony could be developed, giving a more holistic view of the musical information presented and retained. As discussed, the software could be adapted to allow children an alternative means of composition and notation, allowing them to create entirely new music within a familiar setting.

Acknowledgements

The author would like to thank Diarmait Finch, Oscar Mordue, Rei Mordue, and Eve Mordue for continued support and help in delivering this research. This research is dedicated to Gunpei Yokoi, the Nintendo employee who created the D-pad without which this work would have not been possible.

References

Achtman, R.L., C.S. Green, and D. Bavelier (2008). 'Video Games as a Tool to Train Visual Skills'. *Restorative Neurology and Neuroscience*, 26/4–5: 435–46.

Applegate, M.C. (2010). 'Can Children Aged 8–12 become Musically Engaged via the Use of a Re-Purposed Video Game Device?' Unpublished paper.

—— (2011). 'Cultural Perceptions, Ownership and Interaction with Re-Purposed Musical Instruments'. *Journal of Music, Technology and Education*, 3/2–3: 2–3.

Bowman, R.F. (1982). 'A Pac-Man Theory of Motivation: Tactical Implications for Classroom Instruction'. *Educational Technology*, 22/9: 14–17.

BBC News (2008). 'Computer Game Boosts Maths Scores'. <http://news.bbc.co.uk/1/hi/scotland/7635404.stm> (accessed: 20 Oct. 2010).

—— (2009). ' "Brain Training" claims Dismissed'. <http://news.bbc.co.uk/1/hi/health/7912379.stm> (accessed 20 Oct. 2010).

Cooper, N. (1994). 'An Exploratory Study in the Measurement of Children's Pitch Discrimination Ability'. *Psychology of Music*, 22: 56–62.

Cousins, S.B., and Persellin, D.C. (1999). 'The Effect of Curwen Hand Signs on Vocal Accuracy of Young Children'. *Texas Music Education Research*, 6: 17–21.

Denis, G., and P. Jouvelot (2004). 'Building the Case for Video Games in Music Education'. Paper presented at the Second International Computer Game and Technology Workshop, Liverpool.

Driskell, J.E., and D.J Dwyer (1984). 'Microcomputer Videogame Based Training'. *Educational Technology*, 24/2: 11–15.

Edwards, A.D.N., B.P. Challis, J.C.K. Hankinson, and F.L. Pirie (2000). 'Development of a Standard Test of Musical Ability for Participants in Auditory Interface Testing'. <http://www.icad.org/websiteV2.0/Conferences/ICAD2000/PDFs/Edwards.pdf> (accessed 6 July 2010).

Egenfeldt-Nielsen, S. (2008). 'The Legacy of Edutainment'. <http://www.itu.dk/people/sen/papers/The_legacy_of_edutainment.doc> (accessed 26 June 2014.

George, P.H. (2008). *Key Perfect*, vol. 2. East Sussex, UK: Creative Arts Research Foundation

Ghosh, P. (2009). 'Oldest Musical Instrument Found'. *BBC News*, 25 June. <http://news.bbc.co.uk/1/hi/8117915.stm> (accessed 30 Mar. 2010).

Gladwell, M. (2000). *The Tipping Point*. London: Abacus.

Green, C.S., and D. Bavelier (2006a). 'Effect of Action Video Games on the Spatial Distribution of Visuospatial Attention'. *Journal of Experimental Psychology: Human Perception and Performance*, 32/6: 1465–78.

—— and —— (2006b). 'Enumeration versus Multiple Object Tracking: The Case of Action'. *Cognition*, 101/1: 217–45.

Greenfield, S. (2008). *ID: The Quest for Meaning in the 21st Century*. London: Sceptre.

Griffiths, M.D. (2002). 'The Educational Benefits of Video Games'. *Education and Health*, 20/3: 47–51.

—— and N. Hunt (1995). 'Computer Game Playing in Adolescence: Prevalence and Demographic Indicators'. *Journal of Community and Applied Social Psychology*, 5: 189–94.

Harris, P., and R. Crozier (2000). *The Music Teacher's Companion: A Practical Guide*. London: ABRSM.

Heuser, F. (2007). 'A Theoretical Framework for Examining Foundational Instructional Materials Supporting the Acquisition of Performance Skills'. In A. Williamon and D. Coimbra (eds), *International Symposium on Performance Science*. Utrecht: European Association of Conservatoires.

Krakauer, J.W., and R. Shadmehr (2006). 'Consolidation of Motor Memory'. *Trends in Neurosciences*, 29: 58–64.

Leyland, B. (1996). 'How can Computer Games Offer Deep Learning and Still be Fun?' Paper presented as the Ascilite Conference, Adelaide.

Lichtman, M. (2006). *Qualitative Research in Education: A User's Guide*. London: Sage.

MacDonald, K. (2008). 'Computer Games are Put to the Test'. *BBC News*, 14 Mar. <http://news.bbc.co.uk/1/hi/scotland/7295039.stm> (accessed 20 Oct. 2010).

McFarlane, A., A. Sparrowhawk, and Y. Heald (2003). 'Report on the Educational Use of Games'. Education and Employment Ministry. <http://www.teem.org/publications/teem_gamesined_full.pdf> (accessed 4 Oct. 2010).

McGonigal, J. (2010). 'Gaming can Make a Better World'. TED Talks. <http://www.ted.com/talks/jane_mcgonigal_gaming_can_make_a_better_world.html> (accessed 9 Oct. 2010).

Macrae, R., and S. Dixon (2008). 'From Toy to Tutor: Note-Scroller is a Game to Teach Music'. <http://c4dm.eecs.qmul.ac.uk/papers/2008/MacraeDixon08-nime.pdf> (accessed 2 Nov. 2015).

Miller, G.A. (1956). 'The Magical Number Seven, Plus or Minus Two: Some Limits on our Capacity for Processing Information'. *Psychological Review* 63/2: 81–97.

Mithen, S. (2005). *The Singing Neanderthals: The Origins of Music, Language, Mind and Body*. London: Phoenix.

Moshirnia, A. (2007). 'An Assessment of Information Delivery Systems within Modified Video Games'. In *Proceedings of IATED*. Available at <http://iated.org/publications> (accessed 11 Dec. 2015).

Pichlmair, M., and F. Kayali (2007). 'Levels of Sound: On the Principles of Interactivity in Music Video Games'. In *DiGRA '07: Proceedings of the 2007 DiGRA International Conference: Situated Play*. Available at <http://www.digra.org/digital-library/forums/4-situated-play/> (accessed 11 Dec. 2015).

Rogers, G.L. (1991), 'Effect of Color-Coded Notation on Music Achievement of Elementary Instrumental Students'. *Journal of Research in Music Education*, 39/1: 64–73.

Sage, A. (2009). 'Nintendo Brain-Trainer "No Better than Pencil and Paper" '. *The Times*. <http://technology.timesonline.co.uk/tol/news/tech_and_web/gadgets_and_gaming/article5587314.ee> (accessed 20 Oct. 2010).

Sandford, R., M. Ulicsak, K. Facer, and T. Rudd (2006). *Teaching with Games Using Commercial Off-the-Shelf Computer Games in Formal Education*. Bristol: FutureLab.

Schuler, C. (2009). *Pockets of Potential: Using Mobile Technologies to Promote Children's Learning*. New York: Joan Ganz Cooney Center, Sesame Workshop.

Smith, P.K., H. Cowie, and M. Blades (2003). *Understanding Children's Development*. Oxford: Wiley-Blackwell.

Tam, C., H. Schwellnus, C. Eaton, Y. Hamdani, A. Lamont, and T. Chau (2007). 'Movement-to-Music Computer Technology: A Developmental Play Experience for Children with Severe Physical Disabilities'. *Occupational Therapy International*, 14/2: 99–112.

Underwood, M. (2008). I wanted an electronic silence Musicality in Sound Design and the Influences of New Music on the Process of Sound Design for Film. *The Soundtrack*, 1/3: 193–210.

Vose, D. (2000). *The Reading Drummer*. Boston, MA: Berklee Press.

7 Game technology in the music classroom

A platform for the design of music and sound

Andrew R. Brown

Introduction

There is a significant role for sound and music in video games, as there are in other media forms such as film and animation (Collins 2008). Its inclusion in mainstream music educational practices has, however, been slow to gain acceptance. This is most likely to be the result of several factors: a lack of familiarity and expertise amongst educators, a perception that the practice was popularist and therefore trivial and unworthy of a place in the curriculum, and a lack of accessible tools and resources appropriate for students. This chapter will examine how creating sound and music for video games can be part of the music classroom. It will discuss how design patterns in music and audio can be taught using computer-game development as a paradigm.

Game-engine technology, and in particular game-design tools that make those engines available to non-programmers, are no longer just used by game-industry professionals. Software such as Unity has made previously industry-specific knowledge and tools available to amateur programmers. Simpler gaming platforms such as GameSalad provide highly scaffolded environments for game design and easy integration of sound assets. Accessible media-programming environments like Scratch allow students to explore quite advanced concepts such as generative music and interactive audio with relative ease.

These tools are providing new learning contexts that focus on the design of computational artefacts (El-Nasr and Smith 2006) which, from the perspective of music education, can be thought of as new opportunities for learning to create musical and diegetic audio components for game environments. The design (and modding) of video games has been used as an educational context in many disciplines, including computer science and graphic design. The most commonly articulated reasons for engaging with video-game technologies in education include student motivation, vocational preparation, and interdisciplinary integration. It is not surprising that music educators find similar reasons to engage with video-game contexts.

There is considerable activity and research in the use of commercial games in education (e.g. Denis and Jouvelot 2004, 2005). However, this chapter will not be considering the playing of video games, nor the gamifaction of activities to develop musical skills such as aural awareness and rhythmic timing. Instead, it will examine how creative-music tasks can be enhanced by situating them as part of the design of video games.

Three areas of video-game audio are explored in this chapter: sound design, non-linear music, and creative coding. This diversity highlights the richness of opportunities in game music and sound. For each area a related music-education case study is described. These case studies will shed light on the pragmatic reality of how concepts can be put into practice.

Sound design

Sound design for games involves deciding where sound will enhance the game, selecting or creating the sounds, and integrating them into the game play. Audio requirements can include spoken dialogue, sound effects, short musical cues, and atmospheric sonic backgrounds. Sound-design tasks have creative and technical challenges that provide plenty of learning opportunities: some of which will be explored in this section.

Sounds in a video game are described as media 'assets', a series of audio files that can be considered as individual sound objects that need to work together as an integrated whole. Understanding the sound world as an integrated series of sound objects has an interesting intellectual history that can be drawn on. This tradition includes Pierre Schaeffer's notion of sound objects as having sonic, musical, and meaningful characteristics (see Chion 1983), Al Bregman's descriptions of an audio scene as acoustic components and perceptual streams (1990), and Adam Harper's description of musical objects as systems of variables (2011).

Sounds are used in games to reinforce game events and to add depth and build emotion. While they might be dramatic at times, they generally need to integrate seamlessly into the game world and not become a distraction. Their role is important, but as with music and sound for film and other audio-visual projects, sound design can be neglected until the last minute. According to Finnish sound designer Joonas Turner, 'sound still seems to be the underdog, even though it is one third of the overall immersion and feel of the game' however, more optimistically he goes on to comment that 'lately I have been noticing that people have been getting more into sounds through the current rise of indie games' (cited in Rose 2014).

At its simplest, sound design involves the selection of sounds from sound-effects libraries, of which there are an extensive array. Sound-effect libraries are particularly useful for sounds that need to be realistic and would be impractical to record, such as a car's skidding tyres. The creation of original sound effects is a more complex task than sound selection, and involves audio recording, editing and synthesis. There are many techniques to be learned about recoding or synthesising sounds, editing them, combining sonic layers, and so on. Basic recording and editing tools, like Audacity, are easily available for schools and much could be achieved even with a tablet computer and low cost apps.

Given the complexity of creating a game from scratch, it is most likely that sounds will be created for an existing game, usually replacing the existing sounds. Most game development environments include demo games that will suit this purpose. The use of such game modding as a pedagogical activity is relatively widespread, because 'modders [are] able to focus on learning these fundamental design skills because game engines and their tools eliminate much of the overhead

Figure 7.1 Sound selection and playback preferences for a 'sprite' in GameSalad

associated with building convincing products' (El-Nasr and Smith 2006: 1). The process of adding (or replacing) a sound within a game engine usually involves adding the sound to an asset register or folder and selecting it to coincide with the relevant game event or object. As an example, the audio selection dialog for the GameSalad software is shown in Figure 7.1.

Sounds can have behaviours within a game. Behaviours include repetition, variation in loudness, length, pitch, panning location, and the level of effects such as reverb. The method of managing these behaviours differs between game-engine environments. There are some behaviour controls shown in Figure 7.1. It is frequently possible to script additional behaviours where the engines include a coding interface. Having to pay attention to the behaviour of sounds in the game provides a good launching pad for class discussions about how sounds indicate actions in the world, how they are located in space, and what the dynamic changes in sounds indicate about them, their source, or the environment they are in.

There are positive educational reasons for using music technologies to integrate sound and visual media and for including sound design for video games as a valid musical activity. These include the scaffolding, contextualising, and cultural cachet that these technical and media associations bring to music activities. Many of these are discussed by Savage (2005) who reflects upon a composer named Alex who, despite an alienating school music experience quite disconnected from his musical interests, became a successful musician. Savage concludes that 'Alex's work as a sound designer offers an exploration of exciting new notions of artistic practice that integrate rich mixes of subject learning within ICT. This could help us lead music education towards a holistic model of artistic practice mediated through the effective use of ICT rather that traditional or pre-existing musical practice merely done with ICT' (Savage 2005: 8). Imagine the head start students like Alex would have, given a proactive introduction to sound design as part of their music education.

Case study 1: W elementary school in Yongin city

This first case study focuses on the use of digital-sound design for visual media as part of a method to increase student engagement with music and their general sonic awareness. The case is a programme conducted and reported by Eunjin Kim (2013) and involves 16 elementary students in South Korea. It does not specifically use game-development technologies but does reflect the broader objective of using visual and interactive media contexts to support music education.

An after-school programme was conducted for fifth and sixth graders from a small elementary school in Gyeonggi Province in rural South Korea. About half the students had experience playing a musical instrument but none had formal composition training. The programme was started following the release of a new national curriculum in Korea that advocated self-motivation and active participation in contrast to the music appreciation approach traditionally followed in Korean music classrooms. Kim describes the traditional classroom music approach in South Korea as 'teacher-centered, text-based, and knowledge-delivered which, in turn, emphasised "listening to music" and "rote memory of musical knowledge"' (2013: 414). By way of contrast, the experimental programme emphasised a 'technology-mediated teaching and learning approached' (ibid.) that used software including ALSong,[1] Tunearound,[2] and Movie Maker.[3]

The programme featured activities that emphasised sound and music creation for applied contexts that 'were selected because we deemed them most suited to raising the interest of students of the Internet generation' (Kim 2013: 416). The activities included making cell-phone ring tones, sound effects for video, and background music for stories and advertising commercials. Kim describes how sounds were selected and designed to be associated with particular visual materials:

> [Students] were encouraged to organise themselves into teams to carry out the class project. After viewing the image shown by the teacher, the students collected and analyzed music materials such as sound effects and sounds of instruments from the available music software. Following this, students were asked to think about the image and the music materials they had chosen to create their music. Once they had created their musical impression of the image, they presented their work to the class. The teacher then provided feedback.
>
> (Kim 2013: 418)

The participant's response to the programme was monitored through data collected before and after the programme from mind maps, interviews, and questionnaires. Kim reports that the student's liked the activities because, unlike other music-education experiences, they were allowed to 'compose the music', 'use the computer', have a 'practical experience', and 'create something instantly' (2013: 422). She also reports that following the programme participants were 'more aurally aware of their surroundings' and that 'students were enthusiastic about using music technologies in everyday life. They could see the diverse applications of these music technologies in real life situations' (ibid.: 423–4).

These results reflect those experienced by many other educators, including Savage, who have used media-rich contexts for music education and extended the horizons of music to include the broader sonic world.

Non-linear music

At their core, video games are interactive and non-linear storytelling platforms. Whilst the basic structure of the narrative is defined by the designers, the moment-to-moment details and, in some cases, longer-term form are unpredictable and driven by player interactions. This presents a challenge to composers and engine developers alike: how to provide an integrated and temporally coherent musical experience when the emotional arc and the scheduling of events are not known in advance. A variety of techniques and tools have been developed to allow for adaptive and dynamic music that can enable the communication of an appropriate mood to support the story and users actions.

Collins (2008) makes a distinction between two types of non-linear audio in games: interactive and adaptive. She classifies interactive audio as sound events directly triggered by the player's actions, while adaptive audio events are cued according to the current game state, which is always varying. Adaptive music will evolve as the game state changes: the number of enemies, the duration of play, current score, game level, virtual location, and so on.

Simple approaches to managing the unknown duration of game play include infinite repetition of musical material, pausing music playback after a certain period of time, and allowing users to select their own music tracks as background. These techniques are successful in particular circumstances, but as the expectations of game players increase so do the sophistication of compositional strategies and music system design.

A matrix-based approach to managing non-linear music playback is advocated by several authors (e.g. Bernt et al. 2006; Houge 2012). In simple terms the musical score is divided into component parts and the game engine reassembles them on the fly to match the game state. Divisions are made 'horizontally' dividing up the musical parts and 'vertically' segmenting the music into sequential sections. Figure 7.2 is a visual depiction of the results of selecting clips in this way as they might be laid out on a multi-track timeline. Each part has a pool of clips from which to choose. The horizontal location of the clips on the timeline shows the bar position where the selected clips were scheduled for playback. This matrix of segments, or clips, is the basis for algorithmic rearrangements, including repetitions, according to rules specified by the composer or game designer. Composers writing for adaptive conditions need to anticipate the possible combinations and ensure that various arrangements are feasible. Typically, the parts are designed so that they allow for variations in dramatic intensity as the game narrative ebbs and flows.

While game engines are paying increasing attention to music-playback capabilities, more often specialised software, referred to as middleware, is used to manage audio in the game. Applications such as FMod, Miles, and Wwise are widely used in the industry to help manage dynamic audio and music playback. These systems allow playback decisions, such as randomly selecting between alternate clips to add variety, varying the number of loops, triggering alternative assets based on game-parameter values, varying real-time signal processing and effects, and so on.

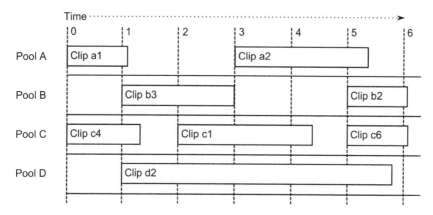

Figure 7.2 Playback matrix of musical clips selected from various pools (Houge 2012)

Some games employ generative music where the score is algorithmically written as the game is played. *Spore*, released by Electronic Arts in 2008 with music composed by Brian Eno is a well-known example of the use of generative music in a video game. Although there are some software systems to support generative music composition (e.g. Noatikl 2), the development of generative music systems requires dedicated software development and integration into the game engine. Generative music will be discussed later.

In educational settings, music students can be introduced to progressively more complex challenges and techniques as their compositional and technical skills develop. The complexity of combinatorial fragments can vary from muting or unmuting parts to on-the-fly reharmonisation of phrases over probabilistic harmonic progressions. The appropriate choice of games to write for and the tools available to manage score integration will also be critical in supporting student learning as they progress.

Regardless of the many clever techniques and tools available to the video-game composer and sound designer, an overriding consideration is to provide a sound world that supports the game narrative, character, and pace. In an article about the meaning of music in games Kanaga suggests 'reading games as scores' (2013). By this he means that a musician should try to apprehend the game's structure, its pace, and internal rhythm and to 'be true to these time-structures' (ibid.) when planning the music and when designing the playback mechanics.

Case study 2: Berklee College

Berklee College is based in Boston, USA, and has a campus in Valencia in Spain. It is a well known music school and has extended its composition and music technology areas to embrace video games in recent years. The topic of scoring for video games is a central part of these programmes and the teaching of non-linear, or interactive, scoring techniques are a significant differentiator of its offerings from other composition courses.

Berklee offers two game-oriented minor studies in its music programmes at Boston – audio design for video games and video game scoring – and a Master in Film Scoring, Television, and Video Games at the Valencia campus. The audio minor focuses on sound design, audio recording and mixing, interactive audio for non-linear environments, and project management. The scoring minor concentrates on the history and analysis of video-game music, digital narrative theory, interactive scoring techniques, digital mock-up, composition, and orchestration. The master's degree has a similar focus to the scoring minor, albeit at more advanced levels, and includes conducting and electronic composition. These programmes reveal the breadth of content involved with music for video games and how this context provides fertile soil for music curriculums.

Looking at the offerings for non-linear music in more detail, there are courses at the undergraduate and masters levels. Titles include 'Interactive Scoring for Video Games' and 'Directed Studies in Linear and Interactive Scoring'. These programmes introduce students to typical game-music workflow and approaches and include linear and non-linear visual content using electronic scoring techniques and/or live-player scoring sessions. Project management and working to deadlines is emphasised throughout. At the bachelor's level activities emphasise regular scoring assignments and at the master's level there is a project focus with students functioning as composer/conductor or composer/producer. The audio minor has a more technological focus on non-linearity with a course titled 'Programming Interactive Audio Software and Plugins in Max/MSP'.

In addition to the teaching activities in game music and sound there are some interesting extra-curricular activities as well. There is an informal Video Game Music Club that holds regular meetings and hosts seminars and panel discussions by leading game professionals. The club also supports an annual concert by the Video Game Orchestra (VGO). The VGO was started by a Berklee graduate in 2008 and is a combined orchestra and rock band that performs arrangements of video-game music. The VGO has developed its own momentum, has held concerts in Boston and around the world, and has been used to record game-music sound tracks. These non-teaching activities, combined with aspects of research by faculty members, amount to a rich culture of video-game music at the institution.

Creative coding

The definition of 'creative coding' or 'creative computing' is contested. Often, in computing circles, it is taken to mean applying computation in novel ways (Zhang and Yang 2013). For this discussion 'creative coding' is taken to mean the use of computer programming for creative arts activities, which is assumed to include video-game development, sound design, and music composition. In educational circles (and beyond) there is a growing movement to empower children by teaching them to programme computers, thus gaining control over them (Rushkoff 2010). In the words of one creative coding instructor, 'when kids realize that by learning to code, they can control computers and make them do their will, they sort of pause for a moment in shock. Then they smile' (Fredrickson 2014: n.p.).

Providing students with the skills to control their computers to make music that responds to interactions such as game play can be similarly empowering.

Game engines often support the use of coding as a method to extend their functionality or to simulate external interactions by users or game elements. These programming systems frequently use interpreted (scripting) languages so that interaction through code is a dynamic process. The Unity game engine, for example, can be scripted using either C# or Javascript languages. The Wwise game audio middleware can be scripted using the Lua language. The differences between these languages is subtle and for the purposes of adding some functionality to sound or music processes, any of them will suffice. What interpreted languages gain in being dynamic they lack in speed and so these scripting languages are primarily used for controlling parameters and triggering functions, not for audio signal processing. A number of game projects have used the Pure Data computer music language, which has a visual programming interface. Commercial music production software are increasingly adding scripting and/or visual programming capabilities too; Abelton Live uses Max for Live and Logic X has the Scripter MIDI plugin. Pure Data and other computer-music environments such as Max for Live operate independently of the game engine or audio middleware and communication between them is required to synchronise activities.

Scripting languages in game-development environments are general purpose. It would be nice to think they were implemented for music and audio purposes, but in reality they are used to automate any aspect of the game. In particular the game logic and character behaviour are often driven by scripted programs, sometimes referred to as artificial intelligence or simply game AI.

Scripting languages can be used to create algorithmic music that is generated on the fly in the game and to allow for a significant degree of musical variability in response to changing game conditions. The musical processes (algorithms) are coded in a programming language and run during game play to generate the score (or parts of it). With the increased computing power of modern game hardware, the use of algorithmic music is expanding. One very notable use of algorithmic music in a major game title is the score for *Spore*, which employed note-based algorithmic music and involved a collaboration between the composer Brian Eno and a team of programmers at Electronic Arts using the Pure Data environment. They found that a set of generative modules that used rules based on music perception and functional harmony was the most successful (McLeran 2009).

Another example is *Escape Point* (Prechtl et al. 2014), a non-commercial game developed in Unity that set out to make extensive use of algorithmic music. The game logic for *Escape Point* was coded in C# in Unity and the musical logic was programmed in Max which controlled sample playback for sound generation through MIDI and communicated with Unity through the UDP network protocol. The developers were interested in coordinating the emotional narrative of the game with the expressive character of the music. To do this they monitored the varying degree of danger in the game as a function of the proximity of enemies to the player's character. This value was passed to the music engine which varied the musical features accordingly.

Educators hoping to incorporate creative coding as part of the game-music and sound projects will need to find suitable software environments that suit their student's capabilities. There are a number of game-oriented programming environments that are designed for use in education, such as. Alice, Scratch, Stencyl, Gamefroot, and GameSalad, but the extent of audio support in these can vary.

Case study 3: Scratch and music

Scratch is a media-rich programming environment designed for young people and inexperienced programmers (Resnick et al. 2009). The current version of Scratch is a web-based application, which means it is widely available. The Scratch website supports creating, sharing, discussion, and remixing of other people's work. Code is written in Scratch by assembling visual code blocks. This visually reinforces code structure with shape and colour while reducing syntax issues by minimising the typing of text. A code example is shown in Figure 7.3.

Scratch is a pedagogical tool, rather than one designed to produce professional quality outputs. Developed at the MIT Media Lab, Scratch builds on a history of constrained programming environments called 'microworlds' where ideas can be explored in code (Papert 1980). The creators state that their 'primary goal is not to prepare people for careers as professional programmers, but rather to nurture the development of a new generation of creative, systematic thinkers who are comfortable using programming to express their ideas' (Resnick et al. 2009: 61).

Enabling the creation of interactive games is a core design goal of the Scratch environment. The starting point for new projects is a virtual canvas and a cat sprite that can be animated. The prominent categories in the editing environment are sprites (characters), scripts (code), costumes (graphics), and sound (audio capture and editing). Although music and sound can be a prominent part of simple animations and interactive programs developed in Scratch, its interest for us in this chapter is that it can be an environment where game design, sound design, and adaptive music can all be undertaken by those with little prior coding experience. Environments like Scratch provide an opportunity for the music student to move beyond being the sound maker with responsibility for the audio, to become a game maker with responsibilities for game design, graphics, and interaction as well. This holistic perspective challenges students to more fully appreciate the role of sound and music in video games.

While the audio capabilities of Scratch are modest, this has not stopped an enthusiastic band of educators from taking full advantage of the combination of computing and music. Chief amongst these are those involved with the 'Performamatics' project lead by the University of Massachusetts Lowell and funded by the United States National Science Foundation. A strong aspect of this project is the combination of computational thinking and music making with Scratch. In this project musical processes are articulated as algorithms and represented as code (Greher and Heines 2014). While many interactive activities that combine music and media are promoted as part of this programme and by the 'Sound Thinking' undergraduate course that preceded it, the orientation is toward physical

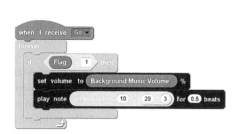 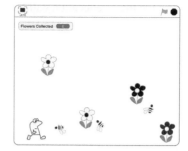

Figure 7.3 Me Bee Flower demo canvas (left) and generative music-code fragment (right)

computing and instrument making. Another source of music projects in Scratch are those by Scratch team member Eric Rosenbaum: aka ericr in the Scratch community. There are also examples of projects in Scratch more directly linked with music and sound for video games.

The *Me Bee Flower* demo game by Alex Ruthmann (2013) is a Scratch project that employs dynamically controlled recorded sound effects and algorithmic background music (see Figure 7.3). The game is built from three characters (sprites): the player (me), bees, and flowers. Each of these have associated sound effects and code to control behaviour for various actions, including walking, flying, stinging, picking flowers, and so on. The stage (canvas) includes code that tracks the game status, plays background music continuously and musical themes when the player wins or loses.

Environments such as Scratch and projects such as *Me Bee Flower* demonstrate that the tools and processes are available to assist music students to engage with all the significant aspects of video games, including dynamic control of sound effects and non-linear music. While code may be an unorthodox representation of music, for many students with little formal music training it may be no harder to grasp than any other notation system. In parallel with traditional music training, the representation of music as code and the video-game context provide for systematic expression of ideas and for student engagement in creative coding tasks. Similar interaction is possible with professional tools such as Unity, however, the degree of sophistication of professional tools may impede access or gratification for inexperienced students (and teachers). The Scratch environment is an example of a growing number of accessible platforms that support creative coding, and music educators are beginning to realise the benefits.

Conclusion

Video games and music are both significant forms of culture and commerce in contemporary society, and there is an increasing degree of interaction between them. The opportunities for music education start with viewing video games as a motivating context for music and sound production. If educators embrace the interdisciplinary nature of video-game practices they can provide a basis for integrating music education with visual art, creative writing, information technology, and more.

There is a range of software tools to support audio for games with applications requiring various levels of engagement and sophistication. Professional game engines such as Unity can be used simply to modify sound and music assets in an existing game project. The final result can look and sound very professional. Professional tools can, of course, also support advanced practices and experimentation; especially when paired with specialist audio middleware such as FMod or Wwise. Fortunately, for educators with younger students or less lofty ambitions, there are a range of simpler game-development tools available. Programs like Stencyl and GameSalad are easy to use and come with many demonstration projects that can be the basis for music and sound projects. Finally, there are media-programming environments like Scratch and Alice that support creative coding where students can both build the game and make the audio and visual materials. In these environments the outcomes may not look and sound so professional but the opportunities for creative agency and expression are high.

This chapter has explored the areas of sound design, non-linear music, and creative coding in some detail and provided a range of case studies that show how varied and interesting the use of game technology can be in the music classroom. It is hoped the ideas, examples and resources outlined here will inspire many more to use game technology in the music classroom.

Notes

1 <www.altools.com>.
2 <www.tunearound.com>.
3 <windows.microsoft.com/en-us/windows7/products/features/movie-maker>.

References

Bernt, A., K. Hartmann, N. Röber, and M. Masuch (2006). 'Composition and Arrangement Techniques for Music in Interactive Immersive Environments'. In *Proceedings of the Audio Mostly Conference: A Conference on Sound in Games*, Piteå, Sweden: Interactive Institute.

Bregman, A.S. (1990). *Auditory Scene Analysis: The Perceptual Organization of Sound.* Cambridge, MA: MIT Press.

Chion, M. (1983). 'Guide to Sound Objects: Pierre Schaeffer and Musical Research', trans. J. Dack and C. North. <http://monoskop.org/File:Chion_Michel_Guide_To_Sound_Objects_Pierre_Schaeffer_and_Musical_Research.pdf> (accessed 11 Dec. 2015).

Collins, K. (2008). *Game Sound: An Introduction to the History, Theory, and Practice of Video Game Music and Sound Design.* Cambridge, MA: MIT Press.

Denis, G. and P. Jouvelot (2004). 'Building the Case for Video Games in Music Education'. Paper presented at the Second International Computer Game and Technology Workshop, Liverpool.

—— and —— (2005). 'Motivation-Driven Educational Game Design: Applying Best Practices to Music Education'. In *Proceedings of the 2005 ACM SIGCHI International Conference on Advances in Computer Entertainment Technology.* New York: ACM.

El-Nasr, M.S., and B.K. Smith (2006). 'Learning through Game Modding'. *Computers in Entertainment*, 4/1: 45–64.

Fredrickson, E. (2014). 'Creative Coding for Kids'. <http://www.creativecoding4kids.com/> (accessed 2 Nov. 2015).

Greher, G.R., and J.M. Heines (2014). *Computational Thinking in Sound*. New York: Oxford University Press.

Harper, A. (2011). *Infinite Music: Imagining the Next Millennium of Human Music-Making*. Alresford: John Hunt.

Houge, B. (2012). 'Cell-Based Music Organization in Tom Clancy's *EndWar*'. In *Proceedings of the Eighth Annual AAAI Conference on Artificial Intelligence and Interactive Digital Entertainment*. Stanford, CA: AAAI.

Kanaga, D. (2013). 'Understanding the Musical Meaning of Games'. *Gamasutra*. <http://www.gamasutra.com/view/news/192212/Understanding_the_musical_meaning_of_games.php.> (accessed 16 May 2013).

Kim, E. (2013). 'Music Technology-Mediated Teaching and Learning Approach for Music Education: A Case Study from an Elementary School in South Korea'. *International Journal of Music Education*, 31/4: 413–27.

McLeran, A. (2009). 'Artists' Statements'. *Contemporary Music Review*, 28/1: 115–28.

Papert, S. (1980). *Mindstorms: Children, Computers, and Powerful Ideas*. New York: Basic Books.

Prechtl, A., R. Laney, A. Willis, and R. Samuels (2014). 'Algorithmic Music as Intelligent Game Music'. In *Proceedings of the 50th Annual Convention of the AISB*. London: ASIB.

Resnick, M., J. Maloney, A. Monroy-Hernández, N. Rusk, E. Eastmond, K. Brennan, and Y. Kafai (2009). 'Scratch: Programming for All'. *Communications of the ACM*, 52/11: 60–67.

Rose, M. (2014). 'Meet Joonas Turner, Vlambeer's Sound Guy'. *Gamasutra*. <http://www.gamasutra.com/view/news/214622/Meet_Joonas_Turner_Vlambeers_sound_guy.php>.

Rushkoff, D. (2010). *Program or Be Programmed: Ten Commands for a Digital Age*. New York: OR Books.

Ruthmann, S.A. (2013). *Me Bee Flower.* Scratch. <http://scratch.mit.edu/projects/10016626/> (accessed 2 Nov. 2015).

Savage, J. (2005). 'Information Communication Technologies as a Tool for Re-imagining Music Education in the 21st Century'. *International Journal of Education and the Arts*, 6/2: 1–11.

Zhang, L., and H. Yang (2013). 'Definition, Research Scope and Challenges of Creative Computing. In *Proceedings of the 19th International Conference on Automation and Computing (ICAC13)*. Brunel University Press: Uxbridge, Middx.

8 Music games

New opportunities for music education

Anna Paisley and Gianna Cassidy

Music games are becoming increasingly pervasive in the wider musical world of the learner. However, the practices and processes of participation and their potential to support and enrich formal music education, has been largely neglected. This chapter presents a case study from a 24-month EPSRC funded project titled 'Music-Games: Supporting New Opportunities for Music-Education', which aims to:

1 Identify educational opportunities and outcomes of employing music games in the classroom and informal learning contexts, highlighting the potential of music games to support and enrich academic, personal, and social development.
2 Present recommendations and materials for educators to guide the effective and innovative employment of music games in and out of the classroom.
3 Highlight music-game processes, experiences, and features that support authentic and inclusive music-making opportunities: game mechanics, narrative, aesthetics.
4 Investigate the flow experience for music-game participation and its relevance to music education and wider academic, personal and social development.

It is asserted that music games are a valuable vehicle to connect formal and informal music participation in the twenty-first century, embodying fundamental musical concepts in game play and authenticating formal participation to the wider musical world of the learner

The power of music games

Music games can be conceptualised as a digital game-based experience that necessitates music performance, appreciation, or creation, including off-the-shelf entertainment such as *Rock Band* (Harmonix, 2010)[1] and music-training games such as *Rock Smith* (Ubisoft, 2014).[2] In particular, rhythmic-based music games have been propelled to the forefront of academic enquiry, with growing recognition of the large proportion of informal music-making practices devoted to music-game play (Missingham 2007). In view of this, Miller notes that one of the foremost attractions of such games is their capacity to create a 'safe' environment in which any given individual can place themselves 'in the virtual shoes of live rock-concert performers' (2012: 85). Accordingly, it may come as no surprise to learn that the origins of *Rock Band* and *Guitar Hero* are rooted in MIT research investigating the need to provide inclusive interfaces to enable all individuals to participate in active music-making (MacHover 2009).

Yet rather than a replacement for conventional music participation, growing evidence suggests that such games may be considered a complementary adjunct to existing practice, providing learners with the confidence and desire to go on to engage in real-world music-making (Cassidy and Paisley 2013). Of the studies that do exist, such findings appear to stem from two experiential outcomes of game play. First, it has been posited that music games provide a gateway into formal music education through the mastery of transferable music skills necessitated by the game, such as dexterity, hand–eye coordination, and rhythm comprehension (Missingham 2007). Second, it has been further suggested that the confines of the music-game context, such as the use of simplified peripherals, create a desire to seek out more authentic music-making to extend one's repertoire of musical experience through formal music participation (Peppler et al. 2011). In sum, the synergistic context of music games appears to present a vehicle to bridge the informal and formal musical worlds of the learner.

Music education and digital literacy

Accordingly, the music curriculum has grown increasingly supportive of the use of music games such as *Rock Band* and *Guitar Hero* (Dillon 2003, 2004). With regard to the latter, UK-based *Guitar Hero* projects have been particularly efficacious, exploring the potential for pupil-led approaches to music education (Consolarium 2010, 2011). However, there is a need for empiricism and contextual implementation in music education and for exploration of the potential of music games to support conventional music education. Nonetheless, despite the paucity of research pertaining to music games specifically, there is a growing consensus that digital games have the ability to motivate learners through the integration of learning and play as a platform for the acquisition of personally relevant and educationally appropriate knowledge and skills (Groff, Howell, and Cranmer, 2010).

Indeed, as a pre-existing, familiar, and personally meaningful context for learners, evidence suggests that games have the unique ability to provide a situated-learning experience to empower the individual to harness a number of curriculum-orientated goals, facilitating personalised, differentiated and self-directed learning (Sandford and Williamson 2005). Such findings are of definitive significance here considering that the autonomy of the individual and centrality of self-directed learning are integral to the efficacy of music pedagogy (Choksy et al. 2000). Furthermore, in consideration of wider, personal, social, and emotional benefits, research suggests that the concept of 'flow' is particularly fruitful in the provision of theoretical insight and robust epistemology in both music and games (Cowley et al. 2008).

Scholars assert that optimal experiences and learning environments occur when the perception of challenge matches that of one's perceived skill, giving rise to an increase in cognitive efficiency, self-esteem, and motivation (Csikszentmihalyi 1992). In game research, the use of 'flow' as a tool to assess player enjoyment and engagement has allowed researchers to elucidate key features and game mechanics, including challenge, immersion, clear goals, immediate feedback, sense of identity, and altered perception of time (Sweetser and Wyeth 2005). Likewise, music research has operationalised the same principles of 'flow', investigating young people's cognitive music-making processes (Custodero 1998) and the relationship between musical creativity and elements of flow (MacDonald, Byrne, and Carlton, 2006). The application of flow to the neglected music-game synergy thus presents a unique, systematic way in which to investigate the relationship between flow and music-game participation in one overarching context.

However, it is with recourse to the underlying premise of using digital games in education where the applicability to music education is undoubted. That is, the unique ability of games to foster links between informal and formal education (Gee 2003). This is particularly timely given growing recognition of the need to authenticate the 'fit' between music education and the musical lives of learners in consideration of the new opportunities and outcomes facilitated by digital music technologies (Hargreaves, Marshall, and North 2003).

New opportunities for music education

To this end, 'Music-Games: Supporting New Opportunities for Music Education' sought to better understand the potential of music games to inspire and engage learners with music. To address this overarching aim, the preliminary phase of the project endeavoured to capture current uses, attitudes, and requirements with music games across age and experience, through a series ($n = 95$) of in-depth usability sessions with *Rock Band 3* (see Cassidy and Paisley 2013). *Rock Band 3* was purposively selected as the most socially inclusive and technologically challenging form of the music game to-date, marked by the introduction of 'pro instruments'. These peripherals are said to simulate real instrumental facility and thus a mastery of 'actual musical skills' to include, a guitar controller modelled on the classic Fender Stratocaster design, with seventeen frets and six strings and a wireless keyboard controller (keytar) that mimics conventional keyboard instruments (Harmonix 2010).

Key findings from this initial body of work indicated that music games represent a timely and relevant platform for learners, spawning a deeper and more meaningful musical understanding and appeared to instil a more positive identity in music. Indeed, the collective findings support the potential of music games to foster an inclusive environment for musical participation within which fundamental musical concepts were embodied. Furthermore, the music-game context was seen to give rise to a myriad of personal, social, and scholastic outcomes that transcended the domain of music, aiding personal recognition of the value of music curricula to one's aspirations and experiences in the wider world (Missingham

2007; Peppler et al. 2011). Such findings thus warranted a need to empirically investigate factors that shape and constrain music-game participation within educational settings.

In the light of this, the latter three phases of the project rested upon the development and evaluation of a co-created scenario of music-game use to scaffold, introduce, and reinforce music-curriculum goals. The results garnered from creation to empirical investigation of this scenario thus formed the evidence-based recommendations for the inclusion of music games as pedagogical tool. The remainder of this chapter will focus upon this sequential body of work where the generation and investigation of a co-created scenario of music participation with music games in the classroom' is outlined, detailing one group of learners encounter with *Rock Band 3*.

Context

The study took place in a non-denominational, co-educational school situated in East Lothian, Scotland, using one Primary 6 class of 33 pupils aged between 10 and 11. This particular school benefits from having a specialist music teacher with tuition provided for cello and violin.[3]

The teacher was female, aged 27 years old and described herself as having a strong background in music education and a keen interest in music from a young age, having performed to a high standard throughout her time at school. In particular she cited her involvement in the Scottish National Youth Orchestra and matched enthusiasm for extra-curricular music activities. Further to this, she was keen to assert that her personal experiences of music education were generally positive; attributing this to the enthusiasm of her previous music tutor.

With regard to teaching methods, the teacher advocated the need to acknowledge the heterogeneity of pupils with regard to musical background and ability and adapt the learning outcomes for each individual in light of this: a practice deemed plausible given the inclusivity and broad nature of the Curriculum for Excellence (CfE) (Education Scotland 2014). Successful progression in one's musical aptitude was thus assessed in light of each child's prior knowledge and experience as a benchmark.

By way of cultivating a sense of enjoyment with, and confidence in, music-making practices, the teacher further endorsed the use of music preferences as a key departure point for engaging children with formal music-making. The teacher felt that the use of *Rock Band 3* would be particularly efficacious in doing so, given an overwhelming penchant for rock music within the classroom. Moreover, a positive attitude towards the use of digital games in education, coupled with a high level of personal involvement with such games, led the teacher to predict a positive outcome for the use of *Rock Band 3*. This pre-supposition was further corroborated by her prior experience of using principles from games within her everyday teaching methods and concomitant desire to increase her repertoire of teaching modes. What follows is a brief overview of the 'scenario of use'[4] co-created by the teacher and researchers.

Co-created scenario of use: *Rock Band 3* in the classroom

Central to the generation of the co-created scenario was the need to devise a method of incorporating *Rock Band 3* within the classroom in line with defined curriculum goals. In order to do so, the following questions were used to guide this process:[5]

1   How will the scenario ensure an 'integrated' (creation, performance, and appreciation) music-making context?
2   How will this support/reinforce/innovate current practice?
3   How will this fit with overall curriculum goals?
4   What other activities will the children be engaged in during this week? How do they relate to *Rock Band 3*? What materials are required?
5   Are there any potential barriers to implementation and how shall these be overcome?
6   What are the predicted outcomes of participation?

At the outset a decision was made to embed *Rock Band 3* within the ongoing term topic of 'Great Britain', a full-term project designed to advance the children's historical and cultural knowledge of Great Britain. Specifically, the teacher opted to use the game as a learning tool to directly cut across at least 7 areas of the CfE applicable to this topic. To this end, a 'Rock Band Activity Pack' was specifically designed to incorporate the following (corresponding areas of the CfE are demarcated in parentheses):

1   Create a band name/logo (expressive arts, languages).
2   Create a personal band member identity and image (expressive arts, languages, health and wellbeing).
3   Design the first album and track listing (languages, expressive arts).
4   Design band merchandise (social studies, numeracy and mathematics, expressive arts).
5   Write a biography (languages).
6   Create a composition (languages, expressive arts).
7   Devise a tour of Great Britain (social studies, sciences).

In keeping with the nature of the overarching topic and to meet with the curriculum goals specific to the area of 'technologies', the pupils were further required to engage with *Rock Band 3* by performing 'Space Oddity' by British recording artist David Bowie from the self-titled album. The implementation of this activity, the choice of an age-appropriate song, and the division of children into working groups of 4 or 5 pupils was considered characteristic of routine classroom practice termed 'structured play' and thus did not predicate any potential disruption to concurrent teaching. To ensure a level of personalisation, the children were free to decide which peripherals to use during game play and the order in which the activities were completed over 5 days.

As a means of measuring the stipulated learning outcomes specified within the CfE (P5–P7; 2nd level), all children were required to complete a 'learning journal' in which they were required to reflect upon what they felt they had learned and to identify the areas of the CfE which they believed they had been embedded in the weeks' activities. Finally, to incorporate an element of both self- and peer-assessment, all children were required to note two things they felt they and their group had achieved and one area their group might wish to improve upon, a pre-existing mode of evaluation within the classroom.

The teacher suggested the proposed scenario would not only meet with 7 of the 8 areas of the CfE, but would help to foster a number of learning approaches considered pertinent to the CfE framework including 'creativity' and 'co-operative and collaborative learning', as well as 'ICT in learning' through their direct engagement with game-based technology. Furthermore, whilst the eighth area of the CfE, 'religious and moral education', was not explicitly addressed by the scenario, the teacher proposed that the mode of peer/self-assessment used here may harvest development in personal reflection, critical-thinking, and evaluation: outcomes considered pertinent to this particular area.

Method

Case

A single, exploratory case study was selected comprising of one group (band) of 2 males and 3 females, aged between 10 and 11, and considered representative of the wider participant pool ($n = 33$). This band were the second to be tested that week and the first to be tested that day, during which the remainder of the pupils in the classroom were required to complete the tasks set out in their 'Rock Band Activity Packs'. All five children were assigned to the group by the teacher in advance of participation, stratifying for an equal gender distribution, across age and experience. No further criteria for group allocation applied.

Design

A sequential mixed-methods paradigm was employed to capture responses from the pupils and teacher through a combination of pre-test, outcome, and post-test measures. Specifically, a pre-test questionnaire sought to capture each individual's prior music and video-game experience and observational methods encompassed a measure of game-play choices and performance and behavioural analysis throughout. A further measure of attitude change towards each child's perceived level of musicality was ascertained through the inclusion of a pre- and post-test item coupled with a post-test questionnaire to address flow experience. A post-test interview marked the final measure to be taken with each group of children and the teacher. In accordance with these proceedings a sequence of quantitative and qualitative modes of analysis were applied.

Equipment

To ensure ecological validity, all testing took place at the rear of the classroom with the game displayed on an interactive whiteboard connected to a PlayStation 3 console (see Figures 8.1 and 8.2). At the outset of gameplay, the game was set-up to ensure the game was in 'no fail' mode[6] with the pre-chosen song ('Space Oddity') ready to be selected on-screen. *Rock Band 3* equipment (peripherals/controllers) were positioned with adequate spacing between each, in such a way as to eradicate potential bias in instrument choice resulting from proximity or location. Recording equipment positioned within the testing area by way of two portable, discrete video cameras captured the on-screen image of game play and real-time feed of the participant.

Figure 8.1 Participants during game play

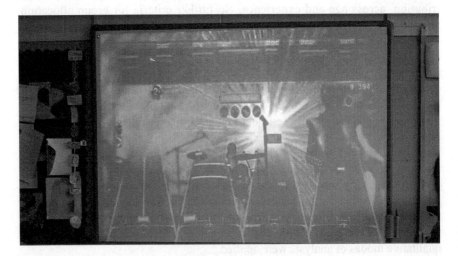

Figure 8.2 Screen capture of game play

Procedure

Prior to commencing the testing sessions, the researchers visited the school and introduced pupils to the study through an informal discussion regarding music and music-based video games. Following this, the pre-test questionnaire, incorporating the pre-test measure of perceived musicality was administered. The three days following marked the testing sessions in which the pupils were required to engage with *Rock Band 3* in their groups (*n* = 7).

At the beginning of each session, participants were informed of the song they would be playing and instructed to use any of the instruments, with assistance provided upon request. The duration of each session was approximately 15 minutes, after which game play was terminated and the participants were immediately invited to complete the flow experience questionnaire and focus-group interview. Completion of this latter phase marked the end of the testing session, which lasted approximately 45 minutes in total.

Following completion of all testing sessions, one researcher re-visited the school to measure perceived musicality following their encounter with *Rock Band 3*.

Materials

Video-game experience and musical background

A purpose-built questionnaire sought to measure each participant's musical background and prior videogame experience. The questionnaire was built by extracting project-specific items from pre-existing music-preference instruments (see Mitchell et al. 2007), adapted for use with children. The resultant questionnaire comprised a series of closed response (yes/no and Likert scale) and open-ended questions that sought to capture music background and video-game experience independently.

Observation: Behaviour and game play

On-screen footage provided data regarding participant and group decisions during game play to include instrument choice and difficulty level as well as game-based features of task duration, accuracy and task completion. The participants' concurrent behaviour was observed, with a focus upon positive and negative non-verbal and verbal interaction with the game and each other. Particular attention was given to facial expression, gesture, and body movement in accordance with usability testing procedure (Van den Hoogen, Ijsselsteijn, and de Kort 2008).

Flow and quality of experience

A post-test questionnaire designed to measure each individuals' subjective account of the experience was immediately administered following termination of game play. This questionnaire was theoretically grounded in literature pertaining to children's experience of flow during music collaboration (see MacDonald, Byrne, and Carlton 2006) and gameplay (Sweetser and Wyeth 2005). The questionnaire itself comprised five key dimensions of flow, including: cognitive efficiency (e.g. 'How well were you concentrating?'), motivation (e.g. 'Do you wish you had been doing something else?'), self-esteem (e.g. 'Did you feel good about yourself?'), challenge (e.g. 'Indicate how you felt about the challenge of the activity'), and skill (e.g. 'Indicate how you felt about your skill in the activity'). Responses were assessed using Likert scales ranging from either 0 (not at all) to 10 (very) or 1 (low/not at all) to 10 (high/very much), in which a high score was indicative of a high level of flow. A further twelve items sought to measure the participants' 'quality of experience' to include six items pertaining to affect (e.g. happy vs. sad) with the remaining six accounting for arousal (e.g. relaxed vs. tense). Seven-point semantic differential scales marked the response mode, with a high score denoting a positive mood throughout.

Perceived musicality

A visual analogue scale item was administered to all children prior to testing and then subsequently re-administered following completion of the study to allow for systematic comparison between scores. This item sought to ascertain each individual's 'perceived musicality' (e.g. 'How musical do you think you are?'). Responses were scored from 0 to 100, a high score being indicative of a high level of musical perceived musicality.

Focus group and teacher interview

Following completion of all post-test questionnaire items, a semi-structured focus group interview was conducted in situ with each group of children and a subsequent one-to-one interview with the classroom teacher following completion of all activities. Both interviews sought to delineate the potential opportunities and outcomes of music-games, alongside any recommendations for effective use within the classroom. A verbatim transcription of each interview ensued, employing the transcription conventions of thematic analysis (Braun and Clarke 2006). To enhance accuracy, transcripts were compared to original recordings and repeated readings of text ensued. From there, inductive, data-driven coding of text and organisation at the semantic level gave rise to recurrent themes later organised into superordinate categories. Results from the teacher interview are considered in the subsequent discussion section.

Results

Video-game experience and musical background

All participants reported having played a musical instrument, with two participants indicating that they currently played drums (male, 10) and piano (female, 11). However, formal music-making was limited to time spent with the music specialist: none of the participants were engaged in any further participation outside school. Interestingly, informal music-making was somewhat more frequent across participants, irrespective of reporting current investment in instrument playing.

All participants indicated a high level of engagement with video games from once per week ($n = 1$) to most days ($n = 2$) and every day ($n = 2$). All except one participant (female, 10) had previously played a music-based video game, including both *Guitar Hero* and *Rock Band*. However, none of the participants had previously engaged with *Rock Band 3*. Irrespective of experience, all participants perceived music-games to be enjoyable, with one participant espousing the potential to 'learn from them'.

Observational: Behaviour and gameplay

Gameplay lasted 16.47 minutes with the group engaging in three separate tasks, with two fully completed attempts and the third terminated. No participant opted to drop-out or change instrument or difficulty and all participants attempted two different peripherals, except Eve who sang throughout, later informing the researchers that this was a pre-planned decision agreed upon by all group members. Indeed, before each attempt, the children had mutually predetermined which instrument they would use.

Most of the children elected to commence the first task at the beginner level (easy), with the exception of Anthony who opted for medium. This, coupled with his eagerness to assist others in the initial set-up ($t = 2.39$ minutes), indicated a high level of confidence in using the game and he continued to emerge as the leader of the group throughout. Following the first attempt, the set-up time dramatically reduced as the children appeared to all grow progressively more self-assured. With the exception of aiding each participant in the location of their instrument on-screen, minimal assistance was sought from the researcher, except in using the Pro-Guitar.

Throughout the session the participants' gaze remained fixed on the screen, occasionally glancing down towards the instrument with mouths open. Such behaviours grew increasingly marked and outward displays of both engagement and positive affect were apparent. In particular, many of the children were seen to shift closer towards the screen and move in time with the rhythm of the song. In addition, the children were seen to smile at each other in instances in which they overcame difficulty or witnessed improvement in their performance. Anthony especially expressed a level of satisfaction in his performance where he was seen to exclaim with pride, pumping his fist in the air and smiling as the task came to a close.

Flow and quality of experience

As illustrated in Table 8.1,[7] a composite (group) measure of flow was calculated, resulting in a mean score of 8.6 ($SD = 0.89$), indicating an exceptionally high level of enjoyment and engagement throughout the session (MacDonald, Byrne, and Carlton 2006). In particular, self-esteem (9.2) and motivation (9.1) were notably high. Furthermore, a closer inspection of each child's individual flow score revealed little discrepancy between these ratings.

A group measure of the overall quality of experience was also derived, pertaining to the participant's psychological state during game play. As shown in Table 8.2, a resultant score of 5.9 (0.87) emerged suggestive of high level of positive affect and concordant level of arousal throughout. Indeed, the participants indicated feeling alert (6.2) and involved (6.0), as well as relaxed (5.6) and happy

Table 8.1 Individual and mean scores across flow dimensions and sub-dimensions

Flow dimension	Flow sub-dimension	Individual score (group mean)	Mean score	Overall mean
Cognitive efficiency	Concentration	8.4 (1.34)	6.5 (2.33)	8.6 (0.89)
	Ease of concentration	6.8 (2.78)		
	Lack of self-consciousness	4.2 (4.92)		
Motivation	Control	8.2 (2.17)	9.1 (0.49)	
	Wish to do activity	7.0 (4.12)		
	Personal expectations	9.8 (0.45)		
	Perceived expectations	8.4 (1.34)		
	Personal importance	9.4 (1.34)		
	Perceived importance	10.0 (0.00)		
	Success	9.2 (1.30)		
	Satisfaction	10.0 (0.00)		
	Goal attainment	9.8 (0.45)		
Challenge		9.4 (0.89)	9.4 (0.89)	
Skill		8.8 (1.64)	8.8 (1.64)	
Self-esteem		9.2 (1.80)	9.2 (1.80)	

Table 8.2 Individual and mean scores across quality-of-experience dimensions

	Affective dimension	Individual score	Mean score	Overall mean
Affect	Happy (vs. sad)	5.8 (1.10)	5.8 (0.78)	5.8 (0.87)
	Cheerful (vs. irritable)	5.6 (1.34)		
	Proud (vs. ashamed)	6.6 (0.89)		
	Sociable (vs. lonely)	4.2 (1.92)		
	Open (vs. closed)	6.4 (0.89)		
	Clear (vs. confused)	6.0 (1.41)		
Arousal	Alert (vs. drowsy)	6.2 (1.10)	5.9 (1.0)	
	Strong (vs. weak)	5.4 (1.67)		
	Active (vs. passive)	5.8 (0.84)		
	Involved (vs. detached)	6.0 (1.41)		
	Excited (vs. bored)	6.6 (0.89)		
	Relaxed (vs. tense)	5.6 (2.19)		

(5.8) throughout. Again, a subsequent breakdown of scores at the individual level showed no disparity within the group ratings.

When taken together, these results, coupled with the non-verbal displays thus indicated a peak flow experience of enjoyment and engagement throughout gameplay.

Perceived musicality and importance of music

A composite measure of the group's 'perceived musicality' before and after the test was derived by combining each individual's score across the two occasions (Table 8.3). Prior to this, the children had been asked to comment upon 'what it means to be musical' with the results thematically based upon musical aptitude. As illustrated in Table 8.3, there appeared to be a dramatic rise in perceived musical ability following completion of the study, with mean scores rising from 41.8 (23.8) to 74.8 (19.5). In particular, Ella showed the most dramatic shift with a pre-test score of 0.0 rising to 64.0. These scores can be considered representative of the wider classroom ($n = 33$), where an independent paired-samples t-test revealed a significant increase in post-test ($M = 71.22$, $SD = 18.68$) from pre-test ($M = 56.84$, $SD = 23.74$) perceived musicality scores ($t(31) = -3.19$, $p = 0.003$).

Table 8.3 Perceived musicality pre- and post-test (individual and group)

Perceived musicality	Anthony (male, 11)	Joseph (male, 10)	Eve (female, 11)	Rachel (female, 10)	Ella (female, 10)	Group
Pre-test	50.0	50.0	60.0	49.0	0.0	41.80 (23.80)
Post-test	73.0	50.0	87.0	100.0	64.0	74.80 (19.49)

Focus-group interview

The focus-group interview lasted approximately 13 minutes. Repeated readings and semantic thematic analysis gave rise to an initial set of recurrent themes ($n = 6$). Further clustering and latent thematic analysis led to the organisation of these themes into two superordinate themes (see Figure 8.3).

Superordinate theme 1: Bridging informal and formal music

Discourse on the potential for music games to provide a gateway into more formal music-making practices saturated the data item. Such talk often manifested itself in an instinctive fusion of music-game participation with that of more formal music-making, to the extent that the distinction between the two almost vanished. For example, when commenting upon his performance within the game, Joe alluded to his lack of prior experience in playing a musical instrument, not a music game:

JOE: I've not got big experience for guitar.

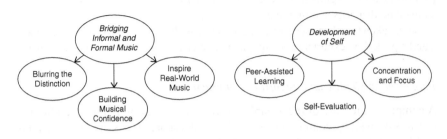

Figure 8.3 Thematic map of recurrent and superordinate themes

Likewise, a close inspection of terminology revealed a marked tendency to adopt language rooted in more formal musical participation, such as Rachel's choice of the word 'notes', as opposed to game-based vocabulary:

RACHEL: I enjoyed doing this on [Pro Guitar]. . . . I felt it was quite hard . . . because it was quite hard to do the notes [*mimics strumming*].

In addition to the seemingly intuitive synergy of formal and informal music, participants further disclosed the potential for the game to incite a desire to engage with music beyond the parameters of game play:

ANTHONY: I was listening to ['Space Oddity'] over the weekend to see, erm . . . what the parts were.

Implicit in subsequent dialogue was a reticent desire to bring formal and informal music together, bearing in mind that the two instruments primarily taught by the music specialist were cello and violin.

JOE: They should make more instruments!
INTERVIEWER: Yeah? What other instruments?
JOE: Like . . . flute or something . . . or a jazz game.
ANTHONY: They should make a jazz game
I: A jazz game?
ANTHONY: A jazz. . . . It's like . . . they should make a cello.
JOE: Or a violin.

Thus, it appeared that the merging of informal with formal through talk perhaps stemmed from an unconscious yearning to do so. The wider implications of this particular finding may go some way as to explaining why many of the children consequently espoused a growth in confidence in their musical ability following participation in music-game play. The quantitative result showed that all of the children reported a definitive increase in their 'perceived musicality' after the test. If the distinction between music-making in the real world and music-making within the confines of game play is somewhat obscured, then it makes intuitive sense to reason that confidence resulting from one's performance within the game context could transition to a wider belief about one's musical ability:

JOE: I showed them, I showed them the drums! [*points towards drum-kit peripheral*]
ANTHONY: There's something else I've learned . . . that I'm awesome!

Given the children's substantial exposure to formal music-making practices through the teacher's approach, the seemingly unique ability of the game to inspire growth in perceived musical ability is interesting. The data set was permeated by references to features and mechanics of the game context that appeared to cultivate a more positive environment for musical participation. In particular, participants highlighted the absence of any negative consequences, because the game was played in 'no-fail' mode, and, perhaps most importantly, the principal mechanic of the game itself: the use of colour to match scrolling 'notation':

ANTHONY: Even though you're quite. . . . Like even though you're not very good at it, it doesn't, erm, fail you.
RACHEL: I thought it was quite good with the colours as well because it was a little bit more easier for us.

Reflection on the learning outcomes of participation led many of the children to allude to the potential of the game to inspire wider musical participation, stemming from the belief that they would be able to transfer into the domain of real-world music making, if not with the immediate skill-set with which to do so, then at least the confidence in to try:

RACHEL: I can play guitar now . . . [*points to Pro Guitar*], because it's quite easy, I've learned how to do it.
JOE: I can probably play the drums and be good now . . . yeah!

Superordinate theme 2: Development of self

The second superordinate theme to emerge, can be thought of in terms of the new opportunities brought forth by the experience that could be extended to the children's wider, personal, social, and academic development that transcend the boundaries of music education. In particular, routine displays of peer-assisted learning were observed throughout the session and were a recurring theme throughout the interview:

JOE: I just held [the Pro Guitar], I didn't hit any of them.
ANTHONY: [*looks at Joe*] You forgot to strum.
JOE: [*looks at Anthony*] You have to strum too?
ANTHONY: Yeah!

EVE: I think the keyboard looks very hard.
ANTHONY: [*looks at Eve*] Well you. . . . What I think what you need to do is put your hands on the colour sections of them.

JOE: [*looks at Anthony*] Actually Anthony the colour sections are [inaudible] the orange is in the green one like that.

ANTHONY: [*shakes his head and looks at Joe*] It's not.

JOE: [*looks at Anthony*] No seriously! . . . I'll show you.

As illustrated in the above quotations and witnessed throughout the session, the music-game context appeared to harvest collaboration, manifesting in a willingness to aid others. Given that such musical participation, game-based or not, is inherently social (North and Hargreaves 2008) this particular finding is by no means novel. However, the potency of a music-game context as a tool in the development of such social skills was somewhat unforeseen, particularly considering that the case study here encompassed individuals who had never worked together as a group and the palpable cohesiveness of this collective towards the end of the study:

I: Who would you play it with?

ANTHONY: This band.

JOE: Yeah! [*smiles*] . . . This band, 'cause we're the Robot Monkeys!

Furthermore, this particular environment appeared to serve as a departure point for further peer-based learning through social comparison of one's performance:

JOE: [*looks at Anthony*] Wait . . . Who do you think did better at drums . . . me or you?

This theme of self-evaluation was further encountered as participants naturally spoke of their ability to monitor their performance throughout game play from the instant feedback provided on the screen, allowing them to each make informed decisions as to which difficulty level and instrument would facilitate attainment of their personal goals:

RACHEL: I just stuck, decided to play it on easy just to get started on it.

RACHEL: We just kind of thought what we're best at . . . and just kind of said what we would rather do and figured it out . . . like when me and Joe wanted to play the guitar . . . erm, we figured it out"

Indeed, latent references to the benefits gained from being able to tailor one's experience in an autonomous fashion were replete. Not only were such utterances indicative of the importance of personalisation to the learning process with specific recourse to self-evaluation, they echoed the predefined expectations of the teacher and the wider curriculum goals in that the children were afforded the opportunity to take ownership of their own aspirations and outcomes.

The final theme to be reported here is that which is considered pertinent to the experience of flow and, specifically, the central element of cognitive efficiency.

That is, when asked to comment upon the global experiences of gameplay, the bulk of participants frequently touched upon the need to fully attend to the game:

RACHEL: How to play focused on the game, keep your eyes on [Cross Talk]
JOE: [*looks at Rachel*] Yeah! Never let anything out your sight

This level of concentration and focus appeared to be engendered by the real-time scrolling 'notation' that characterises the nature of music-based games. Indeed, it appeared that the context of the game appeared particularly efficacious in the personal development of such skills commanding the pupils to continually engage with the task at hand:

RACHEL: We could get the notes quickly then get your fingers on them ready for it.

This latter finding in particular may go some way as to elucidating the relatively high scores obtained for the overall flow experience after the test and concordant behavioural indicators of immersion throughout gameplay.

Discussion

When taken together, the results from this case study empirically support the benefits of music-game participation to inspire, engage, and resonate with young learners (Cassidy and Paisley 2013; Missingham, 2007; Peppler et al. 2011). Crucially, a peak flow experience was evident, indicative of a high level of enjoyment, perceived challenge, and skill (Cowley et al. 2008). Further inspection of the antecedents of this finding elucidated a number of positive social, personal, and scholastic gains, subsequently corroborated by the teacher. Perhaps the most crucial finding to emerge here however, pertains to the significant increase in the extent to which the children perceived themselves to be musical following completion of the study. Indeed, it is well-attested that 'children's self-perceptions of the extent to which they are "good at music" and see themselves as actual, potential or aspiring musicians, can exert a significant influence upon whether or not they do indeed develop as such' (Hargreaves et al. 2007: 666).

Music-game flow: Music and non-music education

In terms of flow, congruent levels of perceived skill and challenge gave rise to an optimum level of flow that appeared to stem from specific experiential features and mechanics of the music-game context, such as the ability to select a particular peripheral (instrument) and difficulty level. Indeed, the benefits of being able to tailor the learning experience were implicit in the children's subsequent dialogue, with putative regard to the efficacy of self-directed learning that echoes the existing music-education literature (Hargreaves, Marshall, and North 2003). Furthermore, this particular facet of the music-game experience may go some way as to explaining the high level of intrinsic motivation observed, given the reliably documented finding that individuals experience high levels of motivation when a sense of autonomy prevails and the opportunity to influence of the quality of their engagement exists (Deci 1995).

Further inspection of this particular dimension of flow revealed a high level of perceived and personal importance of the music-game experience. This finding is somewhat unsurprising given that music games play a prominent role in the informal musical worlds of learners (Missingham 2007) as indicated by the participant's level of engagement with such games prior to commencing the study. What is more, it is entirely plausible that this seemingly high level of intrinsic value of music-game participation arose from the children's recognition of the relevance of music games to real-world music-making. Discourse on the music-game experience lends credence to this supposition, as participants frequently adopted language rooted in formal music education in such a way as to blur the distinction between music-game play and music-making in the wider world. In turn, this may go some way as to explaining the high levels of achievement and satisfaction observed.

Behavioural indices of personal satisfaction with their performances were routinely observed throughout game play, subsequently buttressed by the subjective reports. With regard to the mechanics of the game, the children made use of the immediate feedback from the game and resultant scores in order to gauge personal achievement. In the existing game-based literature, such features are considered fundamental to the experience of flow (Sweetser and Wyeth 2005), especially by allowing individuals to create achievable goals. Research suggests that the attainability of goals rests upon the inclusivity and accessibility of the activity (Custodero 2002).

In the light of this, participants noted two main features of the scenario that afforded the achievement of personal goals. First, in line with the centrality of informal music (see Green 2006), the music-game context was marked by the absence of negative consequences that often permeate formal music-making activities, facilitated by the absence of teacher-based assessment and adoption of the 'no-fail' mode. Second, the children spoke of the inclusive nature of the music game with regard to its fundamental mechanic, the use of colour in the scrolling notation. This particular feature was cited by the participants as engendering wider understanding of the relationship between notated and aural music representation and transferable skills such as dexterity, hand–eye coordination, and rhythm, in line with previous theoretical assertions surrounding the efficacy of music games (Peppler et al. 2011). This ostensible mastery of skill, attainment of goals, and level of satisfaction was met with a concordant high level of self-esteem. Crucially, these resultant levels of confidence coupled with the blurring of real and game-based music may be considered conducive to in the children's desire to go on to engage in more formal music-making.

A further final element of flow worthy of comment is the element of cognitive efficiency and specifically, concentration. As with the multisensory nature of wider-music making, *Rock Band 3* commands full immersion and concentration:

listening to and observing represented notation and responding kinaesthetically (Custodero 2002). As the children remarked, concentration throughout music-game play is reciprocal in nature, in that it is both required and reinforced by the real-time mechanic of the game. Such levels of attentiveness are not only a competency necessary for successful musical learning, they mark an essential 'building block' for wider scholastic success (Arts Education Partnership 2011).

Personal, social, and academic development: Educational opportunities and outcomes

With regard to music education, the chief outcome of this study arose from the children's perceived commonalities between music-game play and formal music-making to the extent that the distinction between the two was blurred. Despite the discrepancies between informal and formal music (see Green 2006), Hargreaves, Marshall, and North (2003) assert that they should be viewed as two poles of a continuum, rather than a dichotomy. In this way, this study suggests that music games present a valuable vehicle to merge the two. By drawing connections between music games and music education the children were able to express levels of confidence in their perceived musical ability, fostering an appreciation of the educational value of such practice and thus a desire to engage in real-world music participation (see Cassidy and Paisley 2013).

In terms of the wider benefits of music-game participation, two definitive outcomes were apparent from the cumulative accounts of both the teacher and children. The observed increase in perceived musicality in the music-game context and related tasks appeared to proffer new opportunities to develop and reconstruct a positive identity in music (see MacDonald, Miell, and Hargreaves 2002). Rather than simply perform a song, the children were encouraged to form a 'band': design a logo, create a band name and 'alter-ego', and assume the role of musician in subsequent tasks such as album artwork and track-listing. In essence, the children were afforded new opportunities to explore and reconstruct their own internal representation of what it means to be a musician and to enhance those creative aspects of themselves; an outcome that epitomises 'best practice' in music pedagogy (Hargreaves, Marshall, and North 2003). This particular outcome has important implications for the future use of music games in determining children's subsequent motivation and performance in music education. 'Studying the way in which children perceive themselves to be musical and the influences of those perceptions on developmental change' will ultimately herald a greater understanding of music education in the twenty-first century (Hargreaves, Marshall, and North 2003: 9). Perhaps the unique capacity of music games provides a particularly fruitful method for doing so.

Inextricably linked to the notion of being in a 'band', the second chief outcome to emerge here lies with the power of music to enhance social inclusion, interpersonal skills, and collaboration (Hargreaves, Marshall, and North 2003; Hargreaves, Welch, and Marshall 2007), a skill-set deemed crucial for music education and wider social, personal, and scholastic development. Prior research indicates that children involved in active music-making often develop a strong sense of belonging, marked by a rise in responsibility, commitment, and respect (Hallam and Creech 2010). Nowhere more so was this evident than in the level of peer-assisted learning observed throughout game play and in the latter phases of the interviews. The teacher was also keen to assert that she felt the use of *Rock Band 3* was particularly efficacious in doing so, as it was a context in which collaboration was commanded. Enthused by the way in which the children adopted this level of social responsibility, the teacher suggested that in addition to the palpable gains for music education, music games should thus be considered a catalyst for social inclusion within the classroom.

Recommendations: Effective and innovative classroom use

Above all, the teacher emphasised the need to contextualise the use of music games, embedding their use within current classroom activities across wider curriculum goals to facilitate pupil recognition of the educational potential of music-games whilst promoting a shared acknowledgement of the personal value of the children's informal music participation. To do so, an activity pack was designed to cut across the main areas of the CfE (Education Scotland 2014), encompassing tasks relevant to being part of a rock band. Integral to this process was the active involvement of the children throughout the design process, in keeping with the notion that educators must strive to integrate structures to informal music that support and enrich it, whilst retaining a level of distance (Hargreaves, Marshall, and North 2003), thus maintaining an optimum level of pupil ownership.

The second chief recommendation was the preservation of pupil autonomy. In particular, the teacher consciously chose not to impose restrictions upon pupil choices such as which instrument to play and which difficulty level to attempt, nor did she dictate the order of activity. Not only is this particular recommendation congruent with the philosophies of democratic education that underscore the CfE (Education Scotland 2014), it is entirely in keeping with the shift in music pedagogy towards student-led learning (Hargreaves, Marshall, and North 2003). This balance between scaffolding and structuring the children's learning, whilst maintaining a level of detachment from the experience itself, fostered the children's sense of autonomy and self-esteem and provided a suitable platform for the development of self-directed / peer-assisted learning and collaboration.

Third, the teacher further indicated that effective employment of *Rock Band* should allow students to acknowledge the wider value of music participation in their overall academic development, to encourage formal music practice. Here, the teacher used 'learning journals' to allow the children to witness the transfer effects of music participation. In doing so, the children were asked to reflect upon their experiences and felt academic gains. This particular ability to engage in self-reflection was believed to influence forethought regarding future learning efforts and willingness to engage in formal music education.

Lastly, the teacher's approach to the overall study revealed a desire to create tasks considered both inclusive and accessible to all. Accordingly, the teacher did not assign children to groups based on any prior experience of music or games. Likewise, the song selected was perceived to be child-appropriate and suitable in light of the general music preferences of the children. Within the wider activities, the teacher further aligned the outcomes of related tasks to the pre-specified learning outcomes for 2nd level (P5–P7) pupils, considering individual differences in the children's typical mode of learning and level of ability.

Conclusion

This study sought to tackle the current call for music educators to harness the opportunities that music games present through the empirical evaluation of a co-created scenario of use of music games within the classroom. In doing so, the authors elucidated a number of key personal, social, and scholastic gains of and concordant recommendations for efficacious and innovative employment of music games in education. Change to music pedagogy is necessary if music participation in the classroom is to keep pace with the wider musical world of the learner (Cain 2004). To this end, it is asserted that the introduction of music-game technologies to the classroom may go some way to bridging the gap between informal and formal music-making, acknowledging the value of learners' informal practice as a catalyst for developing a positive identity in music and subsequent desire to engage in formal music education.

Notes

1 <http://www.harmonixmusic.com/>.
2 <http://rocksmith.ubi.com/rocksmith/en-GB/home/>.
3 The class received music lessons from the Primary 6 teacher, not the school specialist music teacher; however, many of the children attend the school choir run by the specialist.
4 Immediately following completion of the in-depth interview, the generation of a co-created scenario for *Rock Band 3* within the classroom commenced with the both the teacher and lead research assistant present.
5 The teacher was provided with a copy of these questions prior to the interview and scenario generation session.
6 'No-fail' mode allows players to fully perform a track irrespective of their performance level. A decision was made (pre-test) to ensure that the children would only engage with the game using the 'no fail' mode to avoid any distress that may be caused if the participants were to 'fail' at any point.
7 Pseudonyms have been used for confidentiality.

References

Arts Education Partnership (2011). 'Music Matters: How Music Education helps Students Learn, Achieve, and Succeed'. <http://www.aep-arts.org/wp-content/uploads/2012/08/Music-Matters-Final.pdf> (accessed 26 Jan. 2014).

Braun, V., and V. Clarke (2006). 'Using Thematic Analysis in Psychology'. *Qualitative Research in Psychology*, 3/2: 77–101.

Cain, T. (2004). 'Theory, Technology and the Music Curriculum'. *British Journal of Music Education*, 21/2: 215–21.

Cassidy, G.G., and A.M.J.M. Paisley (2013). 'Music-Games: A Case Study of their Impact'. *Research Studies in Music Education*, 35/1: 119–38.

Choksy, L., R.M. Abramson, A.E. Gillespie, D. Woods, and F. York (2000). *Teaching Music in the Twenty-First Century*, 2nd edn. Upper Saddle River, NJ: Pearson.

Consolarium (2010). 'Falkirk Guitar Heroes' [blog entry] (16 June). <http://blogs.educa tionscotland.gov.uk/consolarium/2010/06/16/falkirk-guitar-heroes/> (accessed 2 Nov. 2015).

—— (2011). 'Gavinsburn PS: The Real School of Rock' [blog entry] (25 Apr). <http:// blogs.educationscotland.gov.uk/consolarium/2011/04/25/gavinburn-ps-the-real-school-of-rock/> (accessed 2 Nov. 2015).

Cowley, B., D. Charles, M. Black, and R. Hickey (2008). 'Towards an Understanding of Flow in Video Games'. *Computers in Entertainment*, 6/2: 1–27.

Csikszentmihalyi, M. (1992). *Flow: The Psychology of Happiness*. London: Random House.

Custodero, L.A. (1998). 'Observing Flow in Young Children's Music Learning'. *General Music Today*, 12/1: 21–7.

—— (2002). 'Seeking Challenge, Finding Skill: Flow Experience and Music Education'. *Arts Education Policy Review*, 103/3: 3–9.

Deci, E.L. (1995). *Why We Do What We Do*. New York: Penguin.

Dillon, T. (2003). 'Collaborating and Creating on Music Technologies'. *International Journal of Educational Research*, 39/8: 893–97.

—— (2004). 'It's in the Mix Baby: Exploring how Meaning is Created within Music Technology Collaborations. In D. Miell and K. Littleton (eds), *Collaborative Creativity, Contemporary Perspectives*. London: Free Association Books.

Education Scotland (2014). 'Principles for Curriculum Design'. <http://www.education scotland.gov.uk/thecurriculum/howisthecurriculumorganised/principles/index.asp> (accessed 10 Jan. 2014).

Gee, J.P. (2003). *What Video Games Have to Teach Us About Learning and Literacy*. New York: Palgrave Macmillan.

Green, L. (2006). 'Popular Music Education in and for Itself, and for "Other" Music: Current Research in the Classroom'. *International Journal of Music Education*, 24/2: 101–18.

Groff, J.S., C. Howells, and S. Cranmer (2012). 'Console Game-Based Pedagogy: A Study of Primary and Secondary Classroom Learning through Console Video Games'. *International Journal of Game-Based Learning*, 2/2: 35–54.

Hallam, S. and A. Creech, eds (2010). *Music Education in the 21st Century in the United Kingdom: Achievements, Analysis and Aspirations*. London: Institute of Education.

Hargreaves, D.J., N.A. Marshall, and A.C. North (2003). 'Music Education in the Twenty-First Century: A Psychological Perspective'. *British Journal of Music Education*, 20/2: 147–63.

—— R.M. Purves, G.F. Welch, and N.A. Marshall (2007). 'Developing Identities and Attitudes in Musicians and Classroom Music Teachers'. *British Journal of Educational Psychology*, 77/3: 665–82.

Harmonix. (2010). 'Rock Band 3 Features Set List and More!' [blog] (11 June). <http:// www.rockband.com/blog/rock-band-3-announcements> (accessed 10 Jan. 2014).

MacDonald, R.A.R., C. Byrne, and L. Carlton (2006). 'Creativity and Flow in Musical Composition: An Empirical Investigation'. *Psychology of Music*, 34/3: 292–307.

—— D. Miell, and D.J. Hargreaves, eds (2002). *Musical Identities*. Oxford: Oxford University Press.

MacHover, T. (2008). 'Guitar Hero'. *RSA Digital Journal*. http://www.thersa.org/fellow ship/journal/archive/winter-2008/features/guitar-hero (accessed 2 Nov. 2015).

Miller, K. (2012). *Playing Along: Digital Games, YouTube, and Virtual Performance*. New York: Oxford University Press.

Missingham, A. (2007). 'Why Console-Games are Bigger than Rock 'n' Roll: What the Music Sector Needs to Know and How It can get a Piece of the Action'. Youth Music. <http://www.youthmusic.org.uk/assets/files/Console%20games%20and%20music_ 1207.pdf> (accessed 2 Nov. 2015).

Mitchell, L.A., R.A.R. MacDonald, M.G. Serpell, and C. Knussen (2007). 'A Survey Investigation of the Effects of Music Listening on Chronic Pain'. *Psychology of Music*, 35/1: 39–59.

North, A.C., and D.J. Hargreaves (2008). *The Social and Applied Psychology of Music*. Oxford: Oxford University Press.

Peppler, K., M. Downton, E. Lindsay, and K. Hay (2011). 'The Nirvana Effect: Tapping Video Games to Mediate Music Learning and Interest'. *International Journal of Learning and Media*, 3/1: 41–59.

Sandford, R., and B. Williamson (2005). *Games and Learning*. Bristol: Nesta Futurelab.

Sweetser, P., and P. Wyeth (2005). 'GameFlow: A Model for Evaluating Player Enjoyment in Games'. *Computers in Entertainment*, 3/3: 1–24.

Van den Hoogen, W.M., W.A. Ijsselsteijn, and Y.A.W. de Kort (2008). 'Exploring Behavioral Expressions of Player Experience in Digital Games'. In A. Nijholt and R. Poppe (eds), *Proceedings of the Workshop on Facial and Bodily Expression for Control and Adaptation of Games ECAG 2008*. <http://www.gamexplab.nl/includes/pages/publica tions/articles/ECAG2008.pdf> (accessed 23 Jan. 2014).

Part III

Musical creation, experience, and understanding

9 Music technology and the realm of the hyper-real
Comprehending, constructing, and connecting realities

Phil Kirkman

In this chapter I begin by exploring constructions of 'technology' in relation to a postmodern notion of the hyper-real (Baudrillard 1981). Following this I will form a critical lens through which to view technology as a framework that underpins the formation of new relationships with music and how it functions within time and space, sound and silence. At the same time I will observe key attributes that underpin what we might call the 'synthetic' worlds (Smith, Kisiel, and Morrison 2009) that lie within and in relation to musical technologies. Bringing these aspects together, I will present recent developments in our understanding of individual musical development (Kirkman 2012a) and in the light of these will critically examine the potential and dangers of positioning technology as central in educational spaces which seek to foster ethical and democratic values. I will end by suggesting three ways in which technology-mediated educational spaces may be made 'safe' for learners: comprehending, constructing, and connecting. 'Comprehending' involves understanding the nature of the technologies being used. 'Constructing' is the process of creating novel environments that can allow an individual to build on their existing knowledge and understanding. 'Connecting' means engaging in a meaningful process of dialogue between the members of a community of musicians in order to share creative developments.

Introduction

The idea of 'hyper' is not something too far from our awareness when we consider technology: hypertext, hyperlink, hyperspace. The former describes electronic text with references to ever increasing levels of detail accessed through 'hyperlinks'. The latter, beloved of science-fiction writers connotes travel at speeds in excess of that of light. In both cases these tempt the reader towards exciting new possibilities, ripe with new opportunities for exploration, discovery, adventure, and connectedness. At the same time, in the world outside (or perhaps in the 'real' world?), hyperactive and hypersensitive, hyperinflation and hypercritical, while perhaps sharing tendencies towards abundance, do not hold the same connotations of progress, evolution, advancement, and innovation. Instead, they offer a multitude of concerns to be treated, condemned, devalued, and denounced. Even the promise of the 'hypermarket' is now tainted with the notion of a one-stop shopping experience that threatens to eclipse the diversity of the local and the artisan in a torrent of discount, big-purchase, pre-packaged plastic. In this way, a contradiction emerges between the possible worlds of the future, promised through digital technologies, and our current 'state' in which 'hyper' seems to evoke a dream and appears to enthuse, while simultaneously treating and sentencing the individual. Into this landscape steps the simulacrum: 'The simulacrum is never what hides the truth – it is the truth that hides the fact that there is none. The simulacrum is true – Ecclesiastes' (Baudrillard 1981: 1). The simulacrum is used by Baudrillard to expand a notion of 'the real'. He proposes that just as we have made copies of the world to help us to understand, (perhaps 'control'?) reality, so now we make reality through simulacra which are 'without origin or reality: a hyperreal' (ibid.: 1). In other words we construct simulations which become real. Just as we might simulate illness to the point that symptoms exist (the hypochondriac) or simulate wellness in a patient through the use of a placebo, so too we might simulate inarticulation through digital voicing or treat inaccuracy through autotune.

In her review of technological developments during the 1980s and early 1990s Samantha Bennett draws attention to a tension within this capacity. On the one hand she highlights the 'enabling' features of technology through a 'wealth of time-saving, space-saving, not to mention money-saving systems, bringing with them new working practices and redefining the roles of the producer and engineer' (2009: n.p.). In this sense perhaps technologies are cast in the role of 'hero', bringing greater opportunities for creative exploration and production. It is worth noting that in this sense 'digital' could be seen as 'just what's next' in the development of our capacity to interact with the sonic world. In contrast Bennett notes that pre-digital technologies also helped to shape the production process, citing Albini (2000) as an example of someone for whom traditional practices held comparable 'time-saving' capabilities: 'Working in the computer paradigm is much slower, because no-one knows their computer software well enough to be aware of every single thing it does. In the analogue domain . . . problems are solved instantly' (Bennett 2005: 61). From this perspective digital technologies are cast as the villain, constraining and leading the listener away from the song and instead towards production. From both perspectives, however, it seems that digital technologies offer an opportunity to step outside what has been done before, perhaps positioning 'the producer' as a key voice in the shaping of our sonic (hyper-) reality. Significantly in this context of music education where key values would appear to originate from a curriculum which is 'balanced and broadly based and which promotes the spiritual, moral, cultural, mental and physical development of pupils at the school and of society, and prepares pupils at the school for the opportunities, responsibilities and experiences of later life' (Department for Education 2014), Baudrillard suggests that in the world of the hyper-real 'the only massive affect is that of manipulation' (1981: 69). Thus a music education that fails to subvert the manipulation of learners by the hyper-real would seem to be in conflict with the goal of preparing pupils, in particular, for the democratic responsibilities of later life.

What in this context is musical?

Is health the absence of illness mediated by a concoction of therapy, vitamins, placebos, and Ritalin? Or could it be the presence of illness but the absence of a need to 'treat' ourselves? If disease, war, death pestilence, and failure are part of the human condition then what place does music retain, if we synthesise 'perfection' and 'distort' embodied sound in 'hyper-music? Does it tell us that we have given up on ourselves to find common ground in diversity and discourse, instead retreating into ones and zeros? Perhaps we should instead ask: is a great performance the absence of imperfection or the presence of it? Does it exist in that potential for humanness to strive towards something attainable only through sheer force of will and briefly, for one moment be transported beyond what we can articulate?

It seems that the potential simulated perfections and imperfections of hyper-music challenge us to re-examine the very fabric of music as sound and silence because the dimensions of time and space are now up for grabs. In hyperspace, time and space are now available for manipulation like never before. We can travel at hyperspeed across time and space back and forth across *Longplayer*, Beethoven's Ninth Symphony, or *The Ring* and then split the millisecond as we zoom in to view 1/44100th of a second of bar 2. Paynter and Aston's *Sound and Silence* (1970) just went hyper. A piano no longer has location or action but now has reverb and envelope. A piece no longer has performers and audience but programmers and consumers and remixers. A sine wave and a sample become the elements and frequency and amplitude our core values. With technology, new dimensions bring the whole environment into question; the cultural artefacts as well as the physical reality are subject to change. In their collected volume *Audio Culture*, Cox and Warner bring together 57 essays which explore the theories and practices of 'cultures of the ear' (2004: xiii). They explore what they see as the culture of 'musicians, composers, sound artists, scholars, and listeners attentive to sonic substance, the act of listening, and the creative possibilities of sound recording, playback, and transmission', through a series of themes which work forwards from notions of music into the concept of the 'work' as process and practice then on to culture and aesthetics. While a full discussion of the development or perhaps the deconstruction of 'music' explored in this volume is beyond the scope of this chapter, of note in this discussion are the contributions of three authors.

In 'Rap, Minimalism, and Structures of Time in Late Twentieth-Century Culture', Susan McClary draws on the works of Tupac Shakur and Philip Glass to suggest that the structures within which composers operate (in this case repetition) cease to register as significant as 'they constitute merely the neutral ground of basic assumptions up against which the actual music occurs' (2004: 290). In this way, McClary points towards the challenging notion that the structuring of time according to hyper-music's malleable parameters may be a 'basic assumption' rather than a feature of the 'actual music'. Kodwo Eshun presents a view of the 'black artist' as posthuman cyborg and describes this music as 'from the Outer Side. It alienates itself from the human; it arrives from the future' (2004: 158). Eshun positions 'otherness' or 'difference' as simultaneously futuristic and liberated, a manifesto for self-definition. This appears to be an attempt to bring forward a conception of the human condition that moves beyond restrictions imposed by practices which are underpinned by technological determinism (Mumford 1934; Taylor 2001). In so doing he fosters the idea that the 'basic features' of hyper-music may promote controls that allow for self-determination and the redefinition of unhelpful cultural values, a move towards mediation (Cole 1998; Wertsch 1998) rather than determinism. Finally, in 'The Aesthetics of Failure: "Post-Digital" Tendencies in Contemporary Computer Music', Kim Cascone makes the point that failure is an important feature of the post-digital aesthetic. The ability to zoom in beneath the threshold of perception and detect 'errors' (clipping, aliasing, distortion, quantisation) allows us to see the imperfections of the 'humans who built them'. Drawing on Whitehead (1999) Cascone asserts that 'it is failure that guides evolution; perfection offers no incentive for improvement' (2004: 393). In this way he leads us towards the conclusion that the tool (that is the artefact of sonic manipulation) is now the message and so 'music' now must be expanded to include the 'glitch' within the programming. By extension the musician as programmer (or perhaps the programmer as musician?) may be assumed within this framework. Thus, while McClary encourages us to move beyond the basic assumptions of technology and see the music as what occurs within this context, and Eshun suggests that hyper-music may allow for new movement beyond unhelpful and constraining cultural values, Cascone cautions that such practices and movements are necessarily underpinned by the imperfection of the human condition that can only be attended to if the 'glitches' and the programmer are explicitly acknowledged as hyper-music and hyper-musician respectively.

The changes in the culture of music and musician that have emerged as a result of new technologies include: (1) music is now mass consumed, (2) musical accuracy is potentially (at the level of aural perception) polarised into perfected and uncorrected which is in turn fetishised on YouTube or the *X-Factor*, and (3) music is potentially remote from the music-makers. Throughout the development of recording technology imperfections and inventors can be seen as music and musician. The capacity to capture live sound was first realised with Édouard-Léon Scott de Martinville's phonautograph in 1857 and Edison's phonograph in 1877 (Gelatt 1977). This was developed through the use of electricity and microphones by engineers at Western Electric into the electrical system used to release Alfred Cortot's version of Schubert's *Litanei* for Victor, a company which had grown from the work of Berliner, who invented the gramophone ten years after Edison's phonograph. The early phonautograph could not play back music but instead made visual tracings in response to music performed live. Thus to experience the music as sound the 'listener' had to be in the room for the performance. The phonograph permitted at most a few hundred copies of a performance to be recorded onto phonograph cylinders and so the listeners were limited to the select few who had access to such cylinders and phonographs and the quality of the music was compromised by its limited dynamic range and peculiar timbre. The electrical recordings of the Victor company were of much better quality: there were still pops, clicks, and scratches but there was also an increased dynamic range and they were available to a much bigger market as they could be mass produced. These transitions, along with subsequent evolutions from record to tape to CD to MP3, increased the capacity for sound to be reproduced and distributed more quickly to an expanding audience who are increasingly detached from the context of the 'real' performance (both in space – proximity – and time – history). Thus, as the distance between performer and audience expanded, the contribution of the medium and the inventor, controller, or programmer of that medium became more significant. As a result, the notions of hyper-music and hyper-musicians necessarily encompass both traditional ideas of the work, the performer, and the composer, as well as the tools and the technician and programmer.

Alright that's enough: Get 'reel'!

I should at this point clarify that my point of departure for this chapter is a problem that does not derive from the philosophical minefields of postmodernism but from the perhaps rather less glamorous but (I propose) no less challenging comprehensive-school classroom. How can today's learners possibly compete with the perfection and processing power that assails their musical enculturation in twenty-first-century society?

Today's learners live in a world where technology offers them countless opportunities to engage with music, as creators, consumers, collaborators, and critics. Increasingly sophisticated apps, software, and websites allow learners to construct and reconstruct their own music whether from scratch or recycled. Spotify, iTunes, YouTube, SoundCloud, and a plethora of other portals mean that tracks can be shared, downloaded, compared, and rated with such frequency that it seems the only limits are bandwidth and disk space. Yet, at the same time, this new found freedom puts them at dangerous risk of information overload.

At this point I realise a tension in my own approach to the real as I reach for Wikipedia, which sends me towards Alvin Toffler and his bestselling 1970 book *Future Shock* and the British Education Index via ProQuest which sends me to Niaz and Logie (1993) and in turn to James Clerk Maxwell via Garber, Brush, and Everitt (1986). Information overload is 'a rich metaphor used outside the world of academia' and we are told that 'information technology may be a primary reason for information overload due to its ability to produce more information more quickly and to disseminate this information to a wider audience than ever before' (Wikipedia 2014). But it is also a much more nuanced and complex concept that is beyond the scope of this chapter but which approximates to something like: the limits of mental energy which can be applied to learning or problem solving (Niaz and Logie 1993).

This personal sketch serves to exemplify the way in which the knowledge and understanding constructed in this technology-mediated world can quickly become too narrow, shallow, and self-centred. In his book *The Laws of Cool*, Alan Liu describes this kind of knowledge as 'cool knowledge'. This he proposes is the 'vanishing point' at which contemporary aesthetics, psychology, morality, politics, spirituality, everything' disappears (2004: 3). In this climate, in which the dominant culture is defined by corporate and media conglomerates, he suggests that literature becomes transformed into 'content' and 'the arts' are destined to become 'multimedia entertainment'. The danger hinted at by Baudrillard and articulated by Liu is that in a dominant culture mediated by technology, cool knowledge creates a hyper-real hyper-musical world in which 'content is king' and 'entertainment' is limited only by bandwidth and disk space.

And yet, Liu suggests, as cool knowledge threatens to eclipse 'beauty, sublimity, tragedy, grace' (2004: 3), this hyper-reality can be deconstructed through the authority of history. He suggests that the role of history, in all its forms across the disciplines, is to provide a critical awareness in order to 'de-create' or 'de-art' cool knowledge. The ultimate goal of this de-creation will be to reveal the arbitrary and often subjective nature of the knowledge we hold to be 'true'. So it is from this notion of 'de-arting' or perhaps 'de-musicking' the hyper-real that I borrow a conceptual frame to deconstruct what Smith, Kisiel and Morrison have called the 'synthetic worlds' that lie within and in relation to musical technologies. I take synthetic worlds to mean contexts that inherently comprise metaphors and capabilities which can foster critical thinking (Smith, Kisiel and Morrison 2009: 347).

I suggested that Baudrillard's notion of the hyper-real presents a problem for music education in that notions of sound and silence no longer allow for learners' experiences of working with or experiencing music. Having been encultured into a context where musical perfection is possible and imperfection can be fabricated, the value of music as an essential part of the human condition is called into question. Liu suggests that we can think of this as music becoming 'cool': its value lies in its value as 'content' for 'entertainment' either through consumption or re-construction. And yet in the construction of cool as a hyper-real context it is clear that history has the potential to offer the capacity to 'de-music' this cool knowledge. The synthetic worlds that are constructed by, in this case, music technologies are constructed from metaphors and capabilities which can foster critical thinking when deconstructed through history. Thus the challenge for the music educator is to locate those aspects of history that can allow us to foster learners' consumption or re-construction with and within synthetic spaces and then deconstruct these spaces in order to move beyond the constructed hyper-real into a critical space that allows for reconstruction and reintegration. What Ruskin might call restoration (Liu 2004: 327). With this in mind I will present a framework for musical development that outlines a journey through which learners move towards the deeper knowing hinted at in Liu's critique of cool knowledge. In presenting this framework I hope to work towards an approach by which learners can de-music their enculturation and can reconstruct understanding in such a way that they subvert narrow, shallow, and self-centred 'entertainment content' and construct ethical and democratic musical values (Allsup 2007).

Technology-mediated diagenesis

The following model of diagenesis describes how (secondary) teachers can help to foster learning and development in a way that promises to support the realisation of the potential offered, in particular, by digital technologies. It draws on empirical work with teachers and learners in music classrooms (Kirkman 2009, 2011, 2012X) as well as wider literature on dialectic and dialogic pedagogy and practice.

The notion of diagenesis draws on a metaphor from geology, where the process involves the deconstruction and reconstruction of sedimentary rock to form new rocks. It excludes metamorphic changes and weathering and it is a cumulative process that controls the conservation or destruction of the original material. In a similar way the notion of diagenesis is used here to describe the process of change that an individual undergoes when developmental states are affected by a deconstruction of 'knowledge' (de-musicking). It is distinct from radical life events such as a change of school environment (metamorphic) and change required by external pressure such as parental or teacher rules (weathering) but rather is concerned with learners' interactions with their social and cultural context over time.

Diagenesis builds on current understandings of the potential of digital technologies (Luckin et al. 2012) in two ways. Firstly it builds on the notion that digital technologies offer ways for learners to build on their previous learning and understanding of the world as they discover and then restore knowledge and in so doing liberate themselves from 'cool knowledge' through emancipatory practice (Freire 1968): that is, practice which promotes self-determination and equality. Secondly it draws on our awareness that digital technologies help to foster collaboration and peer support as they facilitate the collective de-musicking of hyper-reality through the explicit mindfulness of the musical metaphors and capabilities of synthetic space, so that they can be examined and then reconstructed in exploratory dialogues between individuals as they are supported, by teachers. Furthermore, the model focuses on the interactions between students, teachers, peers and technologies as they work on exploratory and constructivist learning tasks. In the model, these are mapped onto four spaces or contexts of learning that allow learning interactions to be viewed from different vantage points (Figure 9.1). In each space a different kind of development is made possible as the context is more or less open, dynamic, supported through scaffolding or collaborative through dialogue.

'Institutional space' includes structured classrooms where teachers enable development through scaffolding provided by the digital technologies as well as other pedagogic tools. Learning in this space can be understood to include more static views of knowledge and pedagogy. In this space learning proceeds 'dialectically' (Wegerif 2008) as there is a discourse between the teacher as 'knowledgeable other' and the learner as the one who is questioned in order to foster understanding. In this space the teacher has the role of fostering de-musicking in order to move learners beyond a superficial notion of cool knowledge which acquiesces to a Wikipedia world. While inherent musical meanings (Meyer 1956) may be experienced as sound, silence, time, and space delineated meanings can be challenged as arbitrary and constructed.

'Personalised space' includes individuals' consciousness, where they discover for themselves, because their ability to learn happens to match the design of a lesson. Personalised space is inside institutional space as learners are bound by the rules of learning laid down by the teacher. Development in this space is

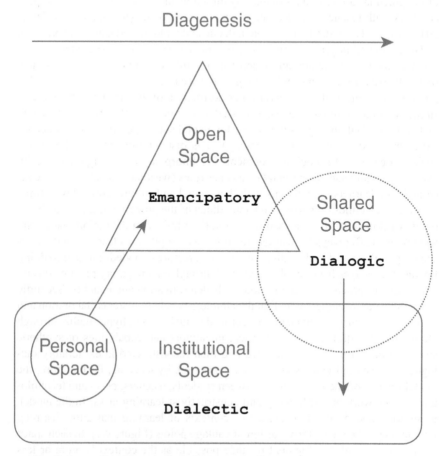

Figure 9.1 Diagenesis: developmental movement between conceptual spaces of learning

serendipitous because the learning and development relies to an extent on a fortunate match between learner and lesson design. When a teacher has structured a
learning context (institutional space) they necessarily introduce both opportunities and barriers to action. This is a key part of structuring the learning. Of course
more expert pedagogy will tend towards a context that anticipates and supports
learners needs and will therefore be 'less serendipitous'. The process of antici-
pating and supporting learners' needs in order to scaffold their development can
be thought of as formative assessment (Black and Wiliam 2001). In this space
the learner begins to find their cool knowledge being deconstructed as they are
pushed beyond the known real and into exploratory open space.

'Open space' describes the contexts in which learners take ownership of their
own learning and their development becomes more exciting, personal, dynamic,
and maximises their potential. It shares features of the open space described by

Harrison (2008), but key differences arise from the significant change in context from his original notion. Individuals are transformed as they work with enabling technologies and shape their own tools and resources. Learners' development into open space is emancipatory, because it relies on them building their own 'computer-mediated environment': that is, a physical and conceptual set of digital technology tools that allows them to build on their previous knowledge and experiences in such a way that they can directly interact with and shape new ideas for themselves. In this context they are agents in their own, learning as they draw on their full range of resources, both inside and outside the classroom, in order to construct understandings in collaboration with others. Development in this space is mediated through interaction with digital technologies as they create a rich context for exploration. In open space the act of de-musicking takes place. Cool knowledge is deconstructed as learners begin to see the musical processes at work behind synthetic perfection and imperfection in the metaphors and capabilities provided by the opportunities presented by the technologies such as quantise or autotune.

'Shared space' describes the contexts where learners share and collaborate through transformed ways of working with their teacher and peers in dialogue. The kinds of interactions that occur within this space are dialogic. Alexander (2008) defines dialogue in contradistinction to casual conversation and informal discussion. Instead he suggests that dialogue encourages the exploration of ideas, questions, pursues evidence, and leads thinking forward. He suggests that dialogue occurs in discussion which challenges and probes ideas and which deepens lines of enquiry in a liberating and safe environment. However, in this context the definition of dialogue must be expanded to include modes of communication other than just talk (linguistic mode). As sound is the primary medium, dialogue in this instance must also include sonic utterances that communicate musical ideas (audio mode) together with other multimodal forms of transmission; gestural, visual, spatial (Gall and Breeze 2005). In this way shared space becomes dialogic in a deeply musical sense, as thinking is driven and shared by sonic, temporal, and spatial features. Through work in this space the whole institutional space (classroom) is ultimately transformed and learners are often seen as creative. In this context learners begin to restore music with the benefit of having understood its nature and synthesis. This act of reconstruction is also one of identity construction as they establish a renewed relationship with the hyper-real and are empowered to become active participants in its destruction and reconstruction. This recursive process becomes an act of democratic participation in the renewal of the institutional space.

Thus, the process of diagenesis describes the movement of learner interactions between dialectic and dialogic forms of interaction through emancipatory 'open space'. Through the process of diagenesis ideas are continually (1) broken apart, as learners are given the tools to examine the nature and scope of ideas; (2) explored, as learners draw on their full range of resources, both inside and outside the classroom, to develop and reconstruct their understanding in the light of new information; and (3) shared, as learners collaborate to examine their new understandings and reach new conclusions.

Potential and danger

There are potential and danger in positioning technology as central in educational spaces which seek to foster ethical and democratic values (Allsup 2007). Within institutional space the potential of technologies has been well explored by music educationalists in recent years (e.g. Kirkman 2012b; Gall 2013; Thorgersen 2012; Wise, Greenwood, and Davis 2011). A recent report from NESTA (Luckin et al. 2012) framed the potential of technologies more generally across eight themes: (1) learning from experts, (2) learning with others, (3) learning through making, (4) learning through exploring, (5) learning through inquiry (6) learning through practising, (7) learning from assessment, and (8) learning in and across settings. However, the same report demonstrates that despite spending in excess of £487 million on ICT equipment and services in 2009/10 alone, there have been no radical improvements in learning experiences or attainment. Thus, the investment in technology-enhanced learning at present appears to dangerously neglect students' learning and development, instead prioritising the development of technology-related business infrastructure. Yet, rather than providing much needed professional development opportunities (Savage 2010), institutions continue to follow a 'cool knowledge' curriculum of the latest gadgets (Jouneau-Sion 2013) and struggle to deal rapidly enough with the cultural changes necessary for innovations to 'take root' (Tondeur et al. 2013).

A further danger is that professional-development models continue to focus on the technology and pedagogy (Wu 2013) while neglecting learners personal spaces (Kirkman and Wilson 2015). In their recent critique of Koehler and Mishra's (2009) widely used model of technological pedagogical content knowledge (TPACK), Kirkman and Wilson (2015) show how, in drawing on Schulman's notion of pedagogy, the TPACK model does not attend directly to the learners themselves. Instead it positions them potentially as 'empty vessels' and leads to a static notion of knowledge. This is inconveniently compatible with cool knowledge and stands in opposition both to the potential of technologies noted by NESTA (Luckin et al. 2012) as well as the notion of education for the responsibilities of later life which underpins democratic notions of education. Furthermore, the TPACK framework does not attend to the dynamic and changing natures of technologies nor the learners themselves. Yet such concerns are central when considering how technology can impact upon learners' development by fostering changes in their relation to the hyper-real and cool knowledge. Thus, while it is clear that technologies hold the potential to liberate learners from hyperspace, so too within a cool knowledge framework of integration they may manipulate the focus away from learning and onto investment in a banking model of education (Freire 1970) which treats learners as consumers to be filled with content.

Alongside this, open spaces are fragile in that what is perceived in the technology is, in a sense, what is reflected in the mirror. Learners are able to engage with and exploit the potential of the technologies that they perceive (Norman 1988). So the act of de-musicking which transpires across this context is an inherently personal process. Learners' views of the metaphors and capabilities of the software

are subject to the potential of the software/hardware environment to allow learners to manage the process of deconstruction and renovation. Yet concerns over e-safety and the potential for misuse can overshadow current discourse about technology integration. While safety must of course be uppermost in our minds, a 'lock it down' culture which prevents exploration and development of learners' own spaces can lead to their open spaces being inaccessible (Thinkfinity 2014; Wikihow 2014). In so doing, learners are limited to engagement within hyper-reality and within synthetic Wikipedia moments of content construction becoming fodder for meaningless assessment exercises bent on demonstrating progress as the creation of 'more cool stuff' that means nothing.

Across shared space one might ask what is being made? What is being explored? What is being renovated? Is it music or perhaps meta-music? If music has something to do with social interactions and community, where are the interactions and where is the community? Are these interactions with the same people? If not, then is the music really serving to bring cohesion to the interactions or is it just a mirror on the classroom wall? Who is giving the feedback? Do they have a stake in the relationship and what is it? Is it sensitive to personality and, as a result, what they need to hear? Or is it damaging? Is this what is meant by cyber-bullying? What is the difference in relationships that are not 'in person'? In this space the rules of engagement are different. The words we use mean different things because they are now reconstructed by everyone in conversation. Cool knowledge exists only as irony and Wikipedia does not satisfy our thirst for difficulty, nuance, disagreement, debate, divergence, and exploration. In this context one must ask to what extent does the loss of a physical and local social context disempower learners as 'too small to matter' or not big enough to be heard in a global environment. In this context the teacher exists to keep dialogue moving back out beyond the local and before the global. The challenge here is that there is no challenge and the potential does not yet exist.

Having intentionally returned to a rather vague conclusion, I will end by suggesting three ways in which technology-mediated educational spaces may be made safe for learners. I choose 'comprehending', 'constructing', and 'connecting' as ideas to frame this section as they emphasise the key points of movement that lead to renovation through diagenesis and which arise from framing digital technologies through Baudrillard's notion of the hyper-real and Liu's concept of cool knowledge. This section is presented as a narrative of considerations for research and practice.

'Comprehending' is the process of understanding the nature of the technologies being used. While progress has been made in this area, much of this remains in the field of research and has yet to be transposed into practice. In some small way this volume addresses this gap. However learners, teachers, managers, and other educationalists have yet to comprehend sufficiently the ways in which different technologies may be placed and employed in the inherently creative acts of learning and development. This is partly due to the rapidity of change and also a result of deficient notions of knowledge and the position of arts as consumer culture as opposed to a democratic imperative. The synthetic worlds have yet to be fully comprehend, and the first thing must be to see the ones and the zeros, to comprehend the medium and see the message for what it is: sound, silence, time, space; a set of symbols to think with. 'Constructing' is the process of creating novel environments that can allow an individual to build on their existing knowledge and understanding. As described above, the act of de-musicking is central to the process of realising emancipation from cool knowledge and its associated narrow, shallow, and self-centred world. Seeing the metaphors in the icons and symbols of digital devices and perceiving musical capabilities that emulate perfection and synthesise imperfection allows learners to see the cool knowledge 'music' processes at work behind the manipulation to perfection of the airbrushed artist. Learners' liberation from cool-fetishised YouTube-prepackaged hypo-music will come as moments of creative destruction as they de-autotune their musical delineations and unquantise their X-factor. Perhaps this will lead to imperfection as a humanising musical aesthetic? 'Connecting' is engaging in a meaningful process of dialogue between the members of a community of musicians in order to share creative developments. This is the ultimate musical renovation. The hyperreal is de-musicked and reconstructed as music, as once again a flawed, diverse, unsanitised, dehomogenised, human condition. Be it remixed, repackaged, unplugged, or debugged, music in shared space is theirs. They own it. But it is not theirs to keep. It is necessarily shared as a symbolic interaction with the world, rich with the potential of rebirth as an act of democratic participation in the renewal of the institutional space as teachers' expand into learners. The realm of the hyper-real only holds us back until we see it.

References

Alexander, R. (2008). *Towards Dialogic Teaching: Rethinking Classroom Talk* (4th edn). York: Dialogos.

Albini, S. (2000). 'Nemesis of Corporate Rock'. In B. Schultz (ed.), *Music Producers: Conversations with Today's Top Hit Makers*. Auburn Hills, MI: Mixbooks.

Allsup, R.E. (2007). 'Democracy and One Hundred Years of Music Education'. *Music Educators Journal*, 93/5: 52–7.

Baudrillard, J. (1981). *Simulacra and Simulation*. Ann Arbor: University of Michigan Press.

Bennett, S. (2009). 'Revolution Sacrilege! Examining the Technological Divide Among Record Producers in the Late 1980s'. *Journal on the Art of Record Production*, 4. <http://arpjournal.com/revolution-sacrilege-examining-the-technological-divide-among-record-producers-in-the-late-1980s/ > (accessed 8 Apr. 2014).

Black, P. and D. Wiliam, (2001). *Inside the Black Box: Raising Standards Through Classroom Assessment*. London: GL Assessment Limited.

Cascone, K. (2004). 'The Aesthetics of Failure: "Post-Digital" Tendencies in Contemporary Computer Music'. In C. Cox and D. Warner (eds), *Audio Culture: Readings in Modern Music*. New York: Continuum.

Cole, M. (1998). *Cultural Psychology: A Once and Future Discipline*. Cambridge, MA: Harvard University Press.

Cox, C., and D. Warner, eds (2004). *Audio Culture: Readings in Modern Music*. New York: Continuum.

Department for Education (2014). *National Curriculum in England: Framework for Key Stages 1 to 4*. <https://www.gov.uk/government/publications/national-curriculum-in-england-framework-for-key-stages-1-to-4/the-national-curriculum-in-england-framework-for-key-stages-1-to-4> (accessed 8 Apr. 2014).

Eshun, K. (2004). 'Operating System for the Redesign of Sonic Reality'. In C. Cox and D. Warner (eds), *Audio Culture: Readings in Modern Music*. New York: Continuum.

Freire, P. (1970). *Pedagogy of the Oppressed*. New York: Herder & Herder.

Gall, M. (2013). 'Technology in the Music Classroom: 2001–2013'. PhD thesis: University of Bristol.

—— and N. Breeze (2005). 'Music Composition Lessons: The Multimodal Affordances of Technology'. *Educational Review*, 57/4: 415–33.

Garber, E., S.G. Brush, and C.W.F. Everitt, eds (1986). *Maxwell on Molecules and Gases*. Cambridge MA: MIT Press.

Gelatt, R. (1977). *The Fabulous Phonograph, 1877–1977*. New York: Macmillan.

Harrison, O. (2008). *Open Space Technology: A User's Guide*, 3rd edn. San Francisco: Berrett-Koehler.

Jouneau-Sion, C., and E. Sanchez (2013). 'Preparing Schools to Accommodate the Challenge of Web 2.0 Technologies'. *Education and Information Technologies*, 18/2: 265–70.

Kirkman, P. (2009). *Embedding Digital technologies in the music classroom: An approach for the new music National Curriculum*. Matlock: National Association of Music Educators.

—— (2011). 'Exploring Contexts for Development: Secondary Music Students' Computer-Mediated Composing'. *Journal of Music, Technology and Education*, 3/2–3: 107–24.

—— (2012a). 'Secondary Music Students' Compositional Development with Computer-Mediated Environments in Classroom Communities'. University of Cambridge, DSpace. <http://www.dspace.cam.ac.uk/handle/1810/244366> (accessed 3 Nov. 2015)

—— (2012b). 'Making New Connections with Digital Technologies: Towards a New Model of Compositional Development in Music'. *Tehnologii Informatice şi de comunicaţie în domeniul muzical / ICT in Musical Field*, 3/2: 7–15.

—— and E. Wilson (2015). 'Learning with Digital Technologies'. In *Las Tecnologías Digitales en la Enseñanza Experimental de las Ciencias: Fundamentos Cognitivos y Procesos Didácticos*. Tizapan el Alto, Mexico: Lito-Grapo.

Koehler, M.J., and P. Mishra (2009). 'What is Technological Pedagogical Content Knowledge?' *Contemporary Issues in Technology and Teacher Education*, 9/1. <http://www.citejournal.org/vol9/iss1/general/article1.cfm> (accessed 7 Apr. 2014).

Liu, A. (2004). *The Laws of Cool: Knowledge Work and the Culture of Information*. Chicago: University of Chicago Press.

Luckin, R., B. Bligh, A. Manches, S. Ainsworth, C. Crook, and R. Noss (2012). *Decoding Learning: The Proof, Promise and Potential of Digital Education*. London: Nesta.

McClary, S. (2004). 'Rap, Minimalism, and Structures of Time in Late Twentieth-Century Culture'. In C. Cox and D. Warner (eds), *Audio Culture: Readings in Modern Music*. New York: Continuum.

Meyer, L.B. (1956). *Emotion and Meaning in Music*. Chicago: University of Chicago Press.

Mumford, L. (1934). *Technics and Civilization*. New York: Harcourt Brace Jovanovich.

Niaz, M., and R.H. Logie (1993). 'Working Memory, Mental Capacity, and Science Education: Towards an Understanding of the "Working Memory Overload Hypothesis"'. *Oxford Review of Education*, 19/4: 511–25.

Norman, D.A. (1988). *The Psychology of Everyday Things*. New York: Basic Books.

Paynter, J., and P. Aston (1970). *Sound and Silence: Classroom Projects in Creative Music*. Cambridge: Cambridge University Press.

Savage, J. (2010). 'A Survey of ICT Usage across English Secondary Schools'. *Music Education Research*, 12/1: 89–104.

Smith, C., K. Kisiel, and J. Morrison (2009). *Working Through Synthetic Worlds*. Farnham: Ashgate.

Taylor, T. (2001). *Strange Sounds: Music Technology and Culture*. London, Routledge.

Thinkfinity (2014). 'Is YouTube Blocked in Your School?' <http://archive-org.com/page/2068525/2013–05–12/http://www.thinkfinity.org/message/69140> (accessed 8 Apr. 2014).

Thorgersen, K. (2012). 'Freedom to Create in the Cloud or in the Open? A Discussion of Two Options for Music Creation with Digital Tools at No Cost'. *Journal of Music, Technology and Education* 5/2: 133–44.

Tondeur, J., N. Pareja Roblin, J. van Braak, P. Fisser, and J.M. Voogt (2013). 'Technological Pedagogical Content Knowledge in Teacher Education: In Search of a New Curriculum'. *Educational Studies*, 39/2: 239–43.

Wegerif, R. (2008). 'Dialogic or Dialectic? The Significance of Ontological Assumptions in Research on Educational Dialogue'. *British Educational Research Journal*, 34/3: 347–61.

Wertsch, J.V. (1998). *Mind as Action*. Oxford: Oxford University Press.

Whitehead, C. (1999). *The Intuitionist*. New York: Anchor Books.

Wikihow (2014). 'How to Access YouTube at School'. <http://www.wikihow.com/Access-YouTube-at-School> (accessed 8 Apr. 2014).

Wikipedia (2014). 'Information Overload'. <http://en.wikipedia.org/wiki/Information_overload> (accessed 8 Apr. 2014).

Wise, S., Greenwood, J. and Davis, N. (2011). 'Teachers' Use of Digital Technology in Secondary Music Education: Illustrations Of Changing Classrooms'. *British Journal of Music Education*, 28/2: 117–34.

Wu, Y.-T. (2013). 'Research Trends in Technological Pedagogical Content Knowledge (TPACK) Research: A Review of Empirical Studies Published in Selected Journals from 2002 to 2011'. *British Journal of Educational Technology*, 44/3: E73–E76.

10 Music technology and special educational needs

A novel interpretation

Evangelos Himonides and Adam Ockelford

The advent of various technologies and technological modalities has, naturally, affected music education, and the way that teachers engage, challenge, and support music students in their musical development. However, it appears that some teachers tend to have a limited view of technology and music, and there is a sense that it would be beneficial for them to see the bigger picture of the potential role of music technology within educational contexts (Himonides 2012a, 2012b; Himonides and Purves 2010). Ironically, the music-educational avenues that technology opens up are wider than ever before, and the distinction between formal and informal learning is becoming increasingly blurred, with the two existing on a fuzzy – if rich – continuum of educational opportunities.

It seems that a particular challenge is that pedagogical development is often driven by manufacturers rather than being initiated and directed by teachers themselves, nor is it based on a critical assessment and understanding of the educators' own needs and aspirations (Himonides 2012b; Purves 2012; Savage 2012). As a result, teachers are often made to feel reliant on particular tools and technological solutions (what the manufacturers and the extended industry wish to sell to them and their schools). This tool-centric modus operandi presents a threat to music education, as Himonides (2016) argues, constraining educators' capacity for reflective practice and making it difficult for them to foster their students' learning and development in creative ways. Music educators' concerns about their practice often pertain to their capacity to use particular software packages (such as Sibelius, Logic, Cubase) and items of hardware (including iPads, proprietary recording and audio interfaces, keyboards, and other MIDI devices).

Similar challenges exist at the intersection of music, education, therapy, and learners with special needs. Although technological developments are continually introducing exciting possibilities for those working in music-therapeutic and special-educational contexts, there tends to be the same focus on the role of 'the tool' itself, rather than looking first at the child and his or her needs and abilities. Particular tools – soft or hard instruments and devices are often presented as 'golden calves', essential to the success of particular music-therapeutic or music-educational interventions. Similarly, in academia, we encounter reports on 'the use of . . .', 'application in . . .' and 'benefits of . . .' given tools in certain contexts, often with little or no assessment of how effectively these tools had actually been used. We seldom find critical studies centring on the understanding of how musical development unfolds, how musical behaviours and musical experiences can be classified, and what the role of technology could be within this dynamic taxonomy. Undoubtedly, particular tools (and tool types or tool 'classes') will have a crucial role within this taxonomy, once it is developed. But it is important to focus on understanding first, before shifting the focus onto the tools themselves.[1]

Such an endeavour is evidenced by the Sounds of Intent project, details of which are presented below. Sounds of Intent constitutes a systematic attempt to map, gauge, and foster musical development using technology. It also presents a unique case of a research-focused exercise within the field of special educational needs that has become the springboard for the development of a similar scheme pertaining to children in the early years of education. Sounds of Intent offers an unusual example of the multidimensional role of technology, providing the wherewithal not only for structuring the understanding of children's musical development, but also as a means of presenting how musical development can be fostered using appropriate technological tools effectively.

Background

In 2000, Adam Ockelford produced a position paper concerning the knowledge and understanding of the provision of music education and therapy for children with complex needs in the UK. This led to the development of a new conceptual framework for practitioners, parents, and teachers working in special needs, and set out suggestions for further research. A number of initiatives followed, including a survey of the music offered in special schools in England (subsequently known as the 'Promise Report' [Welch, Ockelford, and Zimmermann 2001; see also Ockelford, Welch, and Zimmermann 2002); a doctoral thesis by Markou at the University of Roehampton examining the relationship between music education and music therapy for pupils with learning difficulties (Markou 2010; see also Ockelford and Markou 2012); and the establishment of the Sounds of Intent project, whose initial aim was to map the musical development of young people with complex needs (see e.g. Cheng, Ockelford, and Welch 2009; Ockelford and Matawa 2009; Ockelford et al. 2006; Welch et al. 2009).

In the course of the Sounds of Intent research, various ways of depicting putative music-developmental trajectories visually were considered, with the aim of making these readily accessible to teachers. A key consideration was to represent the notion that one developmental stage builds on those preceding without replacing them. The team also wanted the framework to give a general feeling of growth and expansion – of moving out into the world from an inner core. After several attempts, an approach was adopted that used segments within concentric circles (Figure 10.1). This model, including refinements to the wording, emerged over a two-year period (July 2003 to August 2005) in the light of iterative, group-based analyses of video-recorded case-study data from many children with severe or profound and multiple learning difficulties in different schools.

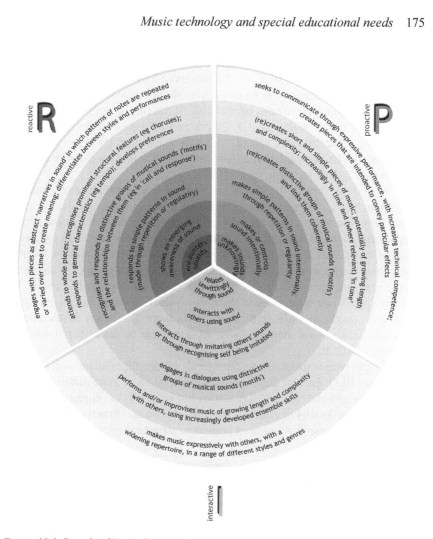

Figure 10.1 Sounds of Intent framework

Upon completion of this mapping exercise, the research team shifted their focus to the design and development of a web-based resource through which the developmental framework would become openly accessible and permit relevant data and illustrative media (videos) to be mapped onto it. The aim was to enable practitioners around the world: (1) to assess the musical engagement and developmental trajectories of children and young people with complex needs, (2) to perform longitudinal assessments of the young people's development, (3) to augment their longitudinal recorded assessments and observations with qualitative data, (4) to access annotated videos in order to be able to compare and contrast their own observations with those of other practitioners and carers, (5) to access all of their pupils' and students' developmental data in a secure, central location, and (6) to share their experiences, engage in critical discourse, and network with other practitioners. A series of research-driven exercises led to the development, by the first author, of the Sounds of Intent online portal, which was officially launched to the public in February 2012.[2] In the two-and-a-half years that followed, the Sounds of Intent online portal received over three million unique visits, with almost half a million downloads of material. At the time of writing, the Sounds of Intent resource was being used by 20 per cent of special schools for children with learning difficulties in England, with nearly 500 practitioners registered on the system, who had created profiles for nearly 2,000 young people with complex needs, in over 5,000 electronic session forms.

The Sounds of Intent framework of musical development covers musical engagement by children and young people with a wide range of musical abilities, ranging from those who show no response to sound to those who demonstrate exceptionally highly developed skills. Hence the framework covers a huge developmental range. This is partitioned into six theoretical stages of musical development, which correspond to core perceptual and cognitive abilities within each of three domains, termed 'Reactive' (how one responds to sound and music; R), 'Proactive' (how one creates sound and music oneself; P), and 'Interactive' (how one creates sound and music in the context of others; I). The six developmental stages – or 'levels' – are shown in Table 10.1: they can be remembered using the mnemonic CIRCLE.

Having six levels across three domains yields 18 'headlines' of musical development (Figure 10.1), Each of these is broken down into four more detailed descriptors termed 'elements' (A, B, C, D), setting out what musical engagement might look like in more detail. For example, the fifth level on the 'Reactive' domain (R5) 'attends to whole pieces: recognises prominent structural features (eg choruses);

Table 10.1 Further conceptualisation of the Sounds of Intent framework (Vogiatzoglou et al. 2011)

Level	Description	Core cognitive abilities
1	Confusion and Chaos	None: no awareness of sound as a distinct perceptual entity
2	Awareness and Intentionality	An emerging awareness of sound as a distinct perceptual entity and of the variety that is possible within the domain of sound
3	Relationships, repetition, Regularity	A growing awareness of the possibility and significance of relationships between aspects of sounds
4	Sounds forming Clusters	An evolving perception of groups of sounds, and the relationships that may exist between them
5	Deeper structural Links	A growing recognition of whole pieces, and of the frameworks of pitch and perceived time that lie behind them
6	Mature artistic Expression	A developing awareness of the culturally determined 'emotional syntax' of performance that articulates the 'narrative metaphor' of pieces

responds to general characteristics (eg tempo); develops preferences' and is broken down into the further four descriptors as follows: 'attends to whole pieces of music, becoming familiar with an increasing number and developing preferences' (R5A); 'recognises prominent structural features (such as the choruses of songs)' (R5B); 'responds to general characteristics of pieces (such as mode, tempo and texture)' (R5C); responds to pieces through connotations brought about by their association with objects, people or events in the external world (R5D). These additional four descriptors are not necessarily hierarchical.

The Sounds of Intent online resource

The framework

From the beginning, the Sounds of Intent team's intention was to produce something that would be intuitive for teachers, therapists, parents, and carers – who were not likely to be music specialists – to use. When the content of the framework was finalised, the development team focused on creating a user-friendly digital equivalent of the initial paper version of the scheme, in which the three domains (Reactive, Proactive, and Interactive) were assigned the colours red, blue, and green, respectively. Initial versions were trialled on personal computer platforms, and early iterations of tablet computers (laptop computers with collapsing and/or pivoting screens that could be used with proprietary styli for note taking). The team's aspiration was to be able to use the technology on keyboard-free portable devices;: subsequently, the iPad and comparable touch-screen tablets enabled this aim to be realised.

The platform

The Sounds of Intent materials were intended to be as inclusive, accessible, and inter-operable as possible. For this reason, the team decided against the development of a stand-alone software application that would have to be installed on teachers', therapists', and carers' personal computers. A web-based solution was therefore sought, through which all materials could be hosted centrally and users could always access the current version of the Sounds of Intent resource without concerns about software updates or whether their personal computers met the technical requirements for the installation of proprietary software. This decision presented some issues, namely the need for practitioners to have a live connection to the internet in order to access the resource, the complicated layers for safeguarding security, issues of intellectual property and copyright that the team had to institute in order to maintain a healthy online presence, and the continual development challenges presented when maintaining an online, dynamic (i.e. database-driven) resource that provides secure access to a large number of users, and that must be fine-tuned in order to guarantee sensitive data recording and retrieval. The Sounds of Intent resource currently provides access to over three hundred digital video examples.

At its core, the Sounds of Intent platform shares fundamental code blocks with one of the popular, open-source, collaborative, online, content management system platforms. On top of the core code layers, the development team has built the final interface with a particular focus on accessibility and interoperability (Bonacin et al. 2010), as outlined by the World Wide Web Consortium's Web Accessibility Initiative and the now completed Website Accessibility Conformance – Evaluation Methodology version 1.0 (WCAG-EM).[3] The WCAG-EM describes an approach to evaluating how websites, including web applications and websites for mobile devices, conform to Web Content Accessibility Guidelines 2.0 (WCAG).

What the platform offers

The Sounds of Intent platform has been developed in order to fulfil the objectives presented in the introductory section, namely:

To assess the musical engagement and developmental trajectories of children and young people with complex needs

Practitioners can simply use the Sounds of Intent online resource in order to gain greater understanding about the person with whom they are working and how their behaviours could be mapped onto the Sounds of Intent developmental framework. All core components of the framework (the six levels inside each domain), as well as the extended elements are presented in an intuitive manner, accompanied by fully annotated headings such as a 'general observation' and an 'interpretation'. Furthermore, each of the extended elements A, B, C, and D is presented with more detailed observations as well as suggested strategies for practitioners to adopt.

For clarity, we present P3 (Proactive, level 3) 'makes simple patterns in sound intentionally, through repetition or regularity' as an example:[4]

GENERAL OBSERVATION

The key here is the intentionality behind the pattern that is made – for example, children and young people may produce a regular beat without being aware of it through motor activity that is not driven by sound. Intentionality can be gleaned through repetition or regularity that occurs in the wider context of variation, or through the alignment of what is achieved through external patterns.

INTERPRETATION

The child or young person can process and reproduce the basic forms of pattern in sound that underlie all music.

P3A: INTENTIONALLY MAKES SIMPLE PATTERNS THROUGH REPETITION

Observation   Children and young people intentionally produce patterns of sounds through repetition – vocal or 'external'. Intentionality in the repetition may be ascertained through the capacity of the child or young person to produce different sounds. For example, on a keyboard, a certain note or notes may be repeated in the context of variation.

Strategies Encourage or model repetition through means which a child or young person can already produce a variety of sounds (vocally or using a sound maker). Recognise and reward repetition that is produced (for example, through praise or imitation)

P3B: INTENTIONALLY MAKES SIMPLE PATTERNS THROUGH A REGULAR BEAT

Observation Children and young people intentionally produce a regular beat, potentially through a variety of means. Intentionality is the critical factor here, and this can be judged by potential or actual variability.

Strategies Encourage or model a regular beat through making sounds which the child or young person is known to enjoy. Reinforce production through praise or imitation.

P3C: INTENTIONALLY MAKES SIMPLE PATTERNS THROUGH REGULAR CHANGE

Observation Children and young people intentionally produce regular change in pitch, loudness, timbre, or to the beat. Changes may occur in isolation or combination.

Strategies Encourage or model regular change using sounds which the child or young person is known to enjoy. Reinforce production through praise or imitation.

P3D: USES SOUND TO SYMBOLISE OTHER THINGS

Observation Given the opportunity, children and young people use sound to symbolise other things. They may use different sounding objects to choose between activities, for example.

Strategies Once a child or young person recognises the symbolic meaning attached to a particular sound, he or she can be encouraged to use this proactively: to communicate decision-making, for example. Use sounds and meanings that the child or young person finds appealing, that they will be motivated to communicate about.

To perform longitudinal assessments of the young people's development

Upon creating a personal account and registering their details with the Sounds of Intent system, practitioners and carers are able to create online profiles for their pupils. The Sounds of Intent database does not record, require or accept pupils' names, addresses or any other personal information that could help identify the individual concerned.

In order to research and monitor development and also maintain a meaningfully coded research database, the following information is recorded:

- pupil's alias (the pupil's real name is known only to the registered practitioner)
- pupil's date of birth
- pupil's ethnicity
- pupil's sex
- pupil's special needs
    - cognition and learning needs specific learning difficulty (SpLD)
        - moderate learning difficulty (MLD)
        - severe learning difficulty (SLD)
        - profound and multiple learning difficulty (PMLD)
    - behaviour, emotional, and social development needs
        - behaviour, emotional, and social difficulty (BESD)
    - communication and interaction needs speech, language, and communication needs (SLCN)
        - autistic spectrum disorder (ASD)
    - sensory and/or physical needs visual impairment (VI)
        - hearing impairment (HI)
        - multisensory impairment (MSI)
        - physical disability (PD)

It is often necessary to assign multiple special needs or disabilities to individual pupils; this is something that the Sounds of Intent database schema fully supports.

Once the pupil's details have been recorded, the practitioner can record session observation data onto the Sounds of Intent system using a dedicated data-entry form (see Figure 10.2).

To augment their longitudinal recorded assessments and observations with qualitative data

The session-data recording form allows practitioners to add narrative to their quantitative assessment for a given session with their pupil. They are able to do so under each domain, recording pupil's reactivity, proactivity, and interactivity, as well as general remarks that are not domain-specific. For example, young people with profound disabilities may experience seizures or be affected by new medication, issues which are likely to have an impact on their participation during a given music session. Over time, practitioners can create and view a developmental profile of their pupils, print longitudinal graphs of their progress, and compare notes regarding their pupils' finer behaviours through particular observation windows.

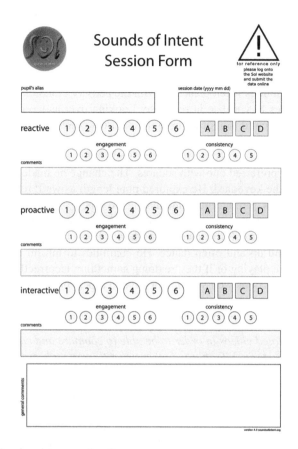

Figure 10.2 Session-data recording form

Some examples are offered below:

RJ singing along with guitar and vocal – joining in with co-worker and singing in context! RJ out of chair and relaxed. RJ recognising different music and listening to known different music – from rock to bhangra to classical. Some vocalisation observed over certain music – but still seems overwhelmed by noise. Recognises song structure and joins in with co-worker. sings with seeming knowledge of song structure and pitch required. Emulates co-workers pitch. Video evidence. RJ is showing increasing recognition of different 'song' structures and different pitches. RJ working well with 'joining in' another performer and structuring voice to match pitch/rhythm and structure of others playing. Video evidence available.

FM seems to recognise outside environment and seems to enjoy different environment. Still restricted in willingness to perform? Outside session – FM seems comfortable in different environment and less distracted than others in group. Reacts in similar way to sounds played – less hearing difficulties than others in group? FM still rubbing drum – allowed drum to be placed on knees without refusal, rubs skin and creates some sound. Outside session seemed comfortable and not as distracting as for others in group. FM comfortable with others around.

Making sounds when presented with the activity of tap/clap and given the opportunities to vocalise in response. Looking over as tap clap was played with another child to request her interest. Looked over at me as the sounds were played and when another student was having their turn.

Using eye gaze to control eye gaze midi thing with squares. Made clear choice that preferred one with squares. The change he made was to slide up and down the keyboard. He explored note length as well; responding to the sliding sounds. Smiled each time that he did this.

N's confidence is growing through each session. He beginning to sing (albeit quietly) to all the songs and when it is his turn to do a solo or lead he will stand up and often dance. He continues to inform children if they shouldn't be playing or if they're doing something incorrectly. He is following my instructions well so I do not have to repeat myself. He is also beginning to keep a regular beat.

To access annotated videos in order to be able to compare and contrast their own observations with those of other practitioners and carers

The Sounds of Intent online resource offers access to over three hundred video recording segments. The digital video-file corpus is hosted on a leading video streaming technology (Vimeo), thus enabling a large number of digital videos to be made available in multiple versions to those who use the resource, depending on their internet connection speed and preferred device. This way, practitioners and carers can access a version of the video that they wish to review without concern for the speed of their internet connection, making it even possible for videos to be accessed on mobile telephones using 3G or 4G cellular networks. Furthermore, each of the continually augmented number of videos available to Sounds of Intent users has been annotated, permitting users to compare, contrast, and identify with specific pupil 'cases', learning contexts and musical experiences.

Some examples:

R4C – Romy's father plays two motifs coherently at the piano, an ascending chromatic scale that transitions into a theme from Aaron Copland's 'Rodeo'. As Romy hears and recognises the juxtaposition of these motifs, she shakes her hands in excitement and laughs. Romy also plays these motifs on the piano, combining them coherently (P4C).

P5C – Michael is thirteen years old. He has absolute pitch, an extremely good musical memory, is able to remember tunes he's heard before in the right key, and can create his own tunes and improvise on them. He has taken the Associated Board Preparatory test. Music is a very important part of

Michael's life. In this clip, Michael is playing, from memory, a piece he previously composed for the piano, in which there are different variations of the main melody. Only one variation is shown here. He also plays in different keys and with further variations of the melody. He plays this piece, maintaining his part, while being accompanied by the music therapist (also I5B).

I1A – As Matthew vocalises his teacher responds empathetically, imitating his vocalisation as well as expanding on it. Mathew's repeated vocalisation, after he has heard the teacher, also indicates that he vocalises in response to what he hears (I2A), demonstrating that his level of musical development lies at and between both Levels 1 and Levels 2 of the Sounds of Intent framework.

I2A – Aisha is thirteen. She loves music, particularly playing the drums and has a good sense of rhythm. She often appears to switch off in class only to show that she has absorbed the content of the lesson, for example, later singing a song. As far as is known, this was the first time that Aisha was presented with a keyboard in this context. On being presented with the keyboard she spontaneously began to play. Aisha pauses during her playing, but comes back to it by hearing and turning towards the sounds made by the teacher, demonstrating that she is responding to the sounds she hears. She produces pure sound for sound's sake, rather than responding in imitation.

I4B – This is a mixed ability class group, ages sixteen to eighteen, in their regularly weekly music lesson. They have been playing drums throughout the term in different ways and are learning about Africa in world studies. The class has been playing simple rhythmic patterns which they have been practising over a few weeks. Here Laura and Nancy are drumming a simple rhythm and an underpinning regular beat. An interaction between the two can be seen here as Laura (seated to the right) watches and listens to Nancy, using imitation in playing and maintaining the pattern.

These examples offer evidence of the work vested in Sounds of Intent by the core team and the wider group of collaborating practitioners, not only into capturing these 'windows' onto musical interventions, but also by providing key information in informing viewers of the significance of each video, which may not be immediately apparent in the case of children with profound levels of disability. This is something further underpinned with the provision of indicators pointing to the Sounds of Intent framework that accompany each individual video. Although the corresponding videos for each part of the Sounds of Intent framework are accessible from within the main framework navigation system (see below), they can also be accessed as a complete list on a dedicated video section.[5]

To access all of their pupils' and students' developmental data in a secure, central location

The Sounds of Intent online resource enables information on children's musical development to be held centrally, without the need to maintain localised files on different computers, and in different classes, schools or other venues. This is particularly useful for practitioners who support young people with special needs within a number of schools or privately. It is, of course, possible for registered practitioners to download their complete recorded datasets for any registered pupil. Instructions are available on the Sounds of Intent website both in textual as well as video format. This has been reported as a valuable option for those practitioners who are required by their schools, local authorities or other funding bodies to maintain assessment data that are compatible with 'P-Scales'.[6]

To share their experiences, engage in critical discourse, and network
with other practitioners

One of the key messages emerging from practitioners' feedback online and at conferences and public presentations is that before becoming engaged with Sounds of Intent they often felt isolated and in doubt about whether their assessments, strategies, and practices were systematic and similar to those of other practitioners in the field. Sounds of Intent has been supporting special needs practitioners in developing a sense of community, online as well as in person, during numerous dissemination activities for which the core team has received funding since the online resource's official launch.[7] Furthermore, and upon request from a large number of registered practitioners for providing a practical 'bridge' between the P-scales and the Sounds of Intent framework, Ockelford published a research-focused paper titled 'Comparison with the "P-Levels" for Music' (2012). This document highlights both the inefficiency of the P-levels as well as the pliability of the Sounds of Intent framework to provide meaningful information micro- and macroscopically. It therefore did not come as a surprise when Britain's Office for Standards in Education, Children's Services and Skills[8] (Ofsted 2012) included Sounds of Intent in a 'good practice case study' conducted at Whitefield Schools and Centre in East London.

Navigating the framework online

Probably the most important part of the Sounds of Intent website is the provision of information, interpretations, strategies, and ways of assessment within the different domains, levels, and sections of the theoretical framework, as presented earlier. The design and development ethos has been to attempt to continually maintain a focus on the Sounds of Intent framework itself whilst a user navigates the information available. Early piloting and user surveys suggested that users wanted to 'always know where they were on the "dartboard" [the graphical representation of the Sounds of Intent theoretical framework as concentric circles]'. Various techniques were employed during the earlier design phases, including the use of different coloured text and text background (according to the dedicated colours for the three distinct domains) without great success. Finally, the team developed a floating navigation panel that would 'follow the user' (i.e. remain within the visible computer screen real estate) on the right-hand side. This special panel (see Figure 10.3) includes a miniature version of the Sounds of Intent graphical framework, where all

You are here

Navigation

[top] [-] [+] [home]

[a] [b] [c] [d]

[R] [P] [I]

Session

Record session

Figure 10.3 Online framework navigation panel (user is in R5)

segments besides the one that the user is focused on appear to be more trans-lucent, therefore continually reminding the user about the framework topology and where they are within it.

Continual piloting of the navigation technology helped the team identify the importance of being able to meaningfully navigate across the different domains, levels, and elements. This led to the addition of navigation shortcuts to the floating panel. These shortcuts enable users to incrementally advance or retract the musi-cal development related information across the domains (for example, a user in P3 will be directly navigated to P4 or P2 by using the '+' or '-' shortcuts, respec-tively). The shortcuts also provide the means for automatically placing the user's focus on the four different elements (A, B, C, D) within the domain and level that they are already in (the highlighted segment of the mini framework [see Figure 10.3]). Therefore, if, for example, a user is accessing information in R5C and clicks on the 'a' shortcut on the floating panel, they will be automatically navigated to the beginning of R5A without having to provide any other information. Finally, the same principle follows assisted navigation across the three different domains. A user accessing information within I4 will be automatically navigated to R4 or P4 if they click on the 'R' or 'P' shortcuts, respectively.

Additional resources

Within each level and element of the Sounds of Intent framework, visitors are provided with meaningfully selected resources and materials that could support their sessions. These include music / accompaniment scores, practitioner word cards and chord sheets, audio recordings, MIDI file versions of the audio recordings, notation files (Sibelius format), and pointers to particular book sections. A fully annotated list of the suggested readings is available on the Sounds of Intent website.[9]

Future developments

There are over three hundred logged requests for future development 'wishes' from practitioners currently registered and engaging with the Sounds of Intent platform internationally. This is a testament to the enthusiasm, dedication, and critical thinking, that special needs practitioners and carers possess, as well as their real need for such a resource in the field.

Overall, the development 'wishlist' can be broadly categorised as follows:

Video uploading / evaluation / voting / sharing

Users would like to be able to upload their own videos onto the platform. At the first instance, in order to enrich their own pupils' portfolios of developmental data, but also, at a later stage, to be able to share those videos with the wider community. This feature is of top priority for the development team, although major challenges exist, such as confidentiality, security, copyright, data integrity, and validity. Ideally, users should be able to upload their own video, choose whether the video should remain private and solely connected to a student's profile, or whether it should be considered for becoming part of the extended Sounds of Intent video database. In that case, practitioners should be able to provide copyright release and ethics information and also some explanatory text that would make the context clear to other viewers. Finally, practitioners should be able to specify where on the Sounds of Intent framework of musical development the video belongs. This should be open to receive popularity ratings from other registered practitioners, thus enabling the practitioner community to scrutinise individual assessment and render the gradually expanding video corpus increasingly valid and robust.

User profile editing

At the time of writing, practitioners were not able to edit recorded pupil and session data. This is an important functionality, an initial pilot for which has started, so that the development team can assess the caveats and potential threats to the validity and robustness of the overall database.

Class addition to database schema

One thing that the development team had not initially anticipated was the overwhelming response that the online resource would receive. Amongst the groups of registered and active practitioners, cases exist where certain practitioners oversee large numbers of young people with special needs (in some cases over 40) in multiple locations. Therefore the need exists for the alteration of the existing, highly complex, database schema and incorporation of pupil classes, groups, and subgroups. Longitudinally, this might also lead to new research findings about commonalities or diversities in developmental patterns within different groups, special needs, other demographic classifications, and practitioners.

More sophisticated longitudinal statistics

The Sounds of Intent resource provides a basic set of statistical graphing tools focusing on the longitudinal mapping of development (on the Y-axis) across time (on the X-axis) for all three domains. Practitioners were also able to plot longitudinal developmental trend lines, for any given time window, computed from the R, P, and I scores. Although this type of longitudinal statistical charting has proven to be very popular with practitioners and was further scrutinised during systematic research focusing on the assessment of the validity of the framework (see e.g. Cheng, Ockelford and Welch 2009; Markou 2010; Ockelford 2013; Ockelford and Markou 2012), the team felt that a new method of longitudinal statistical charting was required. The team wanted to somehow demonstrate that in a highly complex context, such as SEN, a series of 'scores' is something rather too narrowly focused compared with a 'developmental profile'. Various attempts to cater for this resulted in the piloting of novel charting using the complete graphical Sounds of Intent framework as the overall focus, whilst varying how opaque/translucent the individual segments appear, based on frequency of appearance (that is, how many times a pupil had been given a particular R, P, or I score within a given time frame).

The findings of this research were presented in 2012 (see Welch et al. 2012) and form the basis for future developments in statistical charting and developmental profiles and trajectories for Sounds of Intent pupils. More particularly, an analysis of the distribution of the teachers' observational assessment data revealed a wide diversity of musical behaviours in their pupils, but with no significant gender or ethnicity differences. However, analysis by SEN categories suggested that there may be characteristic differences in these group's music behaviour profiles, related to the nature and severity of the disability. Nevertheless, it was extremely rare for any child not to demonstrate some form of engagement with music. Overall, the research indicated that the Sounds of Intent developmental framework was already beginning to assist participant teachers in improving the range and quality of their music education activities. It was also found to be a useful research tool as it will facilitate the building of a much more detailed and complete picture of the nature of musical behaviour and how it can be nurtured and developed for all children.

Classification of software and mapping onto the framework

A common request from Sounds of Intent practitioners has been for the inclusion of a dynamic annotated map of relevant software applications (programs, apps, and utilities) and assessment on where and how they could be used within the overall framework. The first part of this complex exercise has already begun, with help from special needs practitioner and experienced Sounds of Intent clinician Victoria Hubbard. Following this initial map of software and affordances, the team is currently researching the development of a new taxonomy of music technologies within special needs, in order to support practitioners and foster greater flexibility and freedom in the incorporation of technological tools in the special needs musical plateau.

Conclusion

The Sounds of Intent framework and related technologies have been presented in support of our argument that it is important to focus on understanding technology and its role within special needs education first, before shifting the focus onto the tools themselves. Existing and present research evidence from a range of linked studies indicates that the Sounds of Intent framework, being grounded in the rigorous study of a very large number of individual pupil cases, is an appropriate means for tracking musical development in children and young people with complex needs. The latest research suggests that practitioners in the special school sector are able to use the web-based Sounds of Intent technology intuitively in order to track the musical activity of their individual pupils and that this technology is also a useful research tool that can be used to collate such data to provide a larger picture of musical behaviour and development for a wide cross-section of the child population. It is hoped that this information will continue to have a positive impact on how teachers understand and nurture the inherent musicality of their pupils and foster their ability to experience, enjoy, and benefit from music. The Sounds of Intent technology, as a quite novel music technology, will be at the teachers' disposal.

Notes

1 There are parallels with the difference between 'methodology' and 'methods'.
2 <www.soundsofintent.org>.

3 <http://www.w3.org/WAI/>.
4 See <http://soundsofintent.org/sounds-of-intent?level=P3>.
5 <http://soundsofintent.org/videos>.
6 Using P (performance)-scales is statutory when reporting attainment for children with special educational needs (SEN) who are working below level 1 of the national curriculum in the UK (see Standards and Testing Agency 2013).
7 The current list of sponsors and funders is available on the Sounds of Intent website.
8 Ofsted report directly to Parliament and are independent and impartial. They inspect and regulate services which care for children and young people and those providing education and skills for learners of all ages (see <http://www.ofsted.gov.uk/about-us>).
9 <http://tinyurl.com/soi-books>.

References

Bonacin, R., A.M. Melo, C.A.C. Simoni, and M.C.C. Baranauskas (2010). 'Accessibility and Interoperability in E-Government Systems: Outlining an Inclusive Development Process'. *Universal Access in the Information Society*, 9/1: 17–33 (doi: 10.1007/s10209–009–0157–0).

Cheng, E., A. Ockelford, and G. Welch (2009). 'Researching and Developing Music Provision in Special Schools in England for Children and Young People with Complex Needs'. *Australian Journal of Music Education*, 2009/2: 27–48.

Himonides, E. (2012a). 'Commentary: Music Learning and Teaching through Technology'. In Gary McPherson and Graham Welch (eds), *The Oxford Handbook of Music Education*. 2 vols, New York: Oxford University Press.

——— (2012b). 'The Misunderstanding of Music-Technology-Education: A Meta-Perspective'. In Gary McPherson and Graham Welch (eds), *The Oxford Handbook of Music Education*. 2 vols, New York: Oxford University Press.

——— (2016). 'Educators' Roles and Professional Development'. In S.A. Ruthmann and R. Mantie (eds), *The Oxford Handbook of Technology and Music Education*. New York: Oxford University Press.

——— and R. Purves (2010). 'The Role of Technology'. In S. Hallam and A. Creech (eds), *Music Education in the 21st Century in the United Kingdom: Achievements, Analysis and Aspirations*. London: Institute of Education.

Markou, K. (2010). 'Exploring the Distinction Between Music Education and Music Therapy for Children with Complex Needs'. PhD thesis, University of Roehampton.

Ockelford, A. (2012). 'Comparison with the "P-Levels" for Music'. Sounds of Intent. <http://soundsofintent.org/soi_dox/soi_p_levels_ao.pdf> (accessed 4 Nov. 2015).

——— (2013). *Applied Musicology: Using Zygonic Theory to Inform Music Education, Therapy, and Psychology Research*. Oxford: Oxford University Press.

——— and K. Markou (2012). 'Music Education and Therapy for Children and Young People with Cognitive Impairments: Reporting on a Decade of Research'. In R. MacDonald, G. Kreutz, and L. Mitchell (eds), *Music, Health, and Wellbeing*. Oxford: Oxford University Press.

——— and C. Matawa (2009). *Focus on Music 2: Exploring the Musical Interests and Abilities of Blind and Partially-Sighted Children with Retinopathy of Prematurity*. London: Institute of Education.

——— G.F. Welch, and S. Zimmermann (2002). 'Focus of Practice: Music Education for Pupils with Severe or Profound and Multiple Difficulties: Current Provision and Future Need'. *British Journal of Special Education*, 29/4: 178–82.

——, ——, ——, and E. Himonides (2006). ' "Sounds of Intent": Mapping, Assessing and Promoting the Musical Development of Children with Profound and Multiple Learning Difficulties'. In S. Jones, D. Hamlin, and G.S. Rubin (eds), *Vision 2005*, International Congress Series 1282. Philadelphia, PA: Elsevier.

Ofsted (2012). 'Music in Schools: Wider Still, and Wider'. Good practice case study, Whitefield Schools and Centre. <http://www.ofsted.gov.uk/resources/music-schools-wider-still-and-wider-good-practice-case-study-whitefield-schools-and-centre> (accessed 9 Sept. 2013).

Purves, R. (2012). 'Technology and the Educator'. In Gary McPherson and Graham Welch (eds), *The Oxford Handbook of Music Education*. 2 vols, New York: Oxford University Press.

Savage, J. (2012). 'Driving Forward Technology's Imprint on Music Education'. In Gary McPherson and Graham Welch (eds), *The Oxford Handbook of Music Education*. 2 vols. New York: Oxford University Press.

Standards and Testing Agency (2013). 'Teacher Assessment: Using P Scales to Report on Pupils with SEN'. <https://www.gov.uk/teacher-assessment-using-p-scales> (accessed 4 Nov. 2015).

Vogiatzoglou, A., A. Ockelford, G. Welch, and E. Himonides (2011). 'Sounds of Intent: Interactive Software to Assess the Musical Development of Children and Young People With Complex Needs'. *Music and Medicine*, 3/3: 189–95 (doi: 10.1177/1943862111403628).

Welch, G.F, A. Ockelford, and S. Zimmermann (2001). *Promise: The Provision of Music in Special Education*. London: Institute of Education and Royal National Institute of the Blind.

—— E. Himonides, A. Ockelford, A. Vogiatzoglou, and S.-A. Zimmermann (2012). 'Understanding and Nurturing Musical Development in Children and Young People: The Sounds of Intent Project'. In C. Johnson (ed.), *Proceedings of the Twenty-Fourth International Seminar on Research in Music Education*. Thessaloniki: University of Macedonia and ISME.

—— A. Ockelford, F.-C. Carter, S.-A. Zimmermann, and E. Himonides (2009). ' "Sounds of Intent": Mapping Musical Behaviour and Development in Children and Young People with Complex Needs'. *Psychology of Music*, 37/3: 348–70 (doi: 10.1177/0305735608099688).

11 Using experience design in curricula to enhance creativity and collaborative practice in electronic music

Monty Adkins

Creative activity is more than a mere cultural frill, it is a crucial factor of human experience, the means of self-revelation, the basis of empathy with others; it inspires both individualism and responsibility, the giving and the sharing of the experience.

(Tom Hudson, cited in Yorkshire Sculpture Park 2013: 2)

Introduction

This chapter is informed by my work as an electronic music composer and lecturer in the university sector. The chapter does not explore the nature of creativity itself (Burnard 2012) but rather how musical creativities can be facilitated and engendered within academic environments. As a composer interested in engaging students in electronic-music composition at university, rather than a music educationalist, I want to bring students together and develop communities of compositional practice in an academic milieu that is stimulating, relevant, and supportive. I argue that a flipped-classroom[1] approach can facilitate an active learning environment that can transform student experience. As such, I propose the integration of 'experience design' into the creation of new curricula. Through the appropriation of the notion of experience design from business I also demonstrate the importance of the active learning environment in providing a meaningful experience for the student. One of the most important cognitive benefits such scenarios foster is higher mental functioning and learning through 'interthinking' (Littleton and Mercer 2013). This chapter discusses the ramifications of the integration of experience design into educational practice and the possibilities it offers.

Background

When I was a secondary-school pupil, my music lessons involved my tutor writing on the blackboard whilst the students copied this neatly into our class exercise books. As a mechanism for learning it was a complete waste of time. Outside class was where I explored and developed my passion for music, particularly composition, through the scores of Lutoslawski and Stravinsky in our local library or through second-hand books.

As a young student, my most memorable learning experiences were with the piano teacher Charles Watmough. Actually the piano only featured briefly. A nominal half-hour lesson on a Thursday evening could easily and would regularly continue for up to three hours. These classes became a stream-of-consciousness musical adventure as we listened to records and played extracts of orchestral scores on the piano. As a musician eager to absorb as much as I could, these experiences were the highlight of my week. I never knew what was coming and tried to hide my woeful lack of piano practice by getting Charles off-topic as quickly as possible. Such an experience is a continuing feature of many musicians' education. A great deal of 'real' education occurs outside of formal, institutionalised learning mechanisms (Hargreaves 2003). Philip Tagg (2012) writes eloquently about a similar figure in his own musical education, his organ teacher Ken Naylor who encouraged him to explore all aspects of music from the anthems and madrigals of Elizabethan composers to Charlie Parker, Bartok, and Stravinsky, as well as to improvise and compose. Today the role of such inspiring individuals is often replaced by the internet and peer-to-peer social groups.

Despite Charles' inspiring model, my initial classes as a young lecturer at the University of Huddersfield followed the familiar pattern of my own education. As a lecturer on a fast-growing music-technology course, the arguments for one-to-one electronic-music composition classes as opposed to the practicality and financial efficacy of group teaching were soon lost as staff planned classes for increasing numbers, in some instances up to a hundred students. The digital workstation as the de facto tool for acquiring technique and creative learning went unquestioned, despite the fact that such tools often immediately isolate students from one another through the use of headphones in class and often prohibit or make difficult collaborative practice. The model adopted for these computer composition classes was a series of lectures demonstrating sampling, synthesis, and software techniques, and compositional tutorials supported individual assignments. The balance between imparting technical and contextual musico-aesthetic knowledge was, and still is, an oft-discussed topic between the lecturers delivering this course. One of the reasons for this on-going debate is the increasing number of students from diverse musical backgrounds and how to accommodate them within one module.

Such a system, concentrating on the individual acquisition of technical skills and a contextual knowledge of pertinent repertoire, can work. However, one of the things I want to evaluate in this chapter is students' experience of composing within an academic environment and whether this could be enhanced through more practice-centred collaborative activity, and, in turn, how such collaborative environments can shape creative thinking well beyond the academy. Although Paynter and Aston (1970) proposed that education should be about a broadening of perspective and independent exploration whilst also noting that the examination system implies focusing in, the survey of courses undertaken for this chapter demonstrates that there is still an emphasis on the systematisation and division of music studies into history, analysis, composition, and acoustics – a model adopted during the nineteenth century (Golding 2009). There is still an underlying premise in these courses that students will 'join the dots' or 'put the jigsaw together' and that such exploration remains an independent practice outside of formal study time. This chapter challenges this premise. It is informed by cultural historical activity theory (Cole 1996) in which the individual and their interaction with others within a cultural or institutional environment are considered a holistic unit of study. I consider this an example of rhizomatic or nodal thinking (Adkins 2014) about creativity within contemporary culture in which socio-cultural, institutional, interpersonal relationships, and an individual's own practice are all part of a network of interlocking nodes that inform collaborative and educational practice.

Two further experiences underpin this research: firstly, during the summer vacation before the final year of junior school, my middle son's passion for the Khan Academy[2] online maths tutorials saw him develop enough knowledge to finish Year 6[3] by taking the SAT[4] examination for Year 9; and secondly, my own learning of the MAX software from the 'Baz Tutorials'[5] on YouTube. Both of these examples are far from unique and testify to the changing ways in which knowledge is created, distributed, and consumed. No longer is the academy the only access to knowledge. In a constantly shifting digital landscape in which the consumption of knowledge is no longer bound by geographical constraints and the increasing democratisation of technology needed to make electronic music, we are forced to ask what can be gained from going into a university setting to study electronic music at all.

As traditional lectures come to resemble press conferences, with a table littered with all manner of portable recording devices, iPhones, and even a few retro Dictaphones at the front of the lecture theatre, the challenge today is to have classes that offer something unique rather than replicating other forms of knowledge communication and that these classes create a shared and meaningful experience for students. Although music technology and popular music have challenged more canonically restricted forms of music education (Burnard 2012), one of the recurring questions is how educators embrace and encourage nascent artists whose practice and creative work is both diverse and often motivated by personal rather than academic concerns. Their practice, like that of many electronic musicians, often involves individual and collaborative work with a variety of creative tools other than just a computer, often resulting in artefacts that embrace a variety of new media.

In light of current trends in education such as P21[6] in the USA with its emphasis on fusing the '3Rs and 4Cs' (critical thinking and problem solving, communication, collaboration, and creativity and innovation) to ready every student for the twenty-first century, Mark Parkinson[7] challenges teacher-centric and linear learning methods and calls for the emphasis on the interpersonal competition within education to be replaced with collaboration and reflective learning (cited in Chaudahry 2013: n.p.). Royston Soares[8] identifies why teaching methodology needs to evolve:

> The educational industry is challenged because business and organisations are shifting from an industrial word to a communication, service world, and

the economic, political, and social domains impact education. The changes in society have influenced important assumptions about intelligence and knowledge. The specific implication for the classroom and curriculum is that a learner-centred pedagogy is emerging with the role of the teacher changing from a content specialist who transmits knowledge to a facilitator of learning.

(Soares 2013: n.p.)

Parkinson's and Soares' moves away from the teacher-centric approach to learning is akin to Vygotsky's theories of development through social interaction. As our methods of social engagement become increasingly mediated through technology then the roles of the lecturer and student must also be re-evaluated. As lecturers become facilitators of technologically mediated compositional experiences for students, so learning becomes a reciprocal act between peers from which knowledge is gained through retrospective reflection. Vygotsky (1962) considers culture to be a determining factor for knowledge construction. In the academy, the culture in which compositional activity can take place needs to be designed to produce rich experiences for students. Student experience should not merely be an outcome of collaborative activity but something that is consciously considered by the lecturer at the outset. Through reflecting on compositional experiences, be they individual or collaborative, perception, cognitive development, and technical abilities become solidified into new knowledge patterns.

Existing practice

The composition of electronic music has historically resulted from a hybrid of technical and creative knowledge. This hybridity reflects a bi-directional process. Compositional creativity is something that can develop independently of technology, and an understanding of music technology can itself inspire creativity (Nuhn et al. 2002).

For this study, 30 higher education institutes across England and North America were surveyed.[9] The purpose of the survey was to find out:

1   how electronic-music composition teaching was situated within the departments surveyed (as part of a dedicated music technology programme or merely an option within a music degree);
2   how electronic-music composition was being taught (in small or large groups; in studios or workstation rooms);
3   if the emphasis was on individual or collaborative compositional projects;
4   if collaboration was focused on composition or performance of electronic music and to what extent these activities were extra-curricula;
5   what the musical background and literacy of the lecturer and the student's taking the course was.

The prevailing paradigm emerging from this work reveals an approach to composition still predominantly centred on the individual and their creative practice.

Furthermore, although laptop orchestras and hacking groups formed part of extra-curricula activities, the main approach to teaching electronic-music composition was fundamentally no different to those of acoustic composition. In addition, although portable digital technologies such as smartphones and tablets enable more flexible and collaborative working environments (Ruthmann 2007), all 30 institutions still focused their teaching around fixed computer workstations or studio-based practice. One of the reasons cited for this 'traditional' practice was that, at university level, working with portable digital technologies did not encourage the critical listening that lecturers wanted their students to acquire. A generational factor, and one that will certainly change, is that many of the lecturers teaching electronic-music composition came from either a background which privileged Western art music with its inherent 'cult of the Romantic stereotypes of the creator as individual genius' and 'the fetishisation of composition, mythologized as a fixed thing' (Burnard 2012: 2) or a computer science background and had subsequently moved into music technology. The disjunction which occurs in the paradigm that Burnard seeks to overturn is often still relevant for many of the lecturers teaching electronic-music composition. It was found that students on such composition courses came from diverse backgrounds with interests in classical and popular music, music technology, sonic art, or fine art. This is a tendency that will only increase in the future as technology continues to proliferate within educational contexts, particularly music. According to Burnard, 'for new generations, commercial music, web space, and the ever-expanding web world provide a dynamic and complex context wherein all kinds of creativity nestles in the nooks and crannies' and that 'musical creativities assume many forms, and serve many diverse functions, and are deeply embedded in the dynamic flux and mutation of a musician's personal and sociocultural life' (2012: 13). Where group work is encouraged, it often takes the form of performance-based live electronic work and is an adjunct module to those in composition or is an extra curricula activity. Differences in aesthetic approaches are also evident. While some universities teach through the emulation of genres in the manner of a traditional conservatoire, requiring a *musique concrète* etude or a composition made solely with synthesis techniques, others promote a more open approach from the very beginning. Ambrose Field states:

> Students in my classes take part in both individual and group approaches to electronics. The 'doing' of composition is the most important aspect for me not the software or the technology. We don't teach software, our methods are sometimes surprisingly low-tech, but we ask our students to focus on their own individual aesthetics and ideas. No one aesthetic approach is foregrounded as a model – for instance, there is no 'acousmatic class', but instead, a spectrum of practice from independent computer music to alternative computer-based art music is encountered. My only rule is that there is to be no 'pastiche' – everyone must say something individual with his or her music.[10]

This aesthetically open approach is one that has produced much original work from the University of York studios in recent years, particularly that of Radoslaw

Rudnicki (2012), and reflects a growing post-acousmatic aesthetic perspective within academia. Nevertheless, the focus on the development of individual compositional creative practice often results in collaborative composition and the performance practice of electronic music being considered distinct activities. This ethos is evident at the University of Sheffield. Individual electronic-music composition classes form the backbone of the course. In addition, there is a collaborative project, which brings together a composer, performer, and programmer, and a synthesis and programming module, which is partly assessed by group work in a supercollider ensemble. This is the primary model repeated across the institutions involved in this study.

A large proportion of the institutions surveyed have a laptop ensemble or an experimental electronics performance group.[11] These groups take many forms and serve different functions within their respective institutions though many act as an unofficial 'glue' bringing elements of individual courses together. The Dirty Electronics group directed by John Richards at De Montfort University is a non-assessed group. However, parts of the curriculum feed directly into the activities of this group. These include the building of no-input mixers, an optical pianola, hacking and instrument building, and developing an understanding of basic electronics. This interest in performance practice is also reflected in the Concordia University Electroacoustic Studies programme, which includes assignments in Years 1 and 2 in collaborative composition and performance with optional credit for the Concordia Laptop Orchestra (CLOrk) and further performance focused activity in a live digital practices module. The proliferation of the n-Ork laptop model does encourage collaborative practice in which the roles of composer, performer, and programmer are often fluid. However, as Hilliges and colleagues note, 'the user's concentration has to shift away from the group and towards the computer' (2007: 137), often resulting in a composition produced by a collective of individuals rather than truly collaborative experience.

This disaggregation between composition, collaboration, and performance is a common feature of the research findings of this study. Although there is creativity involved in technologically mediated performance it is not necessarily focused on 'compositional' activity – it is the investigation and use of performance technologies that is foregrounded. Diana Salazar notes that the most important element in her teaching is 'to get the students thinking about the performance of electronic music, and collaborative working methods. Skills that I think can sometimes be overlooked in Music Technology degrees that may rely heavily on solitary working methods in studio recording/mixing/composition'.[12]

What clearly arises from this research is that electronic-music composition is seen as a different activity from collaborative work and the distributed creativity (Sawyer and DeZutter 2009) arising from the use of performance technologies. Despite the advent of portable digital technologies and the demystification of creativity and the composer genius (Burnard 2012) through the democratisation of technology, it is clear that this model is still applied (consciously or not) in many institutions. What I conclude from this study is that the pedagogic models used in the teaching of electronic music composition is not viewed significantly differently from acoustic composition, it is merely the tools and the move from notation to a graphical user interface that has changed. What is equally evident is that this compartmentalisation of practice is recognised by students and leads to a schism between their academic work and external artistic practice. Furthermore, students' fears that group work may result in their obtaining a lower mark and, having little relation to their 'real' work outside of the classroom, propagates an unhealthy divide between artistic development and educational practice. Although academia demands quantifiable assignments, in the development of creativity and the creation of musical works there is no ideal production recipe. Creativity is essentially a messy process involving the generation of much redundant material, ideas, and cul-de-sacs that seemed so promising at the time before a final path presents itself.

Whilst many composers and sonic artists still work individually, there are an increasing number for whom the embracing of digital technology is fundamentally changing their approach to the work (Brian Eno),[13] long-term collaborations (@C,[14] Autechre),[15] distributed creativity and audio-visual collaborative practice (Skoltz-Kolgen)[16] or team-based (Kaffe Matthews working with programmer Dave Griffiths, software engineer Wolfgang Hauptfleisch and hardware designer Alexei Blinov). Whilst some still do adhere to the notion of 'spectacle' there is a move away from Bourdieu's 'charismatic ideology of creation'[17] which 'directs the gaze to the apparent producer – painter, composer, writer – and prevents us from asking who has created this 'creation' and the magic power of transubstantiation with which the 'creator' is endowed' (Bourdieu 1996: 167). We need to reflect these contemporary approaches in our teaching and acknowledge that at present the majority of electronic-music composition teaching is being squashed into an old paradigm. We need to question the nature of composition as a tangible artwork. Burnard writing about Margolis (1977), Goehr (1992) and Wolterstorff (1994) states that they all 'considered that a necessary pre-condition for composition was a work-concept that affected the way compositions were judged, valued, and received' (2012: 23). For many current music-technology students the notion of the work-concept is largely irrelevant and something they only encounter when completing academic assignments.

The question I want to address is how an individual's creative practice can be developed through collaborative composition and how experience design can be used to facilitate this. Although informed by Bourdieu's *The Rules of Art* as well as Becker's sociology of art and the Marxian ideologies of creativity put forward by Wolff (1993), I apply these ideas at a more local, individual level. Rather than seeing collaboration as an occasional adjunct to individual compositional work, I argue that it should be regarded as an essential parallel activity through which a symbiotic and richer understanding of creative practice emerges. I acknowledge that collaboration is something that has to be culturally negotiated and learned (Dawes and Sams 2004; Grossen and Bachmann 2000) and that it presents challenges to professional artists as well as to undergraduate students. Nevertheless, the potential pedagogic benefits are significant. More importantly, I want to examine the possible motivations and opportunities afforded to studying electronic music composition at university as the internet becomes ever more a tool for learning.

The social musician

As I am advocating the benefits to individual creativity of collaborative practice (Sawyer 2012), it could be argued that the democratisation and proliferation of technology that has resulted in a plethora of online learning environments and compositional resources becoming available contradicts this position, further isolating the individual from social learning situations. It is readily accepted that information communication technology is driving fundamental change in learning and teaching as well as research practices (Cain 2004; Seddon 2004), and according to John Seely Brown and Richard Adler, social learning areas, including virtual worlds, can 'coexist with and expand traditional education' (2008: 22). It is the 'coexisting' of resources that should be emphasised here. The development of MOOCs (massive open online courses) have 'been hailed as both a revolution in access to information and a harbinger of corporatized educational doom' and that 'MOOCs as a fast, cheap alternative to a traditional college education . . . could result in a two tiered class system in which rich students get face time and poor students get screen time' (McSweeney 2013: n.p.).

As a composer and performer, I want to make music. I want to share music, as I find great inspiration and artistic satisfaction in working with people in the same room at the same time. My learning of Max demonstrates this. Following the acquisition of certain techniques it was only when I came to apply those techniques and faltered that the ability to sit down with colleagues and work through the materials and ask questions solidified my knowledge into a concrete practice. According to McSweeney:

> The crux of the issue is that what one does in a college class is more than acquire content. MOOCs are great for the content part, but the community insights, the ability to synthesize material, those higher-order processes happen because you are studying a common area. They are not themselves the common area of study. And the thing we know from longitudinal studies of students is that they don't remember the content, but they do retain the intuitions that they developed while working through that content. That's the part that we could lose when schools are relying too heavily on digital media.
>
> (McSweeney 2013: n.p.)

There are two elements that can be usefully explored here: the first concerns her notion of community insights and the second the retention of information by students. The first has strong resonances with Etienne Wenger's notion of social learning systems. Wenger posits learning as a fundamentally social act in which we participate through engagement, imagination, and alignment. He observes:

> Our experience of life and the social standards of competence of our communities are not necessarily, or even usually, congruent. We each experience

knowing in our own ways. Socially defined competence is always in interplay with our experience. It is in this interplay that learning takes place.

(Wenger 1998: 226)

Trying to accommodate and assimilate the various competences and stylistic interests that students of electronic music have into a composition course is challenging but not impossible. It involves a refocusing of content to reflect creativity, critical thinking, and the development of knowledge through reflective practice rather than product. For many students, this process-driven approach is a common model through their work in bands – one in which music is essentially collaborative, where a track is developed as a group, often involving the assembling and development of materials and ideas in real time, testing their viability before adding the next element to the song. This model is equivalent to 'devising' in theatre and contemporary dance.

Where collaborative practice takes place within the same discipline, collaborators draw on knowledge of culturally established ways of making work (Green 2002). In collaborative electronic-music composition, two working methods present themselves. Due to the diversity of contemporary electronic music, 'culturally established' working methods differ, as does negotiation of the technology itself. Through the mediation of these practices, new ways of making work may emerge. The second more radical approach is to create or design situations that actively engender a sense of cognitive dissonance (Festinger 1985) in students. It is possible to move outside a student's culturally established means of working through advocating a neutral base where all participants are novices. This can be achieved through the use of graphic scores and improvisatory practices as well as using objects to create sound with which the students have no previous performance practice. Each method aims to promote cognitive growth by means of social interaction through composition. Vygotsky's theories of social learning underpin method 1 and Aronson (1995) has demonstrated that resolving cognitive dissonance (method 2) can have a significant impact on a student's motivation for learning. Vygotsky's theories provide a strong argument for collaborative practice and consider how people interact in cultural, conceptual, and social contexts to create new knowledge. Vygotsky outlined three key principles in his work. Elizabeth Dobson notes that there is

> an emphasis on the socially situated development of knowledge. Interested in the development of higher mental functions, his theoretical position focused on the significance of social interaction in human activity, and the development of socially and culturally mediated understanding (Vygotsky 1978). . . . Vygotsky theorized that human activity, higher mental functioning in particular, is mediated through inter-relationships with social and cultural tools.
>
> (Dobson 2012: 25–6)

This suggests that social interaction and inter-relationships can aid in the development of individual creativity. One of the benefits of collaborative work is in recognising and appreciating the ideas and skills of others and learning from them by appropriating, adapting, and developing them into an individual practice. Here Vygotsky's concepts of the 'more knowledgeable other' (MKO) and the 'zone of proximal development' (ZPD) (Vygotsky 1962) are pertinent. The MKO is defined as someone who has a higher ability than another – a teacher or a student peer. Vygotsky's theory proposes that through dialogue, the development of an individual can be enhanced through the interaction of one who is more experienced. Although various models are proposed this could easily be applied to student groups and the hierarchies that form within them depending on previous experience. According to Dobson, 'Vygotsky describes the ZPD as an area of developmental potential, represented as an elastic area of cognitive difference between what an individual can achieve alone and what can be achieved through interaction with another person (Vygotsky 1978)' (Dobson 2012: 25–6). Further research in this area (Doise and Mugny 1978; Wegerif 2007, 2010), draws much from Piaget's theory of cognitive disturbance, proposing that there is a direct correlation between social interaction, collaboration and the affordance of cognitive development. Extending Vygotsky's ZPD, Neil Mercer developed the intermental development zone (IDZ), 'a dynamic frame of reference which is reconstituted constantly as the dialogue continues, so enabling the teacher and learner to think together through the activity' (Mercer 2002: 143), and later, in collaboration with Karen Littleton, proposed the Intermental Creative Zone (Littleton and Mercer 2013: 114). In electronic-music composition, collaborative work can therefore lead to a questioning of an individual's existing musical practice and prejudices and, through the negotiation of new forms, new methods of sound production or approaches to technical challenges can stimulate the creation of new shared knowledge schemas that result in an active learning framework that extends beyond what the individual alone could achieve.

Active learning and the flipped classroom

A compositional practice that involves both individual and collaborative work for undergraduates and simultaneously using the flipped-classroom approach drives active student learning. This is where specifically designed online tools can facilitate the learning experience rather than leading to an increased sense of isolation. This flipped classroom, as exemplified by the Khan Academy, works well for technology-based music, as software techniques can be contained within TED Talk length screencasts that can be rewound. Kotler and Roberto (1989) recognise that individuals have selective attention, only retaining a small part of any message in memory. Although their work is in the sphere of social marketing, it is equally applicable to other social situations including that of the lecture and resonates with McSweeney's findings in longitudinal studies of students. The flipped-classroom approach allows the use of the classroom time for student-centred collaborative learning activities rather than traditional lectures, which no matter how engaging often engender cognitive overload. Merkt and colleagues observe that 'there is a mismatch of the presentation pace and the recipients' cognitive capacities' (2011: 689). The advantage of the flipped classroom is that it also encourages, through practical activity, a sense of questioning-through-doing. The key point is how information is turned not just into knowledge but into applied-knowledge transferable to a number of situations. According to Cath Ellis:

> Active learning promotes the application of content material while it is still being learned and presented. It engages students more deeply in the process of learning course material by encouraging critical thinking and fostering the development of self-directed learning. Active learning affords the opportunity for application and practice, and the asking of questions. Additionally it is possible to assess and remediate student understanding in real time.
>
> (Ellis 2013: 338)

Designing experience in composition

The flipped classroom allows time for academics to engage with students in potentially new and innovative ways. Through online resources that provide content and a foundation for the acquisition of technical knowledge, academics can use classroom time to provide an active learning environment focused on innovation and experimentation and exploring these through creative activities. This learning environment can be even richer when considering the development of new pedagogic tools in the context of experience design.

B. Joseph Pine II and James H. Gilmore (1998) discuss what they call the experience economy. They chart economic progress through the simple example of the making of a birthday cake for a party: firstly the birthday cake was made from scratch, then with premixed ingredients, then bought from a bakers, then the whole party was outsourced to a play centre or event organiser. Pine and Gilmore describe this as the 'fourth economic offering because consumers unquestionably desire experiences, and more and more businesses are responding by explicitly designing and promoting them' and 'experiences have emerged as the next step in what we call the progression of economic value. . . . Many companies simply wrap experiences around their traditional offerings to sell them better . . . however, businesses must deliberately design engaging experiences that command a fee' (Pine and Gilmore 1998: n.p.).

Traditionally, we think of such experiences as being focused around theme parks, virtual reality simulators, interactive games, and event organisers, such as wedding planners, but rarely education. In considering experience design in education what we are questioning from a pedagogic perspective is the value of going to university and undertaking a course and that the knowledge gained through this experience is as valuable (if not more valuable) than merely the information that is imparted. Experiences can be emotional, physical, or intellectual and cannot be delivered on demand. The ramifications of any given experience only emerge after a prolonged engagement with the activity and the context in which it was undertaken, in this case collaborative electronic music composition. Mihaly Csikszentmihalyi and Michael Rochberg-Halton (1981) consider experience as a transaction and that this process emphasises both the person and the things surrounding the activity, and, as this communicative process unfolds, it results in more knowledge and meaning for the person. Forlizzi notes:

> The process of change shapes the flow of experience into an experience. All of life is a succession of loss and recovery of temporary equilibria, want and fulfilment, doing and not doing. Changes over time bear a new state of harmonious balance. When an organism returns to stability, after having passed through a phase of disruption, Dewey feels the conditions for an experience are in place. A starting point and an ending point define an experience, which is shaped by an aesthetic rhythm, and a unity of action, feeling, and meaning.
>
> (Forlizzi 1997: 12)

In accepting that universities are no longer a service industry for the acquisition of knowledge, experience design offers an alternative for maintaining face time with students. However, the designing of such experiences also has pedagogic worth. In an educational setting, such experience design can be extremely effective in building a community of students and developing learning environments – a balance between subjective experience and objective learning. Experience design does not have the communication of knowledge at its heart but is a means of facilitating this process in the most stimulating manner possible. The aim is to deliver a meaningful experience through a variety of active learning situations that endures and enriches the participant. Where this experience is positive it actively reinforces the concretisation of reflective knowledge. I propose that experience design is essential to twenty-first-century pedagogic practice and will have a significant impact on the design and delivery of courses across music and the arts and will often be in conflict with the current formal and compartmentalised education system, which is bound administratively to courses and modules.

Engendering experiences outside a student's established modus operandi can be as disconcerting as it is positive. Etienne Wenger discusses experiences outside of the known:

> We have an experience that opens our eyes to a new way of looking at the world. This experience does not fully fit in the current practice of our home communities. We now see limitations we were not aware of before. We come back to our peers, try to communicate our experience, attempt to explain what we have discovered, so they too can expand their horizon. In the process, we are trying to change how our community defines competence (and we are actually deepening our own experience). . . . Inside a community, learning takes place because competence and experience need to converge for a community to exist. At the boundaries, competence and experience tend to diverge: a boundary interaction is usually an experience of being exposed to a foreign competence. Such reconfigurations of the relation between competence and experience are an important aspect of learning. If competence and experience are too close, if they always match, not much learning is likely to take place. There are no challenges; the community is losing its dynamism

and the practice is in danger of becoming stale. Conversely, if experience and competence are too disconnected, if the distance is too great, not much learning is likely to take place either.

(Wenger 2000: 232–3)

Designing experience through active learning opens students to possibilities that may inform their ideas or creative process in order to make them better at what they do. In some instances this may result in a broadening of their aesthetic, whilst in others the adoption of a particular technique into a new musical domain. For others it may actually solidify their practice within a small niche genre, happy to do so but now knowing how their work can be contextualised within a wider framework of creative practice. Through considering both the individual and collaborative approaches to electronic-music composition and the flipped classroom to engender this, the aim is for the students to achieve seamless learning. Seamless learning occurs when a student experiences a continuity of learning across a combination of technologies, social settings, times, and locations. As a result of experience design, knowledge is reflectively accumulated largely a posteriori of the activity itself.

Facilitating experience and seamless learning?

The application of the ideas and concepts outlined above has resulted in the rethinking of the delivery of two interconnected first year modules that I was involved in: the practically oriented 'Computer Composition' and the theoretically biased 'Grooves, Glitches, and Crackles', which looks at ways in which technology has changed how we produce, listen, and disseminate music through a number of case studies ranging from Russolo to Fennesz via Jimi Hendrix. The delineation of the content into separate modules and the time allocated to each are now being treated as mere containers for activities to occur within a fluid exploration of theory and practice.

The decision to start in the first year was made to encourage the symbiotic pedagogic value that working individually and collaboratively can have from the start of a student's university education. Furthermore, from a practical perspective, the content of the modules changes little from year to year and is therefore worth investing significant time in ensuring that the online resources are of the highest quality. 'Computer Composition' introduced sequencing, digital synthesis, sampling, more sample-based processing techniques including granular synthesis and FFT based sound transformation. This technical knowledge is supported in 'Grooves Glitches, and Crackles' by discussion of, and listening to, artists as diverse as Steve Reich, Chlorgeslecht, Merzbow, Amon Tobin, Francis Dhomont, Tim Hecker, DJ Shadow, Qbert, Bjork, and Burial and understanding the context in which this work was created. This listening stresses a deliberately rhizomatic or nomadic listening unfettered by stylistic or genre constraints.

We have developed extensive online video materials for Logic, so flipping the classroom. Such bespoke videos whilst serving the same purpose as those on

YouTube enable us to focus more directly on the key skills we wish to embed in our students. This allows the procedural knowledge to be delivered online which results in more individual and collaborative student-led compositional active learning content. Whilst we will continue to make use of Vimeo, iTunes, and YouTube, we are increasingly aware that experience design tells us that the use of bespoke course videos creates more of a brand identity and sense of belonging on the part of students, even a sense of brand loyalty. Often such videos are much shorter than the traditional lecture of one hour. This technique is backed up by research by Demetry who notes that 'two to three microlectures . . . 10–15 minutes in length and tightly focused on a specific instructional objective' are most effective (2010: 1).

Following the flipping of the classroom we created groups within the first year cohort. This allows students to get to know one another quickly rather than sitting in an anonymous lecture and then working in a workstation room individually on a computer using headphones. Also, changing groups regularly for initial small projects allows students to assess each other's skills and interests. As a result, groups start to form naturally so that there is a transition between lecturer-initiated to student-led group formation. Such student-led groups mitigate against the concern many students expressed that such collaborative work might bring their individual mark down. The online sharing of the resulting group and individual work allows a group critique to develop. People take a pride in what they do and as long as properly monitored provides community feedback to the student rather than an individual piece produced in a workstation.

The projects undertaken are varied. Three specific ones are the use of the app Impaktor, which turns any flat surface into a percussion instrument. Interesting musical results emerge when groups of students move beyond the traditional drummer mentality and start using keys, water bottles, and coins to trigger more sophisticated gestures; the creation of live *musique concrète* pieces using objects, microphones and Ableton Live with multiple effects on multiple incoming tracks and mixing between the processed tracks using a Korg NanoKontrol; and the creation of live ambient music with students using ebows on guitars and piano strings, objects (processed in the manner outlined above) and triggered field recordings played through mobile phones and iPads all spatially located around the lecture theatre. The emphasis here is on providing a rich experience, which encourages the student to follow up the class by self- or group-directed learning. Finally we have used Logic and a controller to create live electronic group work in a workstation room using the limitations of the iMac speakers, encouraging students to think about their spatial position in the room. Some choose to cluster in one sport while others spread to the periphery of the room. The examples also draw together different forms of creativity. They demonstrate that composition in the traditional sense is now only one area of digital music making which includes live electronics, adaptive audio for computer games, and composed audio-visual works, as well as sound design. Student feedback from these projects has been overwhelmingly positive.

The purpose of such activities is to propose that electronic music composition moves beyond the fixed. David Tudor had already done this in his live electronic works over 40 years ago, but it is interesting to note that Goehr proposed that 'a function of the composition is to produce an enduring artefact' (1992, cited in Burnard 2012: 29).

In revising our approach to electronic-music composition, modes of assessment have also been reconfigured. We have moved from assessment-driven or outcome-driven models to student-centred assignments. I would argue that at such a stage in a student's career outcome driven models are only useful in marking a student's achievement against prescribed criteria rather than taking into account the growth and development a student may have undergone. If we consider composition as the art of putting things together, then questioning our reasons and motivations for trying unusual or different combinations is as valuable a learning experience as producing yet another work within an established model. Mark Lepper and David Greene carried out an interesting study about extrinsic rewards on intrinsic motivation in 1975. Although their research concerned school children, the results are nevertheless worth considering here. They maintain that:

> In these studies, children in individual sessions either were led to expect and then were given an extrinsic reward for engaging in an activity of initial intrinsic interest; were given this same reward unexpectedly after they had finished with the activity; or were offered no extrinsic reward for engaging in the activity. Subsequently, unobtrusive measures of these children's intrinsic interest in the activity were obtained in their classrooms, in the absence of any expectation of reward. The results in both studies indicated that expectation of a reward while engaging in the activity, relative to the other conditions, significantly undermined the children's intrinsic interest in that activity.
>
> (Lepper and Greene 1975: 480)

Another important assessment development is replacing critical commentaries with an online blog, wiki, or sketchbook containing preliminary audio material and links to video art and other influential material. This acts as a repository that is useful for the student to return to in the future rather than a closed report at the end of the module. The history of music is littered with examples of composers from Beethoven, Elgar, Boulez, and William Basinski returning to musical ideas they developed decades earlier.

Real-world collaborations always bring about new experiences that feed individual creativity. Knowledge construction continues beyond the academy and occurs within Vygotsky's social context that involves collaboration on real world problems or tasks that build on each person's skills and experience shaped by each individual's culture (Vygotsky 1978: 102). An exchange with Miguel Carvalhais, a sound artist, co-director of the Cronica label, and design lecturer highlights this. Carvalhais, who has worked with fellow sound artist Pedro Tudela as @C for over a decade, states that collaboration is the primary means by which he works because:

> I come from a background in communication design for new media and that's increasingly how we tend to work nowadays. Over the years we [@C] have

collaborated more or less regularly with other artists or projects. . . . With Pedro – especially after collaborating on the @c project – we're not only able to maximize each other's potential and creative freedom as we're able to complement them, with respect for each one's individuality, personality and authorship. Collaborations are also constantly challenging, forcing us to negotiate many (if not all) decisions and to permanently broaden our skills.[18]

Conclusion

This chapter has demonstrated that experience design should be considered an essential part of curriculum design in the early twenty-first century. It shows that experience design can enhance a student's learning and engender challenging and stimulating environments for both individual and collaborative creativity. If implemented to the fullest extent, experience design has an impact on curriculum design, teaching methodology and assessment strategy as well as making the approach to composition one that reflects the plethora of contemporary approaches to sound rather than one dominant tradition. As Burnard notes, 'we need to acknowledge the myriad of forms of multiply mediated musical creativities that arise in musical spaces that are deeply influenced by a series of complex factors' (2012: 237).

What I have endeavoured to demonstrate in this chapter is that we are all engaged in local and global communities of practice. We talk and discuss ideas with friends, post on online discussion forums, and even take part in networked performances. Working collaboratively on electronic music composition projects is an essential part of stimulating both the acquisition of core skills and ideas that form the basis of life-long learning and experiences. A university is also a safe environment to experiment, to fail, and then to fail better.

Notes

1 The practice of delivering a lecture online (e.g. as a video-cast) and then using class time to undertake a practical activity based on the material.
2 <www.khanacademy.org>
3 Pupils in Year 6 are 10–11 years old.
4 Standard Assessment Task: an examination for 14 year olds (Year 9) in the National Curriculum.
5 <http://www.youtube.com/user/BazTutorials>.
6 <http://www.p21.org>.
7 Executive director, GD Goenka School, Sharjah, UAE.
8 Principal of GEMS Westminster School, Ras al-Khaimah, UAE.
9 The survey comprised 30 institutions where electronic music composition is taught within Music Departments either as a separate music technology programme or as part of the composition curriculum within a music degree.
10 Private email correspondence with author (1 Aug. 2013). Field is the head of the Department of Music at the University of York.
11 24 of the 30 institutions had an assessed or extra-curricula performance group.
12 Private email correspondence with author (3 Aug. 2013).
13 In generative works such as *Bloom*.

14 Miguel Carvalhais and Pedro Tudela.
15 Rob Brown and Sean Booth.
16 Dominique Skoltz and Herman Kolgen – active as a duo from 1996 to 2008.
17 Through virtual bands such as Gorillaz and the anonymity sought by Burial.
18 Private email correspondence with author (2 Oct. 2013).

References

Adkins, M. (2014). 'A Personal Manifesto of Nodalism'. In M. Carvalhais and M. Verdic-chio (eds), *xCoAx 2014: Proceedings of the Second Conference on Computation Communication Aesthetics and X*. Porto: University of Porto.

Aronson, E. (1995). *The Social Animal*. New York: W.H. Freeman & Co.

Bourdieu, P. (1996). *The Rules of Art: Genesis and Structure of the Literary Field*, trans. Susan Emanuel. Cambridge: Polity Press.

Brown, J.S., and R.P. Adler (2008). 'Minds on Fire: Open Education, the Long Tail, and Learning 2.0'. *Educause Review*, 43/1: 17–32.

Burnard, P. (2012). *Musical Creativities in Practice*. Oxford: Oxford University Press.

Cain, T. (2004). 'Theory, Technology and the Music Curriculum'. *British Journal of Music Education*, 21/2: 215–21.

Chaudahry, S.B. (2013). 'Teaching and Learning with Passion'. *Gulf News*, 4 Aug.

Cole, M. (1996). *Cultural Psychology*. Cambridge, MA: Belknap Press of Harvard University Press.

Csikszentmihalyi, M., and M. Rochberg-Halton (1981). *The Meaning of Things*. Boston: Cambridge University Press.

Dawes, L. and C. Sams (2004). 'The Capacity to Collaborate'. In K. Littleton, D. Miell, and D. Faulkner (eds), *Learning to Collaborate: Collaborating to Learn*. New York: Nova Press.

Demetry, C. (2010). 'Work in Progress: An Innovation Merging "Classroom Flip" and Team-Based Learning'. *Proceedings, 40th ASEE/IEEE Frontiers in Education Conference*. <http://ieeexplore.ieee.org/xpls/abs_all.jsp?arnumber=5673617> (accessed 12 Dec. 2015)

Dobson, E. (2012). 'An Investigation of the Processes of Interdisciplinary Creative Collaboration: The Case of Music Technology Students Working within the Performing Arts'. PhD Thesis, Open University.

Doise, W., and G. Mugny (1978). 'Socio-Cognitive Conflict and Structure of Individual and Collective Performances'. *European Journal of Social Psychology*, 8: 181–92.

Ellis, C. (2013). 'Reflections on the Role of Self-Paced, Online Resources in Higher Education or How YouTube is Teaching Me How to Knit'. In D.J. Salter (ed.), *Cases on Quality Teaching Practices in Higher Education*. Hersey, PA: IGI Global.

Festinger, L. (1985). *A Theory of Cognitive Dissonance*. Stanford, CA: Stanford University Press.

Forlizzi, J.L. (1997). 'Designing for Experience: An Approach to Human-Centred Design'. MA Thesis, Carnegie Mellon University.

Goehr, L. (1992). *The Imaginary Museum of Musical Works: An Essay in the Philosophy of Music*. Oxford: Clarendon Press.

Golding, R. (2009). 'Musical Chairs: The Construction of 'Music' in Nineteenth-Century British Universities'. *Nineteenth Century Music Review*, 6/2: 19–39.

Green, L. (2002). *How Popular Musicians Learn: A Way Ahead for Music Education*. Aldershot: Ashgate.

Grossen, M., and K. Bachmann (2000). 'Learning to Collaborate in a Peer-Tutoring Situation: Who Learns? What is Learned?' *European Journal of Psychology of Education*, 15: 491–508.

Hargreaves, D. (2003). 'Young People's Music In and Out of School'. *British Journal of Music Education*, 20/3: 229–241.

Hilliges, O., L. Terrenghi, S. Boring, D. Kim, H. Richter, and A. Butz (2007). 'Designing for Collaborative Creative Problem Solving'. In *C&C '07: Proceedings of the 6th ACM SIGCHI Conference on Creativity and Cognition*. New York: ACM.

Kotler, P., and E. Roberto (1989). *Social Marketing*. New York: Macmillan.

Lepper, M., and D. Greene (1975). 'Turning Play into Work: Effects of Adult Surveillance and Extrinsic Rewards on Children's Intrinsic Motivation'. *Journal of Personality and Social Psychology*, 31/3: 479–86.

Littleton, K., and N. Mercer (2013). *Interthinking: Putting Talk to Work*. London and New York: Routledge.

McSweeney, E. (2013). 'Music, MOOCS and Copyright: Digital Dilemmas for Schools of Music'. *NewMusicBox* (25 Sept.). <http://www.newmusicbox.org/articles/music-moocs-and-copyright-digital-dilemmas-for-schools-of-music/> (accessed 29 Sept. 2013).

Margolis, J. (1977). *Philosophy Looks at the Arts*. Philadelphia, PA: Temple University Press.

Mercer, N. (2002). 'Developing Dialogues'. In G. Claxton and G. Wells (eds), *Learning for Life in the 21st Century: Sociocultural Perspectives on the Future of Education*. Oxford: Blackwell.

Merkt, M., S. Weigand, A. Heier, and S. Schwant (2011). 'Learning with Videos vs. Learning with Print: The Role of Interactive Features'. *Learning and Instruction*, 21/6: 687–704.

Nuhn, R., B. Eaglestone, N. Ford, A. Moore, and G. Brown (2002). *A Qualitative Analysis of Composers at Work: Proceedings of the International Computer Music Conference, Gothenburg, Sweden*. San Francisco: International Computer Music Association.

Pine, B.J., II and J.H. Gilmore (1998). 'Welcome to the Experience Economy'. *Harvard Business Review*. <http://hbr.org/1998/07/welcome-to-the-experience-economy/> (accessed 19 Aug. 2013).

Paynter, J., and P. Aston (1970). *Sound and Silence*. London: Cambridge University Press.

Rudnicki, R. (2012). 'Portfolio of Compositions'. PhD thesis: University of York.

Ruthmann, A. (2012). 'Engaging Adolescents with Music and Technology'. In S. Burton (ed.), *Engaging Musical Practices: A Sourcebook for Middle School General Music*. Lanham, MD: R&L Education.

Sawyer, K. (2012). *Explaining Creativity: The Science of Human Innovation*, 2nd edn. Oxford: Oxford University Press.

—— and S. DeZutter (2009). 'Distributed Creativity: How Collective Creations Emerge from Collaboration'. *Psychology of Aesthetics Creativity and the Arts*, 3/2: 81–92.

Seddon, F.A. (2004). 'Inclusive Music Curricula for the 21st Century'. In L. Bartel (ed.), *Questioning the Music Education Paradigm*. Toronto: Canadian Music Educator's Association.

Soares, R. (2013). 'The Purpose of Holistic Education'. *Gulf News*, 4 Aug.

Tagg, P. (2012). *Music's Meanings: A Modern Musicology for Non-Musos*. New York and Huddersfield: Mass Media Music Scholar's Press.

Vygotsky, L.S. (1962). *Thought and Language*. Cambridge, MA: MIT Press.

—— (1978). *Mind in Society: Interaction Between Learning and Development*. London: Harvard University Press.

Wegerif, R. (2007). *Dialogic Education and Technology Expanding the Space of Learning*. New York: Springer.

—— (2010). *Mind Expanding: Teaching for Thinking and Creativity in Primary Education*. London: Oxford University Press.

Wenger, E. (1998). *Communities of Practice: Learning, Meaning, and Identity*. New York: Cambridge University Press.

—— (2000). 'Communities of Practice and Social Learning Systems'. *Organization*, 7/2: 225–46.

Wolff, J. (1993). *The Social Production of Art*, 2nd edn. Basingstoke: Macmillan.

Wolterstorff, N. (1994). 'The Work of Making a Work of Music'. In P. Alperson (ed.) *What is Music? An Introduction to the Philosophy of Music*. University Park: Pennsylvania State University Press.

Yorkshire Sculpture Park (2013). 'Tom Hudson: Transitions' [exhibition brochure].

12 Assessment processes and digital technologies

Jonathan Savage and Martin Fautley

Introduction

As explored throughout this book, digital technologies are transforming approaches to musical performance and composition. Digital tools are constantly developed, applied, used, and abused by practitioners, and it can be hard for those of us working in education to keep track of the latest innovations. At any one given moment, a particular instrument, technology, piece of software, or iPad app might be the specific flavour of the month.

There are at least two potential dangers here. Firstly, that it is easy to fall into the trap of presuming that this is an unprecedented situation, something that previous generations of musicians and educators did not have to face. But, of course, this is a falsehood. Change is a constant factor in musical history, performance, and compositional practices, just as it is in educational theory and practice. The pace and nature of change may differ, but every age has its fair share of technological change to contend with. Secondly, there are strong commercial pressures from manufacturers, and broader societal pressures from consumers (particularly students), to keep up to date with what the latest technological innovations are and to adopt them within our classrooms. The uncritical adoption and use of technologies is a constant threat to a high quality music education. We will explore this further in the following discussion, where we consider the importance of critically evaluating the choices made in music technology.

Following Bertrand Russell's caveat that 'the demand for certainty is one which is natural to man, but is nevertheless an intellectual vice' (1950: 26), we would argue that trying to predict the future is a futile task, whether it be the patterns of engagement in how musicians develop their use of technology, or how educators might seek to devise approaches for the assessment the musical outputs that result.

Maybe this is a strange assertion to make at the beginning of a chapter on assessment and music technology. Perhaps, but it should be borne in mind that best way to understand the interrelated issues of assessment and digital technology and thereby prepare for an uncertain future is to investigate, appreciate and understand practices in this area today. With Furedi, we would argue that:

> In the worldview of the educational establishment, change has acquired a sacred and divine-like character that determines what is taught and what

is learned. It creates new 'requirements' and 'introduces' new ideas about learning. . . . Typically change is presented in a dramatic and mechanistic manner that exaggerates the novelty of the present moment. Educationalists frequently adopt the rhetoric of breaks and ruptures and maintain that nothing is as it was and that the present has been decoupled from the past.

(Furedi 2009: 23)

In this chapter we will attempt to provide a narrative about these issues as they are exemplified today. Following a general exploration of four key questions about assessment and music education, we will draw upon a detailed investigation of digital technologies within a particular context to provide illumination and insight into issues relating to the theory and practice of assessment. As with the children and young adults, the process of becoming familiar with the world as it is today provides the best opportunity (and in Arendt's words the 'existential security') to have a chance of attempting something new (cited in Levinson 1997: 7).

Some introductory questions about assessment

As seen throughout this book, digital technologies transform approaches to musical activities. The notion of what constitutes a musical performance, composition, or improvisation; who is doing it; where they might be; how they interact with an audience that may or may not be physically present; the musical skills needed to perform it; and the musical understanding to respond expressively to others are all highly contestable and problematised in different ways by digital technologies.

Within educational settings, the requirements to assess students' work both formally, for external examination, and informally have, perhaps, never been stronger. Yet the systems of assessment in teaching and learning contexts seem peculiarly non-musical, uncreative, and unresponsive to the sweeping array of new musical possibilities that digital technologies have facilitated. In what follows we will explore how assessment processes can, or perhaps should, be developed to provide a more appropriate and critical account of students' musical work with digital technologies. In particular, through the analysis of the work on one contemporary musician and a metaphorical application of key ideas, we will examine how digital technologies themselves can provide a useful framework of ideas for a meaningful and authentic assessment process: one that embraces and values the student themselves and their work, rather than being constructed and conducted as an external processes of testing.

The assessment of a student's work in music, of whatever type, needs to begin by asking a number of basic but very important questions:

- What is being assessed?
- How is it being assessed?
- Why is it being assessed?
- Who is the assessment for? And what will happen to the assessment data produced?

What is being assessed?

At its simplest, the question of what is being assessed is asking the teacher to think about what, from the entirety of musical endeavour available, is the specific focus of the assessment? So, for example, in assessment of composing, what is 'in' and what is 'out' of the assessment? Is it an assessment of a particular skill within the process of composing: for example, the ability to recognise and explore the potential of a musical fragment in a developmental way? Or is it assessment of the product that results from the composition: for example, does the composition as a whole have a meaningful musical structure? If the assessment is focusing on the processes involved in musical composition, how is this undertaken, recognised and communicated to the student?

How is it being assessed?

Addressing the issue of what is to be assessed is only part of the task, as how it is being assessed also has significant ramifications. At its most straightforward, this question could be about the type of assessment process being adopted. The assessment types which are most frequently encountered are:

- formative – an assessment which happens as work is being undertaken and is purposed with improving the work done by the student, often undertaken in dialogic form;
- summative – an assessment at the end of a unit, scheme, term, or whatever, which is designed to summarise student attainment into a mark, grade, or level;
- ipsative – an assessment the student makes against their own prior performance, so that they are measuring their personal progression against their own previous work.

However, there is more to it than this. If the assessment being made is a formative one, then the teacher will want to provide feedback to the student concerning how well they are doing. If it is a teacher-devised summative assessment that is being undertaken (that is, not an externally organised summative assessment), then the immediate question becomes: how will this be done? As we have seen, summative assessment requires a summarising mark. The teacher will need to construct a mark scheme, rating scale, or rubric of some sort that delineates the qualitative aspects of attainment in some sort of quantitative order (marks out of 10, percentages, or whatever). When music technologies are involved, this is not as simple as it might seem.

One of the aspects of assessment of musical process using digital technologies may be, where possible, to distinguish between the human contribution and that of the technology involved. Specific questions may need to be asked about the role of the technology. In essence this is no different from thinking about more traditional aspects of musical performance on, say, a trombone compared with a piano. There is no point in creating a mark scheme for a performance that rates the musician's ability to play beautifully articulated harmonic progressions, as the trombone cannot do this, whereas the piano can. As we will demonstrate later, the limitations and affordances provided by the digital technologies being used do need to be taken into account, although it is the human involvement that should be of prime concern within the processes of assessment. What this means in practice is that the teacher needs to have a detailed understanding of what it is that is being achieved by the student, as well as what the music technology has afforded. This means that evaluating the potential of a piece of music technology is an important educational activity what works closely alongside that of assessing a student's work. We will consider this further below.

Why is it being assessed?

How one might assess the human contribution within any technology-mediated musical activity takes us to the next question to be considered: why is the assessment taking place? This question normally generates one of two responses:

- to help the student improve the work which they are doing;
- to provide a grade or mark for work which has been done.

In the case of the former, these are often formative assessments, whereas in the latter they will always be summative assessments. However, there is also the formative use of summative assessment, where a grade is provided, but the object of providing that grade is to help the student improve their work. Knowing that their work would score a mark of 65% would indicate to the student that there is room for improvement. This becomes formative when the tutor helps the student to realise exactly what it is that they need to do in order to improve.

Who is the assessment for, and what will happen to the assessment data produced?

The question 'why?' clearly has commonality with the final introductory questions: 'who is the assessment for' and 'what will happen to the assessment data?' Perhaps the audience for the assessment is varied, but the two most important constituents are the student and the teacher. In many cases these are also the people who will be end-users of the assessment data. In today's performativity-driven education system however, there are also occasions when assessment data produced is not for the teacher and student but for the systemic purposes of monitoring student progress and ensuring accountability. This sort of assessment data needs very careful handling, as it may not be in the best interests of the teacher or the student to have raw, decontextualised assessment data fed into the system: for example, if the student has done much worse than expected on a summative assessment due to mitigating factors, using this data as a predictor for final outcomes may well not be appropriate.

These general questions frame the work of all music teachers. For a more detailed understanding of how these issues might play themselves out within the context of a technologically rich learning environment, I turn to one study of musical improvisation within such a context – electro-acoustic music. We hope that by presenting this context, we can, through a playful application of metaphor, begin to expand on what an alternative approach to assessment with digital technology might contain.

Improvising machines

Bowers' 'Improvising Machines' (2003) explores the improvisation of electro-acoustic music from various standpoints, including its musicological, aesthetic, practical, and technical-design dimensions. Within it, detailed ethnographic descriptions of the author's own musical performances over a period of years at different concerts across Europe are described, and the various pieces of hardware and software through which these were facilitated are analysed. For anyone with an interest in electro-acoustic music, musical improvisation, the human–design interface, and the wider adoption of digital technologies it is a fascinating and worthwhile read.

Bowers presents an argument that electro-acoustic music is an indigenous 'machine music'. He explores his own experience as an improviser in this idiom, giving special attention to observable variations in the forms of technical inter-activity, social interaction, and musical material which existed across the various musical performances that he gave with fellow performers. He identifies a range of analytic issues drawn from his work as a musical improviser within this idiom of machine music (Bowers 2003: 42–51). These four issues inform his writing in later chapters (notably the exploration and development of a technical design aesthetic in Chapter 3), but are of particular interest for us here in relation to our discussion of assessment and digital technologies.

Contingent practical configurations

> The music has arisen in relation to these contingencies in such a way that, from an ethnographic point of view, it should not be analytically separated from them.
>
> (Bowers 2003: 43)

Bowers defines 'contingent practical configurations' as the technologies used, musical materials and forms explored, performance practices employed, and the specific setting and occasion of, as well as the understanding generated from, musical improvisation. His argument is that the contingencies that occur within his various performance events are not to be seen as problematic obstructions to an idealised improvisational performance. Rather, they are 'topicalised' within the performance itself. They are integral to it and shape the resulting musical statements, interactions, and expressions. Improvised musical conduct of the sort Bowers described is a space in which these contingencies are worked through in real time and in public. The specific contingency of technology-rich musical improvisational conduct is embodied in the relationship between human beings and their machines. You cannot have one without the other. Specifically, 'it is in our abilities to work with and display a manifold of human-machine relationships that our accountability of performance should reside' (Bowers 2003: 44).

Variable sociality

> The sociality of musical production is an important feature of improvised electro-acoustic music. Publicly displaying the different ways in which performers can position themselves with respect to each other and the different ways in which technologies can be deployed to enforce, negate, mesh with, disrupt, or otherwise relate to the local socialities of performance could [again] become the whole point of doing it.
>
> (Bowers 2003: 45)

As with any musical practice, within 'machine music' the social interactional relationships that Bowers and his fellow musicians enjoyed varied over time. There was a deliberate playfulness here. Different alternatives were experimented with, variably and often interchangeably, within the course of a specific musical performance. One particular set of social norms might be disrupted at a particular point, perhaps due to technical issues (cables are not long enough or the monitor is lop-sided) or other factors (the audience begins to leave or the music is too loud and complaints are received from others in the locality). Variable sociality is the different social, interactional relations that are worked out through musical performance. But these social dimensions of musical production are highly important. Within an understanding of improvisational conduct with technology as part of a musical performance, they need to be understood and explored as an integral part of the aesthetic, not as a separate issue.

Variable engagement and interactivity

> Just as performers can variably relate to each other, they can variably engage with the technologies and instruments before them.
>
> (Bowers 2003: 45)

Bower's concept of variable engagement and interactivity facilitates a consideration of the different and varying relations that performers have with respect to their instruments and technologies. In particular, he identifies a number of different patterns of engagement both for the musical performer and for the listener. These have important implications for the ways in which teachers listen to and make judgements about student's work that we will explore below.

His 12-hour musical performance in Ipswich in Suffolk (at which audience members were given a free can of baked beans in return for their attendance), used a range of mechanised musical production technologies that, at particular points, would automatically set new parameters for musical statements or even draw on new source materials from the performers' laptop computers. The pattern of engagement from the performers' point of view was one of initiation, delegation, supervision, and intervention. This process meant that it was not always necessary for one, or both, of the musical performers to be physically present within the space for the whole of the 12 hours.

Alternatively, other forms of musical production within these performance events used more conventional instruments that required some kind of human incitement to action. The pattern of engagement here would be one of physical excitement/incitement and manipulation. Bowers suggests that these forms and patterns of engagement can be further complexified. Firstly, different forms of engagement have different phenomenologies associated with them. How one listens, hears, responds intellectually, or physically acts all effect one's engagement and interaction with sound and its means of production. Furthermore, Bowers raises the issue of intelligibility which does, for us, seem to be closely linked to the transparency of gesture and communication (both between performers and with an audience) within electroacoustic musical performances. His account of one incidence at a concert in Siena (a duet with SOH) is informative:

> My account of how we enacted the planned waves of intensity at Siena should reveal some close co-ordinations between players of bodily gesture with respect to touchpads, keyboards and knobs. I ensured that critical knob adjustments were made visible to SOH by carrying through the local turning at the front panel into a perspicuous whole body movement. In the context of the unfolding music and how it enacted the score, this gestural sequence was legible to SOH as accomplishing the transition into the final section. I assume that, just as my activity was visible to SOH, it would have been to the audience. It would accompany a notable transition in intensity and could be interpreted as bound up with its production. The audience would not have the same resources as SOH, however, for drawing the precise implication that he did (here we are in the score) but my movements would not be meaningless thrashings.
>
> (Bowers 2003: 47)

Of course, there is nothing particularly unique to electro-acoustic musical performance about these points. As many have commented, there is always a frustration associated with performance practices within which 'performers' deliberately mask their identity and bodily gestures. For Buxton, musical performance is a compromise between the presentation of the scored and the improvised, where physical, emotional, gestural, active, and reactive components all have a part to play. He draws up a continuum within which the visibility or invisibility of musical cause and effect outwork:

> I must confess, that I have the same emotional and intellectual response to watching someone huddle over a laptop as I did 20–30 years ago when they were huddled over a Revox tape recorder. The more invisible the gesture and

the more tenuous my perception of the correlation between cause and effect, the less relevant it is to me that a performance is 'live'.

(Buxton 2005: 4)

Musical materials

> To construct workable and intelligible performance environments, I have made various distinctions between these musical materials in terms of their real-world sources, the media by which they are conveyed, the manipulability of those media, the kinds of gestures and devices which are used to realise those manipulations. From time to time, all of those features are seen to be bound up with identifiable forms of social organisation between co-performers, and those forms of interaction have musical-formal aspects to boot. I have tried to reveal these interconnections through ethnographic description of the performance situation.

> (Bowers 2003: 48)

Bowers' sophisticated organisation of musical materials draws on a range of existing methodological strictures for electro-acoustic composition. Whilst he is at pains to emphasise the differences here, his account is illuminating when placed alongside his analysis of Schaeffer's acousmatic composition (and allied practices), Emmerson's distinction between aural and mimetic discourse, and Smalley's spectro-morphological categorisations. These all provide a frame for dialogue and discussion about the sounds that Bowers and his co-performers produced during their improvisations and, importantly for us, about how they reflected on and justified the musical 'product' that resulted at the various concerts.

Central to this discussion (Bowers 2003: 48–50) is the question of how an overall musical structure of 'syntax' can emerge from an improvised performance practice. Drawing directly on Emmerson's work on musical syntax (1986), Bowers states:

> Improvised forms are naturally immanent, ad hoc-ed moment-by-moment on the basis of what has gone before and projecting opportunities for what might come following. In the language I hinted at above, multiple threads of significance may link up several of the elements in play. There may still be singularities and other 'unattached' offerings. The threads may be thin or may be densely interwoven (steady with the metaphor now!). We may have a sense of 'a piece' or a collection of 'moments' or some point in between. These are some of the immanent forms, of abstracted syntax, one can hear generated by electro-acoustic improvisors.

> (Bowers 2003: 50)

It is intriguing that much of this discussion has taken place after the event. In the improvisational moment, the opportunities for this critical and reflective thought are fleeting, but, nonetheless, we agree with Bowers that they do inform, perhaps intuitively, the actions that musical improvisers make. For educators, bringing these 'moment-by-moment' significances to light through a well-designed assessment process is vital.

Developing approaches to assessment with digital technologies

In 'Improvising Machines' Bowers presents an illuminating narrative about the processes and products of his improvisational conduct within the context of electro-acoustic music. It contains a blend of musicological features, technical considerations, and reflective comments, underpinned throughout by a rigorous approach to an ethnographic and critical analysis. How can Bowers' work be applied to assessment?

Assessment takes place within a rich context of contingent practical elements

The contingent practical configurations that Bowers describe are fundamental and integral to his process of improvising with machines. Bowers is able to list them – the technology itself, the musical materials that are generated, the musical forms that emerge, the performance practices that are adopted, the settings within which the improvisations are staged, the occasions of the concerts, and the emergent understandings of the various participants, including the audience, who witness the events.

It is only through a strong commitment to exploring the intricate relationships that develop (both during the process of musical improvisation and retrospectively, through reflective thinking) that a true (or at least defensible) understanding of what has occurred can be established.

This approach is a challenge to teachers, as it raises a number of pertinent questions. To what extent are teachers able to map out the contingent practical elements that are at work within a particular process of assessment? The type and location of these elements might be diverse, extending from the classroom where learning might be initiated to the student's home environment where it continues and develops, from conversations with their friends at school to conversations they have online with others about their work; they may include formal elements, such as the unit of work within which the assessment is based, to informal elements, such as the album that the student listened to yesterday. They will undoubtedly include the quality of relationship that the student has both with their teacher, their peers, their instrumental teacher, or other admired role models.

Unpicking all of these elements is important. To meaningfully assess a student's work requires the teacher to know the student well and contextualise their work within that framework. This further requires a rich understanding of the broad context within which that student's work has been produced. Only then can the teacher understand why that particular student has made the particular musical choices that they have made. The mechanisms by which this broader context can be established are varied, but conversation is at the heart of the assessment process. Skilful questioning, often done in an informal way and at opportune times, can be the most useful assessment skill that a teacher can develop to really understand the broader context of influences that have informed a specific piece of work.

Assessment takes place within a rich social context

Alongside the practical contingent elements that Bowers draws attention to, the exploration of musical improvisation with technology as a metaphor for assessment highlights how it also takes place in a rich social context. Here, Bowers emphasises the strong interactional relationships that take place between musical performers, and between musical performers and their audience. Technologies play an integral role here. They can help enforce the social order, or they can negate it; they can facilitate a meshing of ideas and responses, or they helpfully or unhelpfully disrupt them. The 'interactional' dimension that technology imposes on our relationships is playfully embraced by Bowers, leading to his constant experimentation throughout the various concerts and the establishment of his term of 'variable sociality'.

Within any assessment regime or process there are obvious social norms at play. Work should be handed in at a particular time and in a particular format, teachers rightly have expectations that need to be communicated, students have expectations about what the teacher requires (which might be very different from what the teacher said), the notion of individual student ownership is common as is the strong sense of value that students place on their own work, peer assessment should be done in an even-handed way, and so on. These social norms are a standard part of any educational environment.

Technology can disrupt these social norms. Suddenly, perhaps, it is not obvious who owns a particular musical product. Did the student do that? Or did a machine do it? Does it matter? If student A did that (played a chord on their guitar, for example) and student B did that (manipulated the sound of that chord through a processing unit to great effect), who should get the credit? Or to take another example, within a studio-based teaching session numerous students might be making suggestions, commenting, crafting, and helping to shape a particular mix. Separating out 'credit' for their work in these circumstances is not easy. But Bowers goes on to provide some interesting potential answers.

Thorough assessment depends on understanding a broader process of engagement and interactivity

For Bowers, musical improvisation with machines is a complex business. It builds on numerous contingent practical elements and configurations and is mediated through a process of variable sociality. It demands that a participant is able to diagnose and work within a range of approaches for musical engagement and interactivity. Different technologies demand different approaches. Bowers maps these out. There is little point in trying to force one way of working with one technology directly into another context. Each context, each technology, each machine is very different. For Bowers, one of the key skills that a musical improviser needs is flexibility, a willingness to embrace and respond, intuitively and fluently, to the emerging streams of sound that these instruments produce.

As with improvisation, so with assessment in its most articulate form: skilful teachers recognise that assessment is a broad process of engagement and interactivity. The exact models for such engagement and interactivity are hard to predict in advance. But there are some good starting points. Teachers initiate something. They start students off in a direction. Is that always the right direction? It depends on one's viewpoint. Students may subvert their teacher's expectations. Are teachers happy about that? Is the ability to subvert and play with one's expectations an important musical skill? Perhaps. For teachers, maybe it is important not to be too dogmatic early on. To do so could lead to conformity and dull responses.

Following initiation, there is delegation. Teachers have to transfer ownership and power to their students. Students need space and autonomy. They need time to explore, to experiment, to work with their machines, and to try to obtain outcomes that are of value to them. Delegation might involve handing over significant control to a technology, for a time, to see what emerges. The key here is to consider the human endeavour in equal measure to the technological input. It is the student who will add to and express the value of a technological utterance.

In terms of assessment process, it is important for teachers to spend time observing this crucial 'delegation' stage, watching students working naturally, and not jumping in with comments too soon. Their conversations should be listened to and their actions noted. In particular, care needs to be taken to spot any disruptive moments where they struggle, for whatever reason, to make sense of something. Therein lies an opportunity to assist their progress and development through skilful teaching.

Complacency and disengagement, not just with the task itself, whatever that may be, but also with the critical thought that needs to be maintained when working with music technology also need to be looked out for, and students encouraged not to succumb to the prevailing narratives that technologies impose on their work. They must be critical, abuse technology as well as use it, and always keep their creative options open.

If students are not to continue their work indefinitely, there will come a time when the teacher has to exercise a legitimate supervisory role. Perhaps the time is up for that piece of work, a new direction needs to be taken, or the deadline for submission is near. With supervision comes intervention. Intervention might mean a day of reckoning. However, it could just mean a moment of reckoning or accountability, a pointing in a new direction – a tack, as it were – before the students are off again.

Initiation, delegation, supervision, and intervention: just one potential approach to assessment that is in tune with the ways of working with digital technologies outlined in 'Improvising Machines'. There is, however, another very important issue. Interactivity is equated to intelligibility. What does this mean for teachers wishing to develop a sensitive and informative approach to their students' work with digital technologies? It means a commitment to really listen hard to students' work, not a token listening but a real effort to hear what they are trying to say, to commit to grappling with it until the teacher really understands it and where it has come from. This can lead to sensitive responses and engagement. Assessment is not a tool to bash students with. It is about nurturing and encouraging their musical utterances, whatever stage of development they are at, whilst being completely devoted to understanding them. It is about teachers truly valuing their students' musical voices and finding contexts within which they can be expressed with confidence and the certainty that they will receive a positive and fair hearing.

Finally, it will be very important for teachers to adopt a role as an advocate for their students' work with music technology. As discussed above, the question of what happens to the assessment data that this process produces is a vital one. If summative judgements are to be made by others about a student's work, then it is vital that the teacher has done a detailed job of really understanding their student's work and representing the context within which it has been produced in any submission. An advocate is a defender, and teachers will need to defend their judgements against the blunt and often deconstructive mechanisms of external validation through set criteria.

Assessment must build upon its subject's roots

Finally, in this metaphorical application of lessons drawn from Bowers' 'Improvising Machines', music itself, as a subject, is seen to contain the roots of an assessment practice. For Bowers, the process of improvisation with machines was a journey of discovery. This was a long-term commitment to working with the raw materials of music, to develop an appropriate performance practice alongside the machines that he had chosen (as well as his musical partners), and to uncover, in his words, a syntax of musical expression with which he was able to converse through in various ways.

Music is not a universal language, but, within the specifics of any particular genre or style and the work of performers, composers, and listeners within it, gestures, utterances, shapes, sentences if you like, that carry meaning can be recognised. These elements get exhibited and approved in all kinds of ways. It might be a glance, a nod of the head, a tap of a foot, a smile across the studio, an affirmational vocalisation, a positive comment, or something else entirely. Whatever these 'in the moment' and 'of the moment' validations of a musician's work are, and whenever they occur, they are what really count.

Assessment, as a practice, needs to be more musical. First and foremost, it needs to be developed through a musical language (and we do not just mean sounds) that is authentic to the context within which it occurs. By language we mean the spoken, written, gestured, and musical iterations and interactions that occur between individuals in a musical group. For teachers, the key is finding a way to be part of these musical conversations in a way that does not interrupt or stifle students' creativity. Like researchers, teachers will need to recognise that they will have an impact on any situation that they are part of, but this should not stop them putting themselves in those positions. Teachers will need to analyse and reflect carefully on the impact that their presence has though and this will need to be accounted for in the assessment process and any judgements that arise from it.

Put simply, skilful teachers take time to stop and listen. They resist the urge to jump in, offer opinions, or interrupt the flow of a musical exchange. If things are not working, for whatever reason, these teachers use skilful questions or prompts to help their students find their own way through, solve the technological difficulty they are facing, or encourage them to use their instruments in a new way to stimulate a different creative direction.

A quick note about evaluating technologies

> Evaluation is always based on data. Avoid evaluations which start with a judgement about whether a project was good or bad, whether it worked or not. In good evaluations, judgements grow out of that data. . . . Evaluation usually settles for something that is persuasive.
>
> (Kushner 1992: 3)

As with projects, the same can be said about 'products'. The prospect of evaluating a specific music technology and its use may seem daunting, but there are many benefits in considering which technologies have been successful, what might need to be developed further, what can be re-purposed perhaps, and what should not be used again. Some of this work might relate directly to the process of assessment: for example, the teacher may want to explore whether their students could have achieved similar results had a particular piece of technology not been used.

Kushner's reference to the importance of data in making evaluative judgements prompts an obvious question: what types of data should the teacher be using to make judgements about the effectiveness of the music technologies that are being used in their classroom? Kushner would argue for the benefits of naturalistic evaluation. Principally, this generates data drawn from observation of educational exchanges and discussion with the participants within these settings. Given that most teachers will be acting in the dual role, of teacher and evaluator, we would argue for the pre-eminence of the teacher's voice alongside that of the student's voice.

Some key questions that teachers might consider as they begin to evaluate the specific music technologies that they are using in their teaching are:

1   what values underpin this particular piece of music technology, and how do they relate to the teacher's own musical values and those of the students?
2   how have the students learnt with this piece of technology, in what ways have they learnt differently compared to a more traditional approach, and what has the teacher learnt by the whole experience?
3   who have been the winners and losers with this piece of music technology?
4   how would they describe their teaching approach with this piece of music technology – authoritarian or democratic, formal or informal – and what aspects, if any, of their pedagogy have changed or developed?

5 were their original aims, objectives, and activities for this piece of music technology appropriate, and how did they change and develop?

6 whose knowledge really counts when using this piece of music technology, and how did its use relate to the broader subject knowledge base that they are trying to infuse throughout their teaching?

Conclusion

Assessment contains within it the notion of evaluation, of endeavouring to determine the qualitative aspects of a piece of student's work and make judgements about them. Saying how good something is in the arts can be difficult and clearly, simply liking something is not enough. Teachers and students need to work hard at really understanding their musical engagements and products.

Early, in considering the four simple questions about assessment, we discussed the use of assessment criteria. These can certainly help in focussing attention on a particular aspect of a student's work. They can also help students prioritise their activities in a particular creative task. What also needs to be done in order to use assessment in a more holistic way is to endeavour to ascertain students' understandings of what they want to do, and how this fits with what they are required to do. As one of the early writers on formative assessment observed, 'the student comes to hold a concept of quality roughly similar to that held by the teacher' (Sadler 1989: 121). Clearly, this is a double-edged sword (depending on the concept of quality that a teacher has), so, as we have emphasised throughout this chapter, the teacher needs to enter into a dialogue with the students concerned and find out what they are doing and why. This will mean that the students' own views on quality need to be taken into consideration. As Hickman observes:

> If criteria are considered to be necessary . . . the community decides on criteria for assessment, but we need to determine the size of the community; I would advocate that the learner's own criteria be used, which means that the community is a minimum of two people.
>
> (Hickman 2007: 84)

Taking into account the views of the learner is not simply about privileging the learner's voice, but about ascertaining what they are doing and, importantly, why. As Hickman goes on:

> It is concerned with the evaluation of personal achievement rather than an individual's relationship to local or national norms. . . . Students' self-assessment provides teachers with insights into students' understanding of their own progress. . . . It is concerned with individuals' growth and development; because developmental or ipsative assessment is intrinsically learner-centred, it is made by negotiation between teacher and taught and often takes the form of students self-assessment.
>
> (Hickman 2007: 79)

In considering any creative work, whether using music technology or not, it is useful to think about what the student concerned thinks about their own attainment and how this relates to what they were hoping to achieve in the first instance. In the case of music technology, the additionality offered by the technology also needs to be considered within the context of the specific work of the student. Rich accounts of musical performance, improvisation, and composition can provide illuminating insights into the reflective, critical, and analytical thinking that inform them. These insights can be harnessed and adopted within a teacher's pedagogy and result in a more skilful model of music teaching. We hope that our analysis of Bowers' work and more general exposition of educational assessment will help teachers move their work forwards in this important area.

References

Bowers, J. (2003). 'Improvising Machines: Ethnographically Informed Design for Improvised Electro-Acoustic Music'. *ARiADAtexts*. <http://cid.nada.kth.se/pdf/CID-195.pdf> *(accessed 13 Dec. 2015)*.

Buxton, B. (2005). 'Causality and Striking the Right Note'. In *Proceedings of the 2005 International Conference on New Interfaces for Music Expression. Canada, Vancouver, BC.* <http://www.nime.org/proceedings/2005/nime2005_004.pdf> (accessed 13 Dec. 2015).

Emmerson, S. (1986). 'The Relation of Language to Materials'. In S. Emmerson (ed.) *The Language of Electroacoustic Music*. London: Methuen.

Furedi, F. (2009). *Wasted: Why Education isn't Educating*. London: Continuum.

Hickman, R. (2007) '(In Defence of) Whippet-Fancying and Other Vices: Re-evaluating Assessment in Art and Design'. In T. Rayment (ed.), *The Problem of Assessment in Art and Design*. Bristol: Intellect Books.

Kushner, S. (1992). *The Arts, Education and Evaluation: An Introductory Pack with Practical Exercises*. Norwich: University of East Anglia.

Russell, B. (1950). *Unpopular Essays*. London: George Allen & Unwin Ltd.

Sadler, D. (1989). 'Formative Assessment and the Design of Instructional Systems'. *Instructional Science*, 18: 119–44.

13 Performing with the Music Paint Machine

Provoking an embodied approach to educational technology

Luc Nijs and Marc Leman

Introduction

From existing literature overviews (e.g. Frankel 2010; Webster 2002, 2011) and from a growing number of books devoted to technology in music education (e.g. Bauer 2014; Finney and Burnard 2009; Manzo 2011; Rudolph 2005; Watson 2011), it becomes clear that computer-based applications are playing an increasingly important role in the field of music education. Software and hardware developments have led to numerous explorations in the music curriculum. In the domain of instrumental-music education, applications are developed, for example, to monitor musical parameters such as pitch, timbre or dynamics (e.g. WinSingad [Howard et al. 2004], Seeing Sound [Ferguson, Moere, and Cabrera 2005], InTune [Lim and Raphael 2009]), to monitor musical expressiveness (e.g. PracticeSpace [Brandmeyer et al. 2006]), to monitor body movement such as bowing gestures or pianists' elbow-movement (e.g. AMIR [Larkin et al. 2008], MusicJacket [Van der Linden et al. 2011]), to provide intelligent tutoring (e.g. Imutus [Schoonderwaldt, Hansen, and Askenfeld 2004], Vemus [Fober, Letz, and Orlarey 2007]) or to support the development of improvisation skills (e.g. Miror Impro [Addessi and Volpe 2011], MIMI [Schankler et al. 2011]).

However, despite the appeal and the oft-proclaimed added value of such applications for music learning and teaching, scholars have raised various issues, such as: Are music educational technologies really challenging traditionalist approaches and promoting new possibilities and forms of expression (e.g. Beckstead, 2001; Hennessy, Ruthven, and Brindley 2005)? Are they really pedagogy-driven or rather a mere celebration of new technological possibilities (e.g. Manzo 2011)? Is the role of technology in music education well understood (e.g. Himonides and Purves 2010)?

In this chapter we present our research with the Music Paint Machine (MPM), an interactive music-educational technology that has been developed to support the acquisition of music-performance skills and, in particular, of musical creativity and expressiveness. Driven by pedagogy and inspired by technology, the development of the MPM envisioned the creation of interesting opportunities for learning to play a musical instrument.

After presenting an overview of the application, we discuss the MPM's pedagogical background, which is based on a combination of the theory of embodied music cognition and educational constructivism. Next, we discuss the characteristics of the application through which the pedagogical foundations are implemented. These characteristics are then elaborated on with regard to the MPM's potential of inducing an optimal – flow – experience. Finally, we discuss these aspects in the context of a longitudinal case study in which children (1st and 2nd grade) learned to play the clarinet with the support of the application. We present an overview of the main results and discuss them in the light of the presented background.

The Music Paint Machine

The Music Paint Machine is an interactive music educational technology that allows a musician to make a digital painting by playing music and by making various movements on a pressure sensing coloured mat.[1] The system monitors and analyses the musician's sound and movements and translates low-level features of music (duration, pitch, loudness) and movement (direction) into the visual domain (see Figure 13.1).

The music is recorded with a single microphone. Depending on the educational context, a clip-on microphone, headset, or directed room microphone can be used. The movements of the musician are tracked in two ways. First, feet movements are tracked with a custom made pressure-sensing mat. The sensors (pairs of load cells to create a Wheatstone bridge) are positioned under a replaceable colour wheel. Depending on the educational goal, different colour wheels (with a different number or combinations of colours) can be used. Second, upper body movements are tracked with a Kinect motion sensor. To accurately track and analyse

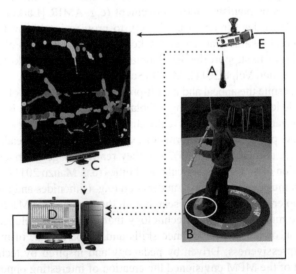

Figure 13.1 Music Paint Machine: (A) microphone, (B) pressure-sensor mat, (C) Kinect camera, (D) computer with custom-made software, (E) projector

these movements (without being disturbed by the movements of other learners in the classroom), the system can be calibrated enabling the motion sensor to only track movements within a certain area of the room (when standing on the mat).

Incoming data (sound, movement) are processed in real-time, based on custom-made software, programmed in Max/MSP (version 5.0, IRCAM, 1990–2010)[2] and Java. Pitch and amplitude of the music are processed using the Sigmund-object (Puckette, Apel, and Zicarelli 1998). Duration is processed on the basis of a user-defined amplitude threshold: at the beginning the player plays a very soft and a very loud note to define the loudness range. When playing within this range, the system tracks pitch and transforms pitch, loudness, and movement into a drawing. Pitch is also processed on the basis of a user-defined range: at the beginning the player plays the lowest and highest note they can play on their instrument. In this way the system can adapt the screen resolution to accommodate the range of notes a learner can play (see Figure 13.2). Notes outside this range are not processed.

The raw feeds of the Kinect sensor are processed on the basis of Microsoft SDK skeleton tracking (Webb and Ashley 2012). At present, the system only uses the shoulder joints of the skeleton in order to process the movement of the torso. Movements of the feet are determined on the basis of variations in voltage. The sensors placed under the colour circle convert the weight of a foot into an electrical signal.

Originally, the transformation of music and movement data into the visual output was based on a fixed one-to-one mapping: the same performance parameter (music, movement) was always used to control the same synthesis parameter (visual). However, in view of the didactic implementation of the system, the mapping was rendered flexible through the use of a grid (see Figure 13.3). In this way it became possible to implement different mapping strategies (one-to-one, one-to-many, many-to-one [see Hunt and Wanderley 2002]), to change the mappings themselves (what-to-what) and to adjust the ranges or characteristics of mapped input and output values (how-much-to-how-much). In addition, it became possible to define the instrument played, the individual pitch range (few notes for beginners, all notes for experts) and the individual dynamic range of a player

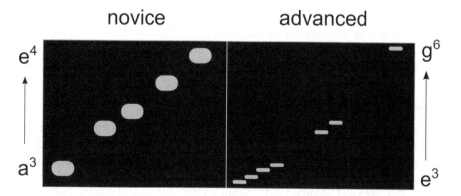

Figure 13.2 Screen resolution of the Music Paint Machine adapted to player's range

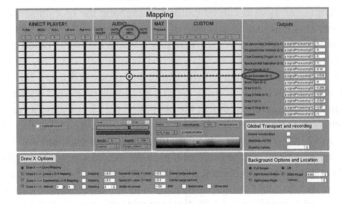

Figure 13.3 Control interface of the Music Paint Machine: the grid allows mapping of
sound and movement to visuals (e.g. note amplitude to brush diameter) for
specific goals (e.g. learning to use different dynamics)

(minimum and maximum dB), to add backgrounds, to split the screen (teacher,
student), to show a representation of the chosen colour on the screen, to show vertical lines as the representation of beats, to add a metronome, and to use functional
movements (e.g. raise left arm to clear the screen). These features were added on
the basis of a study on user experience and didactic potential (Nijs et al. 2012).
A final important feature of the system is its ability to save mapping configurations as presets in order to facilitate their re-use.

Pedagogical background

The idea of the Music Paint Machine originated from a theoretical investigation of
the musician–instrument relationship (Nijs, Lesaffre, and Leman 2013) and was
further developed on the basis of an iterative process between (1) a theoretical/
pedagogical framework, (2) a technological framework for the development of
the software and hardware, and (3) an experimental framework.

In this section we elaborate on the pedagogical framework, which is based on
educational constructivism, on the paradigm of embodied music cognition, and
the daily practice of teaching.

Educational constructivism

Constructivism is an important force in contemporary thinking on education
(Webster 2011). It is a theory about knowledge and learning that goes back to
the writings of Dewey, Piaget, Bruner, and Vygotsky. Today a variety of beliefs,
approaches, and strategies exist under the umbrella of constructivism (Maréchal
2009; Pritchard and Woollard 2010; Schunk 1991). Here we elaborate on some of
the common underlying principles: the construction of knowledge, the learner's
active role, and the importance of the (social) learning environment.

Constructivism argues that learning is based on the construction of knowledge through the learner's interaction with the environment. The mechanism that underlies the construction of knowledge is based on the acquisition and automation of mental schemas, the cognitive structures that provide a context for the processing of novel information by guiding the selection, organisation, and integration (in prior knowledge) of new information (Chandler 2005; Moreno and Mayer 2007; Paas, Renkl, and Sweller 2003; Sweller, Van Merriënboer, and Paas 1998). Evidently, the nature of instruction (what information is provided and how it is presented to the learner) has an impact on schema acquisition and learning (Van Merriënboer and Sweller 2005). For example, presenting learning content in different modalities (auditory, visual, kinaesthetic) helps build a variety of neural connections that integrate stimuli in different sensory modalities with one another and with relevant prior knowledge. As such it can help learners to more effectively process this content (De Jong 2010; Mayer et al. 1999; Sweller, Van Merriënboer, and Paas 1998).

In a constructivist approach, the learner takes a central position and plays an active role in the construction of knowledge. In contrast to a teacher-centred approach in which knowledge is mainly transmitted through the verbal description and aural modelling of musical learning content, a constructivist approach to music teaching and learning fosters a learning process in which learners become responsible for the inquiring and ultimate musical meaning making (Custodero 2010). As such, learning becomes – to an important extent – a self-regulatory process in which goal setting, self-monitoring, self-assessment, self-reinforcement, and self-instruction take a prominent place. Consequently, exploration and experimentation by the learner are essential components of the learning process. Both activities provide a creative space in which goal imaging, motor production, and self-monitoring can be developed autonomously. Research on expertise identifies these skills as basic for performance (e.g. Ericsson and Lehmann 1996).

For learners to effectively take control of their own learning process, it is necessary to create a learning environment in which they are provided with options and opportunities to decide on different elements of the learning process. This is far from being an 'anything goes' pedagogy in which the learner does whatever they want. Rather, the teacher acts as a facilitator by carefully selecting content and designing tasks in order to scaffold the choices that are given and, as such, to model the learner's decision-making processes (Wigfield, Tonks, and Klauda 2009). According to Bransford (2000), an effective learning environment is learner-centered (e.g. it connects to the learner's knowledge, skills, believes, and interests), knowledge-centered (e.g. it establishes clear goals, uses multimodal presentation, and develops self-monitoring), assessment-centered (e.g. it provides frequent formative feedback), and community-centered (e.g. it fosters collaboration and dialogue). Furthermore, it is characterised by a balance between discovery learning and personal exploration on the one hand, and systematic instruction and guidance on the other hand (Schelfhout, Dochy, and Janssens 2004). Finally, a powerful learning environment promotes the occurrence of an optimal – or flow – experience by fostering its conditions, which are a balance between skills and challenge, unambiguous feedback, and clear goals every step of the way (Chen, Wigand, and Nilan 1999). Such a flow experience, when one is completely absorbed by the task at hand, positively affects the learner's engagement by stimulating the intensity of the learning (concentration, interest, attention) and a positive response (esteem, enjoyment, intrinsic motivation) (Shernoff and Csikszentmihalyi 2009).

Embodied music cognition

At the heart of instrumental music education is the development of a relationship with the musical instrument. In our view, an optimal relationship is one that allows an embodied musical interaction: that is, a musical experience in which the musician participates in a direct and engaged way in the musical environment that is created while playing (Nijs, Lesaffre, and Leman 2013). In this view, learning to play a musical instrument involves the process of developing an intimate relationship between musician and instrument in which the instrument is experienced as a natural extension of the musician. This occurs when the musical instrument is integrated in the bodily coordination system and, as such, has become like an organic component of the body (Nosulenko et al. 2005; Zinchenko 1996). When this happens, instrumental gestures (sound-producing and sound-facilitating [Jensenius et al. 2010]) can become constituents of the dynamic structure of the body (body schema) and thereby part of the somatic know-how of the musician (Baber 2003; Behnke 1989). Because of the integration of instrumental gestures into the musician's repertoire of bodily dispositions, the musician can spontaneously and intuitively respond to the affordances and constraints of the musical world that is created throughout the performance.

This account of the musician–instrument relationship is fundamentally embedded in the paradigm of embodied music cognition, in which the body is conceived of as the natural mediator of human experience (Leman 2007). It is assumed that musical experience has a firm and indispensable corporeal ground that goes beyond a merely sensual 'response' to an auditory 'stimulus' and that functions as a fundamentally constitutive element of the musical signification process (e.g. Bowman 2004; Leman 2007). This corporeal ground enables a behavioural resonance with the music on the basis of a pre-reflective attunement to the music during which the physical energies of the music (e.g. frequency, amplitude) are turned into an 'intentional world, in which inert sounds are transfigured into metaphorical gestures in a metaphorical space' (Scruton 1983).

An essential element of this pre-reflective attunement and crucial to the possibility of freely resonating with the music is the body's original motility, that is, the ability of the body to move spontaneously (Behnke 1989; Merleau-Ponty 1945). We believe that the flexibility and spontaneity of artistic expression is highly dependent on the degree to which the body can play its role as a natural mediator and freely articulate the perceived intentions in the music. In our view, learning to play a musical instrument is therefore regaining the 'original motility' that is more or less blocked when novice musicians (and their teachers) initially focus attention mainly on the sound-producing gestures such as posture, fingerings, bowing, or embouchure (see Davidson and Correia 2002). Therefore, we advocate an approach to instrumental music learning and teaching that promotes the development of a 'motile' body instead of a 'docile' body. The latter focuses on shaping the body into templates of right postures and correct sound-producing gestures to be deployed for reproducing the music according to a disembodied (often master-dictated) model of the music. The former, in contrast, allows and stimulates the merging of sound-producing gestures with expressive articulations and personal movement style into an integrated movement repertoire. This repertoire functions as a frame of reference for the musical signification process and facilitates the corporeal resonance with the music. This means that learning and teaching to play a musical instrument are not only concerned with the technical perfection of sound-producing and sound-facilitating (supporting sound production) gestures but actively exploit the sound-accompanying (corporeal attunement to the music) and communicative gestures (Jensenius et al. 2010). Consequently, exploring music also becomes a question of exploring the body, preferably in conjunction with the musical instrument but also without.

The daily practice of teaching

An important source of information for the development of the pedagogical framework that underlies the Music Paint Machine was the daily practice of teaching. Being a clarinet teacher, the first author developed an early intuition about using visual feedback and movement (non-instrumental gestures) in the instrumental-music classroom. The potential contribution of visual feedback to the development of a sense of musical feeling and to the development of listening and playing skills were first explored in the classroom by using waveform visualisation in Audacity.[3] It was found that visual feedback can reinforce the verbal and gestural feedback of the teacher by providing images that display information on what the student actually played (as sometimes opposed by what they think they have played). Furthermore, colours were used in the score to highlight different (levels of) performance cues (Chaffin and Logan 2006). Next to the use of visual feedback, body movements and postures (e.g. moving the torso to learn about phrasing, moving the feet to learn about strong and weak beats) were used to learn specific musical and instrumental aspects of performing.

Basic features of the Music Paint Machine

This section elaborates on the four main features of the system: the creative use of visual feedback, the active use of movement, the variety of possible uses, and the ability to control conditions for an optimal experience.

The creative use of visual feedback

A first feature concerns the use of visual feedback. The system provides concurrent visual feedback about the musician's performance. For example, when mapping pitch to vertical position on the screen the system provides information on the degree to which intonation is steady when dynamics change (e.g. pitch lowers when loudness increases). However, the visualisation of music and movement is more than the mere provision of information to enable performance monitoring in function of 'correct' playing (e.g. comparing results to the master's model). By turning the screen into a canvas of exploration and experimentation, the Music Paint Machine invites musicians to use music, movement, and visuals creatively and to travel into unknown territories of music-making in order to obtain a personalised outcome: the digital 'painting'. Consequently, the visualisation can be considered a creative output that results from the expressive intentions of the musician (for examples, see Figure 13.4; www.musicpaintmachine.be).

Because the emphasis is no longer on the cognitive control of the music based on iconically or symbolically represented information but on the physical, auditory, and visual experience of the music, we believe this approach may bypass possible pitfalls of concurrent visual feedback, such as cognitive load, internal focus, and dependency (Nijs and Leman 2014). Future experiments will address this aspect of visual feedback.

Body movement as an active controller

A second feature concerns the way body movement is integrated in the interaction with the system. The MPM monitors the player's movements but goes beyond merely providing knowledge of performance. By inviting players to actively use body movements in order to generate a desired effect (e.g. drawing from right to left instead of drawing from left to right by turning left with the upper body), the MPM integrates movements that differ from the habitual gestures (Jensenius et al. 2010) and, as such, stimulates musicians to creatively use the body while playing the musical instrument. In this way, the system introduces a variability of movement, the deployment of which is believed to stimulate the development of body awareness and to increase enactive knowledge: knowing in and through the body (Juntunen and Westerlund 2001). This approach to the body is related to the idea of differential learning (Schöllhorn 2000) and to the variability of practice hypothesis (Schmidt 1975). Using this approach, the system goes beyond the corporeal dimension of merely instrumental gestures (sound-producing and sound-facilitating [Jensenius et al. 2010]).

We believe that by intensifying bodily involvement during performance learners can develop a 'motile body' that facilitates an embodied interaction with the music while playing their instruments. By establishing a creative space in which learners can experiment with movements that go beyond the conventional ways of moving while playing, the MPM promotes an approach in which the body is no longer detached from the musical signification process. This is radically different from the master–apprentice model in which templates of right posture and instrumental technique are deployed to reproduce the music according to a disembodied (master's) model of the music.

A broad spectrum of possible practices

These features show that the MPM is a highly flexible, versatile, and adaptable system. The main source of its 'protean' nature (Mishra and Koehler 2003; Papert 1980) is the ability to customise the system's configuration (e.g. mappings, fine-tuning of user-settings) to achieve specific educational content and goals. For example, one educational goal might favour the mapping of pitch to vertical position (e.g. matching melodic patterns), while another educational goal might favour the mapping of pitch to colour transparency (e.g. when the goal concerns intonation).

The broad spectrum of possible uses can be subdivided into two principal modes: the *explorative mode* based on discovery learning (experimentation with music, movement, and visuals) and the learning-path mode based on guided instruction and modelling (methodically organised exercises) (Nijs and Leman 2014). Furthermore, the system can be used online and offline. The former focuses on engaging in a closed loop with the digital painting under construction (process). The latter focuses on the digital painting as pedagogical documentation (product) for further reflection and dialogue between learners and teachers in order to build understanding on a collaborative basis.

We are aware that the protean nature of the system might – to a certain degree – impede its broad integration into the instrumental classroom. After all, teachers are obliged – at least at this moment – to design themselves proper levels to suit the learning content. However, we believe this feature is at the same time a strength, because it challenges teachers to reflect carefully on the design and implementation of the different practices in order to empower learners to find new forms of musical expression. The MPM's features allow teachers to create a powerful learning environment that is tailored to a specific context.

Stimulating an optimal experience

A fourth feature concerns the control of the conditions for an optimal – or flow – experience, using the features defined above. Flow is defined as an optimal experience that occurs when a person experiences a balance between the perceived challenges of a situation and his or her skills or capabilities for action (Csikszentmihalyi 1990). It implies that the subject is completely and from moment-to-moment involved in the ongoing activity to the point of forgetting everything else (time, personal concerns, instrument) except for the activity itself. Attention is given to the task at hand, and the person functions at his or her fullest capacity.

We considered flow experience to be an important construct to guide the design of the MPM. Aimed at facilitating its occurrence, particular attention has been devoted to three flow dimensions: the balance between skills and challenges, immediate and unambiguous feedback, and clear goals (Chen, Wigand, and Nilan 1999; Csikszentmihalyi, 1990). The features of the MPM facilitate each of the conditional flow dimensions. First, the adaptability of the mapping and the ranges of the measured values allows the teacher to create a learning context that appeals to the current skill level of the learner. An example is the ability to adapt the screen resolution to the range of notes a learner can play. But at the same time the learner's skills can be challenged too. For example, it can be challenging to paint complex, beautiful, or funny pictures by playing the musical instrument. Second, what appears on the screen is based on the objective measurement of the learner's playing (sound and movement). Therefore, the visualisation of movement and sound provides immediate and unambiguous feedback on one's playing. For example, if a learner wants to play crescendo (louder and louder) on the clarinet but intonation changes because of low lip pressure, this will be reflected on the screen by a slightly curved line. Third, the system allows activities that are characterised by clear goals. For example, playing a long note by drawing a line from one side of the screen to another, using a predetermined combination of colours or drawing a specific shape. Learners can define their own goals or teachers can design tasks that provide clear goals every step of the way towards an educational goal.

Measuring flow: A study on user experience

Based on the pedagogical framework and its technological implementation, we assumed that the possible effectiveness of the MPM depends to an important degree on its ability to provide learners with a powerful learning environment that stimulates learning by invoking an optimal experience (e.g. Shernoff and Csikszentmihalyi 2009). Therefore we conducted a study on user experience in which the subjective experience while engaging with the MPM was measured on the basis of flow and presence, two constructs that define optimal experience. The measurement of flow has already been used to probe the subjective experience of young learners when using technological applications (e.g. Addessi and Pachet 2005; Denis and Jouvelot 2005; Kiili 2005). With our study (Nijs et al. 2012), we also introduced the concept of presence into the domain of music-education-technology research. Presence, mainly used to denote optimal experience in virtual reality, is conceived of as a layered process that relies on a coherent collaboration of bodily sensations, perception, and cognition to keep attention focused on an activity and to pre-reflexively monitor actions in order to achieve an intended outcome (Riva et al. 2010). Because the MPM creates an augmented musical environment that affects a musician's involvement in this environment at the level of sensation, perception, and cognition, we hypothesised that the MPM affects the musician's sense of presence while painting through movement and sound.

In our study, 65 musicians (amateurs and professionals) participated and interacted with the MPM. To measure the subjective experience of the participants, we used a questionnaire on flow (Flow State Scale [Jackson and Eklund 2004]), on presence (in-house designed, based on Witmer and Singer's Presence Questionnaire [Witmer and Singer 1998]) and on the didactic potential of the system (in-house designed).

The results of this study suggested that the MPM has indeed the hypothesised potential to elicit an optimal experience (Nijs et al. 2012). In particular the flow dimensions of 'balance between skills and challenge', 'concentration on task' and 'autotelic experience' had high scores. This indicates that the MPM has the potential to elicit a fun experience that fully captures the musician's attention. However, the results also revealed a low score on the flow dimension of 'clear goals'. A possible explanation is the explorative character of the task. Taking this result into account, the implementation of clear goals (e.g. specific exercises, levels of difficulty) has been a major concern in follow-up studies with the MPM.

Results also suggested an intrinsic relationship between flow experience and presence, as argued in the literature on presence (e.g. Riva 2008). Statistical analysis (canonical correlation) revealed a cluster between the presence principal components (agency, interface quality) and flow dimensions (sense of control, merging of action, and awareness). This finding is important for the design of interactive music systems such as the MPM. It indicates that the quality of the subjective experience is determined by the quality of bodily engagement as reflected in the degree to which action and perception match.

Because the meaningfulness of an activity is important for both flow and presence (Csikszentmihalyi 1990; Witmer and Singer 1998), we also sought participants' views on the didactical potential of the MPM. Participants estimated the MPM's didactic potential as high. In particular they agreed on its potential to stimulate exploration and experimentation with body movements, music, and visual output. They also recognised that the MPM could be helpful for learning to improvise. Because exploration, experimentation, and improvisation are often neglected in traditional musical-instrument lessons (e.g. Scott 2007), the MPM can play a complementary role by providing an engaging and motivating experience that invites teachers and learners to leave the beaten track and explore new ways of teaching, learning, and playing music.

Learning to play the clarinet: Longitudinal study with the Music Paint Machine

Based on the user study, major software and hardware changes were made to optimise the MPM in function of its didactic integration. We then set up a 9-month longitudinal study in which 12 children (1st and 2nd grade) learned to play the clarinet (Nijs and Leman 2014). The researcher (first author) was the teacher. The overall goal of the study was (1) to integrate the MPM into instrumental-music instruction in order to develop good practices and (2) to investigate the effect of instruction with the system on the learning process.

Children attended class in groups of three and received instruction for 1 hour. The learning content for all groups was kept the same as much as possible. Lessons were based on an aural approach in which the children were guided from sound to sign on the basis of a carefully designed learning path that integrated exploration, experimentation, and direct instruction. The children learned to play by ear, starting with well-known children's songs. Both improvisation and composition were an integral part of the lessons. The weekly lesson preparations and the experience of using the system during instruction led to different practices – free exploration (learners were free to make whatever painting they wanted), guided exploration (learners were free to make a painting within certain limits [e.g. using certain movements]), and direct instruction (learners received specific tasks [e.g. duplicate a certain pattern starting on a different note]) that were carefully designed for specific learning goals (see Figure 13.4). In this way the use of the MPM was often guided by clear goals, every step of the way. These practices were tested and refined throughout the study.

To measure the possible effect of the MPM's didactic integration on the learning process, the study adopted a non-equivalent control groups design with the primary and intermediate measures of music audiation (PMMA, IMMA [Gordon 1986]) before and after the test. It was hypothesised that, due to its specific use of visual feedback (e.g. pitch, note duration) and on its potential to stimulate playfulness with musical parameters, the MPM could contribute to tonal and rhythmic discrimination skills, which are important components of musical aptitude (Gordon 1986, 2007). The results of this study did not reveal a significant difference between the control group and the treatment group. Yet, statistically significant correlations were found between the PMMA pre-test results and aspects of musical home environment (e.g. singing behaviour at home) and personality (e.g. anxiety, perseverance [Mervielde and De Fruyt 1999]). These results suggest that the use of Gordon's measures of music audiation needs to be reconsidered. However,

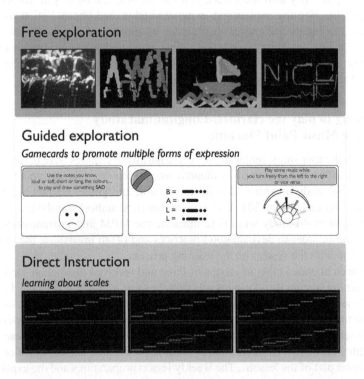

Figure 13.4 Different practices on the Music Paint Machine

due to the teacher/researcher approach, we acquired throughout the study important 'inside' knowledge about the potential of the MPM for music education (see Campbell 2011; Rod 2011; Woodside 2004). This knowledge concerned (1) the transformative impact (see Kiesler 1992) of technology integration on different aspects of the lesson (e.g. proxemics, pacing, timing), (2) the didactic benefit of the creative visualisation (e.g. finding patterns), and (3) the attention and motivation of the children. Here it also became clear that technology integration has a profound impact on teacher reflectiveness. To further elaborate on these insights, the systematic observation of the video footage (132 hours) of the lessons is needed. A coding system is currently being developed on the basis of the work of different scholars (Colprit 2000; Custodero 2005; Duke 1999a, 1999b; Duke, Prickett, and Jellison 1998; Flanders 1970; Heikinheimo 2009; Karlsson and Juslin 2008; Rostvall and West 2003, 2008; Zhukov 2004).

Furthermore, in dealing with the complexity of a real-life educational setting and with the requirements of the quasi-experimental design, this study has provided insights on methodology (design, measures, analysis) in music-educational-technology research. For example, our study made clear that this design is a viable way to investigate transformative impact of (technology-supported) music instruction (see also Welch et al. 2005).

Conclusion

In this chapter we presented our work with the Music Paint Machine, an interactive music system that allows a musician to make a digital painting by playing music while making various movements. Grounded in an in-depth investigation of the musician–instrument relationship, the concept and development of the MPM were shaped by an embodied constructivist approach to music teaching and learning and by an elaborated empirical framework (user study, study on didactic integration).

Although the MPM is similar to existing music-educational technologies (monitoring the musician's playing based on the objective measurement of sound and movement, providing visual feedback), it differs from most of them with regard to the nature and use of the visual feedback (creative), to the role of body movements (active controller), and to the different possible practices (a multitude).

We believe that, based on these features, the MPM creates an open framework that challenges certainties, invites learners and teachers to use technology creatively to foster a multitude of engaging learning opportunities, and, as such, promotes an emergent curriculum towards new ways of performing with technology and possibly even to new forms of musical expression.

Notes

1 <http://www.musicpaintmachine.be>.
2 See <http://cycling74.com/; <http://www.maxobjects.com>.
3 <http://audacity.sourceforge.net>.

References

Addessi, A.R., and F. Pachet (2005). 'Experiments with a Musical Machine: Musical Style Replication in 3 to 5 Year Old Children'. *British Journal of Music Education*, 22/1: 21–46.

—— and G. Volpe (2011). 'The Miror Project'. In Towards Ubiquitous Learning. Proceedings of the Sixth European Conference on Technology Enhanced Learning. Berlin: Springer-Verlag.

Baber, C. (2003). *Cognition and Tool Use: Forms of Engagement in Human and Animal Use of Tools*. London: Taylor & Francis.

Bauer, W.I. (2014). *Music Learning Today: Digital Pedagogy for Creating, Performing, and Responding to Music*. New York: Oxford University Press.

Beckstead, D. (2001). 'Will Technology Transform Music Education'. Music Educators Journal, 87/6: 44–9.

Behnke, E. (1989). 'At the Service of the Sonata: Music Lessons with Merleau-Ponty'. In H. Pietersma (ed.), *Merleau-Ponty: Critical Essays*, Lanham, MD: Rowman & Littlefield.

Bowman, W.D. (2004). 'Cognition and the Body: Perspectives from Music Education'. In L. Bresler (ed.), *Knowing Bodies, Moving Minds: Towards Embodied Teaching and Learning*. Dordrecht: Kluwer Academic.

Brandmeyer, A., D. Hoppe, M. Sadakata, R. Timmers, and P. Desain (2006). 'PracticeSpace: A Platform for Real-Time Visual Feedback in Music Instruction'. Paper presented at the Ninth International Conference on Music Perception and Cognition, Bologna.

Bransford, J. (2000). *How People Learn: Brain, Mind, Experience, and School*. Washington DC: National Academies Press.

Campbell, K.H. (2011). 'Teacher as Researcher: An Essential Component of Teacher Preparation'. *Northwest Passage*, 9/2; 23–34.

Chaffin, R., and T. Logan (2006). 'Practicing Perfection: How Concert Soloists Prepare for Performance'. *Advances in Cognitive Psychology*, 2/2: 113–30.

Chandler, P. (2005). *Music and Schema Theory*. <tzone.org/~okko/html/documents/music_and_cognition.pdf> (accessed 6 Nov. 2015).

Chen, H., R. Wigand, and M. Nilan (1999). 'Optimal Experience of Web Activities'. *Computers in Human Behavior*, 15/5: 585–608.

Colprit, E. (2000). 'Observation and Analysis of Suzuki String Teaching'. *Journal of Research in Music Education*, 48/3: 206–221.

Csikszentmihalyi, M. (1990). *Flow: The Psychology of Optimal Experience*. New York: Harper & Row.

Custodero, L.A. (2005). 'Observable Indicators of Flow Experience: A Developmental Perspective on Musical Engagement in Young Children from Infancy to School Age'. *Music Education Research*, 7/2: 185–209.

—— (2010). 'Meaning and Experience'. In H.F. Abeles and L. Custodero (eds), *Critical Issues in Music Education*. New York: Oxford University Press.

Davidson, J., and J. Correia (2002). 'Body Movement'. In R. Parncutt and G. McPherson (eds), *The Science and Psychology of Music Performance: Creative Strategies for Teaching and Learning*. New York: Oxford University Press.

De Jong, T. (2010). 'Cognitive Load Theory, Educational Research, and Instructional Design: Some Food for Thought'. Instructional Science, 38/2; 105–34.

Denis, G., and P. Jouvelot (2005). 'Motivation-Driven Educational Game Design: Applying Best Practices to Music Education'. Paper presented at the 2005 ACM SIGCHI International Conference on Advances in Computer Entertainment Technology, Valencia.

Duke, R.A. (1999a). 'Measures of Instructional Effectiveness in Music Research'. Bulletin of the Council for Research in Music Education, 143: 1–48.

—— (1999b). 'Teacher and Student Behavior in Suzuki String Lessons: Results from the International Research Symposium on Talent Education'. Journal of Research in Music Education, 47/4: 293–307.

—— C.A. Prickett, and J.A. Jellison (1998). 'Empirical Description of the Pace of Music Instruction'. Journal of Research in Music Education, 46/2: 265–80.

Ericsson, K., and A. Lehmann (1996). 'Expert and Exceptional Performance: Evidence of Maximal Adaptation to Task Constraints'. *Annual Review of Psychology*, 47/1: 273–305.

Ferguson, S., A. Moere, and D. Cabrera (2005). 'Seeing Sound: Real-Time Sound Visualisation in Visual Feedback Loops used for Training Musicians'. Paper presented at the Tenth Symposium on Information Visualization, London.

Finney, J., and P. Burnard (2009). *Music Education with Digital Technology*. London: Continuum.

Flanders, N.A. (1970). Analyzing Teaching Behavior. New York: Addison-Wesley.

Fober, D., S. Letz, and Y. Orlarey (2007). 'Vemus: Feedback and Groupware Technologies for Music Instrument Learning'. Paper presented at the Fourth International Music Conference, Lefkada, Greece.

Frankel, J. (2010). 'Music Education Technology'. In H.F. Abeles and L.A. Custodero (eds), Critical Issues in Music Education: Contemporary Theory and Practice. New York: Oxford University Press.

Gordon, E.E. (1986). Manual for the Primary Measures of Music Audiation: And, The Intermediate Measures of Music Audiation. Chicago: GIA Publications.

—— (2007). Learning Sequences in Music: A Contemporary Music Learning Theory. Chicago: GIA Publications.

Heikinheimo, T. (2009). *Intensity of Interaction in Instrumental Music Lessons*. Helsinki: Sibelius Academy.

Hennessy, S., K. Ruthven, and S. Brindley (2005). 'Teacher Perspectives on Integrating ICT into Subject Teaching: Commitment, Constraints, Caution, and Change'. Journal of Curriculum Studies, 37/2: 155–92.

Himonides, E., and R. Purves (2010). 'The Role of Technology'. In S. Hallam and A. Creech (eds), *Music Education in the 21st Century in the United Kingdom: Achievements, Analysis and Aspirations*. London: Institute of Education.

Howard, D.M., G.F., Welch, J. Brereton, E. Himonides, M. DeCosta, J. Williams, and A.W. Howard (2004). 'WinSingad: A Real-Time Display for the Singing Studio'. *Logopedics Phonatrics Vocology*, 29/3: 135–44.

Hunt, A., and M. Wanderley (2002). 'Mapping Performer Parameters to Synthesis Engines'. *Organised Sound*, 7/2: 97–108.

Jackson, S.A., and R.C. Eklund (2004). *The Flow Scales Manual*. Morgantown, WV: Fitness Information Technology.

Jensenius, A.R., M. Wanderley, R. Godoy, and M. Leman (2010). 'Musical Gestures: Sound, Movement, and Meaning'. In R. Godoy and M. Leman (eds), Music, Gesture, and the Formation of Embodied Meaning. New York: Routledge.

Juntunen, M., and H. Westerlund (2001). 'Digging Dalcroze, or, Dissolving the Mind–Body Dualism: Philosophical and Practical Remarks on the Musical Body in Action'. Music Education Research, 3/2: 203–14.

Karlsson, J., and P. Juslin (2008). 'Musical Expression: An Observational Study of Instrumental Teaching'. Psychology of Music, 36/3: 309–34.

Kiesler, S. (1992). 'Talking, Teaching, and Learning in Network Groups: Lessons from Research'. In A. Kaye (ed.), NATO Advanced Workshop on Collaborative Learning through Computer Conferencing. Heidelberg: Springer-Verlag.

Kiili, K. (2005). 'Digital Game-Based Learning: Towards an Experiential Gaming Model'. *Internet and Higher Education*, 8/1: 13–24.

Larkin, O., T. Koerselman, B. Ong, and K. Ng (2008). 'Sonification of Bowing Features for String Instrument Training'. Paper presented at the Fourth International Conference on Auditory Display, Paris.

Leman, M. (2007). *Embodied Music Cognition and Mediation Technology*. Cambridge, MA: MIT Press.

Lim, K.A., and C. Raphael (2009). 'Intune: A Musician's Intonation Visualization System'. *Computer Music Journal*, 34/3: 45–55.

Manzo, V. (2011). Max/MSP/Jitter for Music. New York: Oxford University Press.

Maréchal, G. (2009). 'Constructivism'. In A.J. Mills, G. Durepos, and E. Wiebe (eds), *Encyclopedia of Case Study Research*. London: Sage.

Mayer, R.E., R. Moreno, M. Boire, and S. Vagge (1999). 'Maximizing Constructivist Learning from Multimedia Communications by Minimizing Cognitive Load'. Journal of Educational Psychology, 91/4: 638–43.

Merleau-Ponty, M. (1945). Phénoménologie de la perception. Paris, Edition Gallimard.

Mervielde, I., and F. de Fruyt (1999). 'Construction of the Hierarchical Personality Inventory for Children (HiPIC)'. Paper presented at the Eighth European Conference on Personality Psychology, Tilburg, The Netherlands.

Mishra, P., and M.J. Koehler (2003). 'Not "What" but "How": Becoming Design-Wise about Educational Technology'. In Y. Zhao (ed.), What Teachers Should Know about Technology: Perspectives and Practices. Greenwich, CT: Information Age.

Moreno, R., and R. Mayer (2007). 'Interactive Multimodal Learning Environments'. Educational Psychology Review, 19/3: 309–26.

Nijs, L. and M. Leman (2014). 'Interactive Technologies in the Instrumental Music Classroom: A Longitudinal Study with the Music Paint Machine'. *Computers and Education*, 73: 40–59.

—— M. Lesaffre, and M. Leman (2013). 'The Musical Instrument as a Natural Extension of the Musician'. In M. Castellengo and H. Genevois, *Music and its Instruments*. Sampzon: Editions Delatour France.

—— P. Coussement, B. Moens, D. Amelynck, M. Lesaffre, and M. Leman (2012). 'Interacting with the Music Paint Machine: Relating the Concepts of Flow Experience and Presence'. *Interacting with Computers*, 24/4: 237–50.

Nosulenko, V., V. Barabanshikov, A. Brushlinsky, and P. Rabardel (2005). 'Man–Technology Interaction: Some of the Russian Approaches'. *Theoretical Issues in Ergonomics Science*, 6/5: 359–83.

Paas, F., A. Renkl, and J. Sweller (2003). 'Cognitive Load Theory and Instructional Design: Recent Developments'. Educational Psychologist, 38/1: 1–4.

Papert, S. (1980). Mindstorms: Children, Computers, and Powerful Ideas. New York: Basic Books.

Pritchard, A., and J. Woollard (2010). *Psychology for the Classroom: Constructivism and Social Learning*. New York: Routledge.

Puckette, M.S., T. Apel, and D.D. Zicarelli (1998). 'Real-Time Audio Analysis Tools for PD and MSP'. Paper presented at the International Computer Music Conference, San Francisco.

Riva, G. (2008). 'Enacting Interactivity: The Role of Presence'. In F. Morganti, A. Carassa, and G. Riva (eds), *Enacting Intersubjectivity: A Cognitive and Social Perspective on the Study of Interactions*. Amsterdam: IOS Press.

—— J.A. Waterworth, E.L. Waterworth, and F. Mantovani (2010). 'From Intention to Action: The Role of Presence'. *New Ideas in Psychology*, 29/1: 24–37.

Rod, M. (2011). 'Subjective Personal Introspection in Action-Oriented Research'. Qualitative Research in Organizations and Management: An International Journal, 6/1: 6–25.

Rostvall, A.L., and T. West (2003). 'Analysis of Interaction and Learning in Instrumental Teaching'. Music Education Research, 5/3: 213–26.

—— and —— (2008). 'Theoretical and Methodological Perspectives on Designing Video Studies of Interaction'. International Journal of Qualitative Methods, 4/4: 87–108.

Rudolph, T.E. (2005). Technology Strategies for Music Education. Milwaukee, WI: Hal Leonard.

Schankler, I., J. Smith, A. François, and E. Chew (2011). 'Emergent Formal Structures of Factor Oracle-Driven Musical Improvisations'. Paper presented at the International Conference on Mathematics and Computation in Music, Paris.

Schelfhout, W., F. Dochy, and S. Janssens (2004). 'The Use of Self, Peer and Teacher Assessment as a Feedback System in a Learning Environment Aimed at Fostering Skills of Cooperation in an Entrepreneurial Context'. Assessment and Evaluation in Higher Education, 29/2: 177–201.

Schmidt, R.A. (1975). 'A Schema Theory of Discrete Motor Skill Learning'. Psychological Review, 82/4: 225–60.

Schöllhorn, W. (2000). 'Applications of Systems Dynamic Principles to Technique and Strength Training'. Acta Academiae Olympiquae Estoniae, 8: 67–85.

Schoonderwaldt, E., K. Hansen, and A. Askenfeld (2004). 'Imutus: An Interactive System for Learning to Play a Musical Instrument'. Paper presented at the International Conference of Interactive Computer Aided Learning, Villach, Austria.

Schunk, D.H. (1991). Learning Theories: An Educational Perspective. New York: Macmillan.

Scott, J. (2007). 'Me? Teach Improvisation to Children?' *General Music Today*, 20/6: 6–13

Scruton, R. (1983). The Aesthetic Understanding: Essays in the Philosophy of Art and Culture. London and New York: Methuen.

Shernoff, D.J., and M. Csikszentmihalyi (2009). 'Cultivating Engaged Learners and Optimal Learning Environments'. In R. Gilman, E.S. Huebner, and M. Furlong (eds), *Handbook of Positive Psychology in Schools*. New York: Routledge.

Sweller, J., J.J.G. Van Merriënboer, and F.G.W.C. Paas (1998). 'Cognitive Architecture and Instructional Design'. Educational Psychology Review, 10/3: 251–96.

Van der Linden, J., E. Schoonderwaldt, J. Bird, and R. Johnson (2011). 'Musicjacket: Combining Motion Capture and Vibrotactile Feedback to Teach Violin Bowing'. IEEE Transactions on Instrumentation and Measurement, 60/1: 104–13.

Van Merriënboer, J.J.G., and J. Sweller (2005). 'Cognitive Load Theory and Complex Learning: Recent Developments and Future Directions'. *Educational Psychology Review*, 17/2: 147–77.

Watson, S. (2011). *Using Technology to Unlock Musical Creativity*. New York: Oxford University Press.

Webb, J., and J. Ashley (2012). *Beginning Kinect Programming with the Microsoft Kinect SDK*. New York: Apress.

Webster, P.R. (2002). 'Computer-Based Technology and Music Teaching and Learning'. In R. Colwell and C. Richardson (eds), *The New Handbook of Research on Music Teaching and Learning*. Oxford: Oxford University Press.

—— (2011). 'Construction of Music Learning'. In R. Colwell and P. Webster (eds), *MENC Handbook of Research on Music Learning*, vol. 1. New York: Oxford University Press.

Welch, G.F., D.M. Howard, E. Himonides, and J. Brereton (2005). 'Real-Time Feedback in the Singing Studio: An Innovatory Action-Research Project using New Voice Technology'. *Music Education Research*, 7/2: 225–49.

Wigfield, A., S. Tonks, and S.L. Klauda (2009). 'Expectancy-Value Theory'. In K.R. Wentzel and A. Wigfield (eds), *Handbook of Motivation at School*. New York: Routledge.

Witmer, B., and M. Singer (1998). 'Measuring Presence in Virtual Environments: A Presence Questionnaire'. *Presence*, 7/3: 225–40.

Woodside, A.G. (2004). 'Advancing from Subjective to Confirmatory Personal Introspection in Consumer Research'. *Psychology and Marketing*, 21/12: 987–1010.

Zinchenko, V. (1996). *Developing Activity Theory: The Zone of Proximal Development and Beyond*. Cambridge, MA: MIT Press.

Zhukov, K. (2004). 'Teaching Styles and Student Behaviour in Instrumental Music Lessons in Australian Conservatoriums'. PhD thesis: University of New South Wales.

14 Big data and the future of education

A primer

Evangelos Himonides

It is often stimulating to try and forecast what the future of something is going to be, even more so for an educator or educational researcher. It seems that things are vastly more difficult to predict when education comes to the discussion. How are education, music education, and music-technology education going to be any different in 10, 20, or 100 years time? One way to engage with the question would be to look at how education changed over the past 10, 20, and 100 years and assess the outcome of the changes or, more efficiently, the 'types' of changes that occurred. This is obviously not a deterministic assessment: opinions would vary. But some agreement would probably be made that matters have shifted from the old-fashioned notion that a student comes to the educational context as an 'empty vessel' apprentice into which the master pours his wisdom. Another established accord would probably be that learning is usually socially located and very rarely able to occur in a vacuum. Over the years, these continually scrutinised assessments led to the understanding that the 'acquisition of knowledge', although extremely important, is something very different to the 'communication of knowledge', and a step further to the 'fostering of the acquisition of knowledge', and, ideally, the 'enabling of the creation of new knowledge'. This progression is by no means an established model to be found in a textbook about the evolutionary sociology of education; it is, rather, a summative way to look at the shift of focus from 'learning' (the acquisition of knowledge), to 'being taught' or 'trained' (the communication of knowledge), to 'becoming a learner within a group where learning is constructed' (the fostering of the acquisition of knowledge), and, finally, to 'acquiring critical thinking in order to be able to contribute to knowledge' (enabling the creation of new knowledge). This latter focus on critical thinking is what I believe to be the one most defining (but not immediately obvious) difference between past and contemporary educational foci. What makes critical thinking relevant in a chapter about music, technology, and education, is, admittedly, not clear at this juncture. Hopefully, this will be resolved once my views (and some evidence) are presented demonstrating the strength of these entwined concepts. Before such an attempt, however, it is essential to acknowledge that forecasting the future of education is also challenging because of what we and our past experiences bring into this discussion, both individually, and as a whole, socially. This is not only because people's present (and future) attitudes are strongly interwoven with and shaped by their experienced level, quality, and access to education, but also because education is believed to be a mirror of past and present collective (i.e. societal) attitudes and social ethics. This might appear to be a somewhat vicious circle, or a chicken-and-egg problem, especially when we are reminded by key stakeholders in the media (see e.g. NACCCE 1999; Robinson 2011; Robinson and Aronica 2013) that we are now preparing students for jobs that do not yet exist, to serve industries yet to be defined. How do we educate the future workforce for these unidentified industries, how do we prepare people to carve the uncarved niche, and how do we foster the opening of the unopened pathway?

I believe that we do so by being critical and by enabling others (students) to develop critical-thinking skills. One could argue that this is not a new realisation: the ancient Greeks were quite passionate about developing thinking and being 'critical'. They were drawn to forming solid conclusions by being analytical about information to which they had access. This is evident in the works of Socrates, Plato, Aristotle, and their contemporaries, intellectual offspring, and so forth throughout the centuries. But somehow, this early-established awareness about the need to be critical did not necessarily infuse mainstream public educational models across the world. In a Royal Society for the Encouragement of Arts, Manufactures and Commerce (RSA) Edge lecture titled 'Changing Paradigms', Robinson (2010) proposed that the current educational system was designed, conceived, and structured for a different age. It was conceived in the intellectual culture of the Enlightenment and the economic circumstances of the industrial revolution. He then, quite colourfully, demonstrates how parallels could be drawn between industrial production models and public schooling, even arguing that children and learners are not that far from being seen and treated as manufactured 'products' that come to the end of a conveyor belt. Although reality might not be quite so disturbing, Robinson's concerns are sound and invite further discourse. The central point for such a dialogue would probably be how to assess the established educational plateau critically and understand how things could improve. Himonides (2016) raises homologous concerns with regard to teacher development and accreditation and invites us to consider the reincarnation of evidence-based education in an era that is now mature enough to consider the assessment of the whole picture, instead of carefully selected snapshots of reality, upon which research in the social sciences is often based, including education, as an applied social science. In Chapter 10 of this volume, Himonides and Ockelford also invite the reader to view technology as a much broader concept and not just as a set of useful tools that the industry has gradually orchestrated for the dependence of educators. In doing so, they invite us to envisage the use of technology as shaping education in the core and not just employed by education on the surface.

I believe that this needed shift in how we view the world of education comes with the establishment, and gradual engrainedness of 'big data'. There appears to be some ambiguity about the use of the term 'big data' in the literature and media. It is not always clear whether we are referring to classes of technologies generating vast sums of data, technologies responsible for the storage of large datasets, or technologies that are in place for 'making sense' of these big datasets. Here I will be referring to all three of the above categories but will focus more closely on the first and last of them. The storage of vast datasets is, of course, a vital part of big data, but we will be focusing more on heuristics, acknowledging the importance of data storage as part of the big-data ecology.

But what exactly is big data? In an attempt to provide an interpretation that is not going to be obsolete before even the present chapter goes to press, I could try to be 'meaningfully vague': big data refers to datasets of any kind (telecommunication, statistical, ethnographic, genomic [Bolouri 2014], medical [Barrett et al. 2013; Boyd and Crawford 2011], financial [Provost and Fawcett 2013], neuroscientific, behavioural [Davenport, Barth, and Bean 2014], meteorological, geological [Bozdag et al. 2014], astronomical, and so on), that are typically expanding rapidly (IBM 2014) and are almost certainly impossible to store, manage, and process using mainstream, standalone computers and software applications. Practically, the size of big datasets can start from tens of terabytes to hundreds of petabytes (one thousand terabytes or one quadrillion bytes). One important fact about big datasets is that they normally cannot be stored in conventional 'relational' databases:[1] they are stored in hundreds, even thousands of machines (computers), and processed in parallel (or in chunks or segments) across the different machines.

In order to understand big data and begin the 'cognitive pondering' about their potential use in education, I need to challenge some certainties and overcome certain obstructions. The greatest obstacle in doing so is probably the realisation that big data is a 'messy' phenomenon. Big datasets are not neatly organised (Koch 2013) in the way that most learners or researchers are used to dealing with data. Most 'interactions' with datasets entail an organisation of data into some kind of tabular form, regardless of whether they be numbers, text, or, frequently, both. Since the early days of their systematic acquaintance with and attempts to understand the world, people learn to organise data by thinking about different categories, entities, classes, or groups of information as 'columns'; and different 'cases', 'instances', 'occurrences', or 'records' of those as 'rows'. Further to this established organisation, analysis of the data, uses established statistical procedures that rely on 'tidiness' and usually discard records (or instances) that do not conform, in order to perform assessments about whether there are significant differences (or similarities) within and across different groups; about whether particular 'behaviours' can be observed within particular groups; about whether particular behaviours can be 'forecast' or predicted, and about whether particular behaviours might be linked (or completely irrelevant) to others. Again, usually, there is some kind of 'hypothesis' to be tested using these established statistical methods. Frequently, hypotheses are tested in order to understand the 'greater world' by looking into miniscule subsets of it, hoping (or often somehow 'providing statistical evidence') that the miniscule subsets are 'representative' of this greater world. This is a concept commonly known as 'sampling,' which is also a very important (and sometimes ambiguous) one in the field of music technology (if one really thinks about it, in one sense people do assess whether the amount of digital information that they use is 'adequate' to describe the rich analogue phenomenon that is 'sound'). This is an established approach that tries to satisfy the human hunger for 'causality', the inherent inclination to try to identify what-ever is happening as a direct result of a particular (and fully 'describable') action. Mayer-Schönberger and Cukier (2013) provide a very comprehensive portrayal of the established 'causality-centric' reality and also refer to Nobel laureate Daniel Kahneman's work (2012) in which the symbiosis of the rational mind versus the impulsive mind and the numerous underlying dynamics are explored. Dealing with big data requires performing a substantial leap from 'causality'. The new big-data approach is strongly aligned with the notion of how different things 'cor-relate' and how strong the different correlations are. Analyses of big datasets are not usually triggered by underlying hypotheses, but rather by systematic mining and identification of strong correlations between different variables (behaviours, metrics, trends, scores, indices). This approach has already provided groundbreak-ing paradigms of scientific and social change: the examples are numerous, from how people shop online and how online retailers attract customers, to how people engage with media and technology (Manyika et al. 2011), behave as a crowd (Hill, Merchant, and Unger 2013), experience health care (Murdoch and Detsky 2013), and travel, to how global markets behave and how investors are likely to invest or behave financially at certain junctures. A very powerful example of the use (as well as potential) of big data is that provided by Mayer-Schönberger and Cukier (2013) relating to the 2009 H1N1 virus crisis. The authors provide evidence that Google was able to track where the flu had spread in real time, as opposed to the one- to two-week lag that was needed for the United States' Centres for Disease Control and Prevention to be able to gain similar insight.

> All their system did was look for correlations between the frequency of cer-tain search queries and the spread of the flu over time and space. In total, they processed a staggering 450 million different mathematical models in order to test the search terms, comparing their predictions against actual flu cases from the CDC in 2007 and 2008. And they struck gold: their software found a combination of 45 search terms that, when used together in a mathemati-cal model, had a strong correlation between their prediction and the official figures nationwide. Like the CDC, they could tell where the flu had spread, but unlike the CDC they could tell it in near real time, not a week of two after the fact.
>
> (Mayer-Schönberger and Cukier 2013: 2)

Similar information is presented by Barrett and colleagues (2013), who also dem-onstrate that big data is often discussed in the context of improving medical care. They suggest that big data has a less appreciated but equally important role to play in preventing disease.

Regarding Robinson's view of the general design of educational provision and how this has changed (or not) since its establishment mentioned above, I believe that humanity is at a turning point. Big data, artificial intelligence, and the rapid growth of technology have the potential to change the face of education dramati-cally. Here, a primer is offered, with the intention of performing an initial rough sketching and rehearsal of a number of themes that might be highly relevant to the big-data educational revolution. Although this primer concerns education in general, a sharper focus will be on music education, mainly in order to address the additional demands of the field.

Qualitative research

Lesson observation

A plethora of studies based on the analyses of lesson observations have been published. In the early days of educational and socio-scientific enquiry, research-ers relied on note-keeping, journals, diaries, mapping, photography, and audio recording to generate data. The field later benefited from the advances of video-recording technology and, more recently, from the practically mainstream avail-ability of digital video technology. Nowadays, it is not surprising for a telephone (smartphone) to have the ability to record digital video in high definition. Tools that can record and produce broadcast quality media are available constantly within arm's reach. The use of this technology in order to conduct qualitative research is already well established. Researchers, teachers, and students conduct classroom observations throughout the world, in order to be able to assess various aspects of their educational contexts in depth. The cost of doing so, however, is more than substantial. Qualitative datasets require major investments in time and resources for their transcription. This often equates to real-time assessment and re-assessment of the observational material with the intention to code, recode, and further classify meaningful 'snippets', in order to later perform quantitative assessments about the frequencies of their appearance and/or their cumulative contribution to a whole session. Given the challenging logistics of this type of research, we face some substantial impediments. Coding and analyses are often highly subjective, with only very small subsets of the coded corpus being scruti-nised, validated, or reviewed independently. Findings from this type of research are potentially feeble, due to the fact that only a very small number of data-rich cases can be thoroughly assessed and transcribed. An additional challenge is that the whole coding framework and the amount of work invested in the actual cod-ing of the qualitative datasets is customarily inaccessible to anybody else who would like to perform similar analyses, assess the original coding, repeat similar analyses, or replicate the original research (a fundamental component of scientific enquiry in other fields).

A big-data approach has immense potential. Extensible frameworks and sche-mata can be established so that qualitative data coding can be governed (or at least informed) by standardised coding structures. Where new evidence emerges suggesting that these structures need to be revised, the extensible character of the frameworks could cater for the systematic documentation of the introduced changes. Observation data analyses can be supported by adaptive/dynamic learn-ing analytics, where learners, educators, and their similarly dynamic contexts could support and feed into automated analyses of recorded observational material.

Verbal aspects of these materials could be fed into natural language processing (NLP) engines and simultaneously triangulated with further audio-visual feature extraction analyses (e.g. subject motion analyses during a music performance or instrumental rehearsal session). The material assessment schemata can be openly accessible, therefore enabling other researchers and practitioners to benefit from studying the datasets at their core, instead of relying upon subjective assessments of individual snapshots. One might argue that what is being presented negates the very nature of 'qualitative research'. I disagree, profoundly; I believe that the qualitative essence of the research lies in the focus of the enquiry not on the established subjective methods for conducting such enquiry. A systematic approach that is open to scrutiny, open to refinement, designed to be extensible, and capable of adapting to specific contexts will probably become the established norm in qualitative research. Furthermore, individual researchers' contributions to the model will have the potential to continually refine it. This is not possible with the existing modus operandi, even within its oft-disguised incarnation of 'multimodality' and 'multimodal research'.

Discourse analyses, interviews, personal journals, and narrative enquiry

The transcription, coding, analyses of qualitative datasets, and further synthesis from those in order to test hypotheses and form conclusions or suggestions for further research or practice is also a highly convoluted objective. Besides the logistical constraints that usually limit the depth of field, similar caveats must be raised regarding subjectivity of judgement, scrutiny, replicability, as well as implications regarding how representative the chosen foci could be in helping us gain greater insights about particular contexts.

A big-data approach to natural language processing has already provided clear evidence about where the future lies. A very strong example is Google's massive undertaking to digitise the 'written word'. According to Google, their 'ultimate goal is to work with publishers and libraries to create a comprehensive, searchable, virtual card catalogue of all books in all languages that helps users discover new books and publishers discover new readers'.[2] What might not be immediately obvious behind this otherwise 'noble cause' is what Google might make out of being in possession of such a dataset. The key word in Google's statement is 'searchable'. Google did not simply aspire to produce digital photographic copies of each page of each book that has ever been published in order to altruistically offer a photographic archive of the printed word to humanity. Google have started scanning and 'recognising' each page of each book that has ever been published, therefore generating a massive dataset of actual 'meaningful' text (as well as their original graphical representation – the scanned copy of each book page). Access to this enormous resulting dataset, in tandem with the fact that the 'text' is meaningful (that is, not the random or noisy text encountered on the internet – which Google thoroughly scans and crawls anyway), allows Google to have access to 'meaning'. Further to this, sales metrics, bookmarking metrics, citation metrics, and so on provide a second tier of 'refined meaning' (or meta-meaning) to the already meaningful published word. This might seem far-fetched, but it is well-established fact. The usage of a particular term (or n-gram)[3] over the years can be seen, and searches can be refined within different idioms or even different genres or vernacular ('British English', 'English fiction', 'French'). The power and potential of this technological breakthrough is obvious in Google's automatic language translation technology, which has gradually become more successful, and is still continually improving. Will it ever be foolproof? This is somewhat unlikely. Language is a rich and labyrinthine concept. But the embarrassing mistakes and automatic translation frivolity and nonsense generated on some occasions will come to a negligible point, compared to the immensity of the meaningful, automatically rendered results.

Similarly, with qualitative research, the quality of the analyses of one or a dozen interview transcripts by the critical mind of a trained researcher would probably be unsurpassed. But what would be the insights gained from relying on this approach (or investing in funding this approach) exclusively, instead of using big-data analytics for the processing of a billion conversations a day for a year or a decade or a century? Even if big-data analytics (Siemens and Long 2011) never managed to derive 'proper' meaning from the spoken or written word, this approach would surely provide benefits and novel insights? I believe that since people can already ask their mobile phones whether they should wear a raincoat before leaving home and have their phone automatically assess what the weather is going to be and then assess whether a raincoat would be an appropriate garment for the given weather, the potential of NLP and big-data and the implications for education and educational research should at least be considered.

Social media

There is a continually augmented body of evidence that highlights the incredible power, as well as potential, of social media. The past decade has witnessed the establishment and rapid growth of social media like Twitter and Facebook. Many scholars, educators, general practitioners, but also policy makers, have realised that these new technological affordances can have an immense impact on education, learning, development, and notions that are either fundamental components of these (like social dynamics, self esteem, sense of self and social inclusion, engagement or disaffection, identity) or naturally cascaded effects (like professional development, vocation, formation of synergies, alliance, continual professional development, networking). What appears to be somewhat paradoxical, though, is that most of the studies focusing on social media and their strong potential appear to be either very limited in scope or highly qualitative. It is important to note that the term 'qualitative' is not used as a derogatory term here: it is simply interesting to witness how the established practices mentioned in the previous sections are rehearsed within these novel contexts, often with disregard for the new ecologies brought by these novel contexts.

The prospective adaptation of social-media paradigms within education and music education brings very exciting possibilities for the future. These possibilities only partially revolve around the new media and communicative channels to which learners might have access: having access to social networks is exciting; having access to synchronous and asynchronous conferencing is exciting; having access to rich educational media is exciting, but we are at a juncture where a metaphorical line needs to be drawn and a shift of focus needs to be established. We need to relinquish our sorcerer's apprentice syndrome in this new social web *Fantasia* and develop critically informed structures for harnessing this technology in order to first understand, and consequently develop, the tools for monitoring social dynamics and socially located learning. This needs to occur in a comprehensive, systematic, and extensible manner, and not within studies of limited scope that report on a small number of people's 'attitudes towards' or 'personal views about' exciting new media.

Conferences

The notion of big data can have a strong presence within conferences in education and music education. This is an important niche upon which to focus as conferences offer unique opportunities for networking, and introduction and exposure to contemporary empirical knowledge and cutting-edge research. Existing practices, internationally, appear to be remarkably parochial when it comes to the planning, organisation, development, implementation, assessment, communication, and dissemination of conferences and conference-related information. More or less, we are still using sixteenth- and seventeenth-century models, simply supported by computers and the internet. A new praxis could involve bringing scholars and practitioners from around the world together in developing an extensible schema (or schemata) for:

- the classification of conference foci;
- planning and logistical management with date and time optimisation based on international professional timetables, academic and teaching diaries, and other logistical factors;
- the meaningful, but also standardised, syndication of conference contributions, using multiple channels, media, and modalities;
- the development of core conference team structures, based on mining big data and the use of key metrics that will enable teams to get together in more efficient and effective ways (for example, based on output, documented practice, professional social-media endorsement, accreditation, general social-media interactions and synergies, online activity trails, and so on);
- the systematic review and dissemination of conference publicised output and its integration into established scholarship metrics systems and technologies; and
- the establishment of unified conference evaluation frameworks that will be able to feed back into the dynamic quality assessment and assurance

provision, bringing practitioners', researchers', and scholars' developmental needs into focus.

Assessment, analytics, and big data

Assessment is undeniably a very important part of education. Whatever our moral ground or beliefs about whether assessment should be a formal part of the educational ecosphere, it is strongly interwoven with how educational provision is funded, teacher training, educational policy, curriculum design, future planning about the workforce, societal and further cultural dynamics, as well as the relations with the industry and global markets.

Besides certain failed attempts to introduce 'evidence based education' (see Himonides 2016), it is quite rare to come across established practices where the power of big data has been used in educational assessment. It is anticipated that, in the near future, big data will redraw the map of assessment in multiple ways. Natural language processing will provide incredible new tools for the assessment, appraisal, engagement, and appreciation of learning, as well as educational practice. This, in tandem with the real affordability of recording, storing, and accessing high-quality media, will introduce new contexts within which interactions between learners and educators could be systematically and continually assessed by computers. This assessment will be multimodal as well as multilevel in its core: different qualitative data streams (speech, movement, text, affective response, real time and post hoc evaluation, social evaluation, and voting) could be analysed, and triangulated. These datasets could further become mapped onto educational 'deliverables', 'products', produced work, and portfolia. Most importantly, these assessments could be conducted within systematically described extensible schemata and therefore be open to revision, augmentation, and improvement by future stakeholders.

As Himonides (2016) suggests, in regard to evidence based education, the metrics, participation, popularity, design, and delivery of massive open online courses (MOOCs) will become dominant contexts within which novel assessment frameworks can be researched, rehearsed, and developed. Humanity has never had such an opportunity to test assessment and other educational hypotheses so rapidly, systematically, and by such vast numbers of willing and actively engaged participants. New opportunities for introducing carefully designed, fully randomised trials for the assessment of different models of assessment (meta-assessment) are being introduced. There is still a certain naivety about how sophisticated educational assessment may become through adopting big-data frameworks. Although it has been stressed that it is important to employ extreme caution in adopting data-driven decision making in education (see e.g. Marsh, Pane, and Hamilton 2006), I envisage a new era of assessment within which artificial intelligence in the big-data era will help produce genetic algorithms for educational assessment, therefore continually working towards the establishment of the 'fittest survivor' assessment model for any given context.

Additional possibilities and thoughts

Big data will provide new possibilities in the development of dynamic 'learning trajectories', adaptive and responsive educational pathways (or walk-throughs), which will become available to learners based on the dynamic assessment of their needs. This assessment will be the result of multidimensional big dataset analyses (behavioural, affective, longitudinal, ethnographic).

Big data is likely to help address the imbalance between particular foci of educational curricula, globally. For example, in music education, western classical music's role is distinct from other musical genres. This is not necessarily something that is closely aligned with what the established musical-genre taxonomy might be in terms of policy-making, funding, community, industry, media, consumer metrics, or streaming metrics. A relevant example is offered by the IFPI (International Federation of the Phonographic Industry, a non-profit organisation representing the recording industry worldwide).[4] According to their latest press release 'globally, digital now accounts for 39 per cent of total industry global revenues and in three of the world's top 10 markets, digital channels account for the majority of revenues' (IFPI 2015: n.p.). Classical music represents less than 5 per cent of this revenue. Nevertheless, at the time of writing, IFPI's chairman was the renowned tenor Plácido Domingo. Big data might be able to help form a more systematic understanding about why a small number of upper- and middle-class, predominantly white, Christian, classically trained, intelligentsia are responsible for the development, assessment, experience, and future occupation of generations of learners that have none of these characteristics in common – what are the frameworks in place for fostering the development of the working class, mixed-race, Jedi Knight,[5] Gabber musician, for example, and, most importantly, how can we ensure that these frameworks are systematic, reliable, and open to continual scrutiny?

Further, big data could help establish a pragmatic framework for understanding how education (and music education) sit within different countries and social contexts. This could lead to the design and development of societal context-sensitive educational systems, as opposed to the somewhat popular practice of 'young' governments of adopting facsimiles of 'established' or 'successful' educational systems.

Focus on music

The 'other than musical' benefits of music have been exciting foci of numerous studies over the past two decades. The current face of education and music education and the numerous challenges that music and the arts in general are facing are now more than ever presenting the need for the systematic research and mapping of how musical development fosters the development of other skills, expertise, and abilities. Big-data methods can support us in assessing how this is being researched, how this is being assessed, and how the findings of these feed, or should feed, into policy, educational practice, and curricula.

Very few examples worldwide provide systematic accounts of how musical development is evidenced outside the mainstream (special needs, music therapy). The Sounds of Intent project (Himonides and Ockelford, this volume) is a powerful example of how big data could support the development of children and young people with complex needs. The augmented evidence base can inform policy and help schools, carers, and parents provide more meaningful and rich experiences for pupils in need.

Big data can play a significant role in the preservation of culture, tradition, and the provision of meaningful access to other people's cultures, traditions, and musical wealth. This could be achieved in a number of ways, either by providing the analytical tools to study forms, structures, and design of particular cultural artefacts (e.g. Music XML, systematic musicological analyses) or by providing access and means for the preservation of musics that are under threat of extinction, such as the online Afghan Rubab tutor (OART), created by John Baily, head of the Afghanistan Music Unit at Goldsmiths and developed by Himonides.[6] OART is particularly powerful, because it celebrates the multifaceted nature of musical culture and cultural dynamics. Besides the value inherent in the provision of the OART resource itself, it is interesting to witness the extremely powerful social network elicited by this resource, with countless musicians, even from within Afghanistan, finding numerous channels through which to express their gratitude for the preservation of their music and cultural heritage (something that had been in serious jeopardy under the Taliban regime and the ban of music). The systematic tracking and triangulation of people's engagement with such a resource, their learning interaction profiles, their social interaction profiles, as well as pure statistical and ethnographic data and usage metrics is a big-data plateau that could offer valuable insights.

Big data can also support systematic, analytic, and empirical musicology in advancing understanding of how music works. This is a continually augmented big dataset. Increasing understanding about music can develop discernment about how people engage with it and are affected by it. This, triangulated with vast arrays of neuroscientific datasets, can broaden understanding about how music is processed in the brain. Consequently, this could lead to the establishment of an extensible schema for mapping the musical brain.

Last but not least, big data will have an impact on research, publications, citations, and other metrics. The systematic recording of public output and the organisation of how this has been assessed, communicated further, syndicated, and adopted is an already established necessity, and almost all publishers, commercial, academic, or other, have subscribed to this notion. Big-data techniques will support the development of even more sophisticated neural networks for the curation, presentation, and assessment of the evidence base (Howe et al. 2008). This way, research can become more effective and help develop more successful quality assurance frameworks, thus safeguarding transparency and democracy of knowledge and education. Big data will help us bring Postman's discussion (1986) about whether the future is likely to be Huxleyan or Orwellian to a conclusion. Current reality suggests that Huxley was somewhat more prophetic about the future. He believed the problem would be the overabundance of information, as opposed to censorship (Orwell's fear). Big data can help us find meaning in vast pools of information.

Epilogue

It is not easy to predict what exactly is going to happen in education (and music education) in the years to come. This becomes a much harder endeavour, when particular disciplines – such as music education – are under very serious threat by the myopic policies, blurred vision, and lack of understanding demonstrated by some governments, funding bodies, policy-makers, and even higher education institutions about the wider benefits of the arts (and, dare we say, music in particular) in the development of human beings and the enhancement of their lives. There never has been an advanced 'civilisation' that did not have an active engagement with the arts; there never has been a paradigm of a society or group of people possessing high levels of life satisfaction that was not multidimensionally creative; and there never has been an educational system that succeeded by ostracising the arts. Even if my 'guesswork' about the future roles of big data in education proves to be far fetched, inaccurate, romantic, or naive, stakeholders should at least take advantage of this new reality in order to assess how important the arts, and music in particular, are to people all over the world. This extensible map of global human artistic ecology could form the basis for education and music education in the big-data era.

What has been presented throughout this chapter does not really constitute a framework for educational reform. It rather roughly sketches some fairly inevitable future shifts and developments in thinking about the role of technology in education. With any 'mellontological' (i.e. talking about the future) approach comes the potential risk of being accused of possessing an anti-humanistic view about education or research in the social sciences. This is a risk worth taking, as long as we understand that, in this context, the celebration of humanism is the betterment of the education and general development of humans, not the specificity of the tools used in doing so. If systematic research has already demonstrated that big data can be invaluable for the safeguarding of humanity's physical health and well-being, the future can only be exciting for education and humanity's intellectual health and well-being.

Acknowledgement

I wish to thank Dr Tammy Jones for reading this work and providing valuable feedback.

Notes

1 Relational databases have been around since the 1970s. In relational databases, information (i.e., different types of data) are stored in tables, with additional information

regarding how the different data types relate to each other also being stored within the database schemata.

2 <http://www.google.co.uk/googlebooks/library/>.
3 See <http://en.wikipedia.org/wiki/N-gram>; <https://books.google.com/ngrams/info>.
4 <www.ifpi.org>.
5 Although not an officially recognised religion in the UK, more than 390,000 people (almost 0.8%) identified their religion as Jedi in the 2001 UK census.
6 <www.oart.eu>.

References

Barrett, M.A., O. Humblet, R.A. Hiatt, and N.E. Adler (2013). 'Big Data and Disease Prevention: From Quantified Self to Quantified Communities'. *Big Data*, 1/3: 168–75 (doi:10.1089/big.2013.0027).

Bolouri, H. (2014). 'Modeling Genomic Regulatory Networks with Big Data'. *Trends in Genetics*, 30/5: 182–91 (doi:10.1016/j.tig.2014.02.005).

Boyd, D., and K. Crawford (2011). 'Six Provocations for Big Data', Paper presented at A Decade in Internet Time: Symposium on the Dynamics of the Internet and Society, Oxford. <http://papers.ssrn.com/abstract=1926431> (accessed 13 Dec. 2015).

Bozdag, E., M. Lefebvre, W. Lei, D. Peter, J. Smith, D. Komatitsch, and J. Tromp (2014). 'Big Data and High-Performance Computing in Global Seismology'. In *EGU General Assembly Conference Abstracts*, 16: 16606. <http://adsabs.harvard.edu/abs/2014EGUGA.. 1616606B> (accessed 13 Dec. 2015).

Davenport, T.H., P. Barth, and R. Bean (2014). 'How "Big Data" is Different'. <http://sloanreview.mit.edu/article/how-big-data-is-different/> (accessed 6 Nov. 2013).

Hill, S., Merchant, R., and Ungar, L. (2013). 'Lessons Learned about Public Health from Online Crowd Surveillance'. *Big Data*, 1/3: 160–67. doi:10.1089/big.2013.0020

Himonides, E. (2016). 'Educators' Roles and Professional Development'. In S.A. Ruthmann and R. Mantie (eds.), *The Oxford Handbook of Technology and Music Education*. New York: Oxford University Press.

Howe, D., M. Costanzo, P. Fey, T. Gojobori, L. Hannick, and W. Hide (2008). 'Big Data: The Future of Biocuration'. *Nature*, 455/7209: 47–50.

IBM (2014). 'What is Big Data?' <http://www.ibm.com/big-data/us/en/> (accessed 6 Nov. 2015).

IFPI (2015). *The Recording Industry in Numbers: The Recorded Music Market in 2014*. <http://www.ifpi.org/news/IFPI-publishes-Recording-Industry-in-Numbers-2014> (accessed 6 Nov. 2015).

Kahneman, D. (2012). *Thinking, Fast and Slow*. London: Penguin.

Koch, C. (2013). 'Compilation and Synthesis in Big Data Analytics'. In G. Gottlob, G. Grasso, D. Olteanu, and C. Schallhart (eds), *Big Data*. Berlin: Springer-Verlag. <http://link.springer.com/chapter/10.1007/978–3–642–39467–6_2> (accessed 6 Nov. 2015).

Manyika, J., M. Chui, B. Brown, J. Bughin, R. Dobbs, C. Roxburgh, and A. Byers (2011). 'Big Data: The Next Frontier for Innovation, Competition, and Productivity'. Mckinsey & Company. <http://www.mckinsey.com/Insights/MGI/Research/Technology_and_Innovation/Big_data_The_next_frontier_for_innovation> (accessed 13 Dec. 2015).

Marsh, J.A., J.F. Pane, and L.S. Hamilton (2006). 'Making Sense of Data-Driven Decision Making in Education'. Rand Education. <http://www.rand.org/pubs/occasional_papers/OP170.html> (accessed 13 Dec. 2015).

Mayer-Schonberger, V., and K. Cukier (2013). *Big Data: A Revolution that will Transform How We Live, Work and Think*. London: John Murray.

Murdoch, T.B., and A.S. Detsky (2013). 'The Inevitable Application of Big Data to Health Care'. *Journal of the American Medical Association*, 309/13: 1351–2 (doi:10.1001/jama.2013.393).

NACCCE [National Advisory Committee on Creative and Cultural Education] (1999). *All our Futures: Creativity, Culture and Education*. London: HMSO.

Postman, N. (1987). *Amusing Ourselves to Death*, new edn. London: Methuen.

Provost, F., and T. Fawcett (2013). 'Data Science and its Relationship to Big Data and Data-Driven Decision Making'. *Big Data*, 1/1: 51–9 (doi:10.1089/big.2013.1508).

Robinson, K. (2010). 'Changing Paradigms' [video]. RSA <http://www.thersa.org/events/video/archive/sir-ken-robinson> (accessed 6 Nov. 2015).

—— (2011). *Out of our Minds: Learning to be Creative*, 2nd edn. Oxford: Capstone.

—— and L. Aronica (2013). *Finding your Element: How to Discover your Talents and Passions and Transform your Life*. New York: Viking Adult.

Siemens, G., and P. Long (2011). 'Penetrating the Fog: Analytics in Learning and Education'. *Educause Review*, 46/5: 30–32.

Index

Note: Page numbers in *italics* indicate figures and tables.

For Product Safety Concerns and Information please contact our
EU representative GPSR@taylorandfrancis.com Taylor & Francis
Verlag GmbH, Kaufingerstraße 24, 80331 München, Germany